Norwegian Americans
and the
Politics of Dissent
1880–1924

Lowell J. Soike

1991
The Norwegian-American Historical Association
NORTHFIELD • MINNESOTA

Foreword

The essential story of *Norwegian Americans and the Politics of Dissent, 1880–1924* by Lowell J. Soike bears upon the nature of the immigrant political experience in general. Soike directs his attention specifically, however, to Norwegian-American political behavior in the states of Wisconsin, Iowa, and Minnesota during an era of dissidence and third-party movements in order to test the limits of an ethnocultural and ethnoreligious interpretation of a manifest Norwegian-American reformist proclivity. The study defines and weighs the broad array and complexity of the interrelated causal forces that determined Norwegian-American response to the public issues of the day and concludes that nationality and differing Lutheran positions were at best only unpredictable determinants of political action.

This volume is a revised version of Soike's doctoral dissertation of the same title in the Department of History at the University of Iowa in 1979. Interested scholars are directed to this work for a complete discussion of those sources and methodologies employed that are not included here. The Association is pleased to make available under its imprint Soike's challenging and compelling analysis of the political culture of the Upper Midwest. It is a significant contribution to the historical literature on the democratic processes as these played themselves out in an immigrant and multiethnic environment.

Lowell Soike is Chief of Historical Surveys in the Bureau of Historic Preservation in the State Historical Society of Iowa. Soike

has published one book-length study and several essays on rural ar-
chitecture and preservation projects. He is preparing an article for the
Association on the Otter Tail county, Minnesota, politician Haldor
Boen.

It is again my privilege to acknowledge with much gratitude the
superior and dedicated work of my efficient assistant, Mary R. Hove,
in the editorial and production stages of the present publication. She
also prepared the index.

Odd S. Lovoll
St. Olaf College

Acknowledgments

It might well be said that a person never knows the patience of family and friends until he writes a book. This lengthy study, taking far more years to complete than ever anticipated, mixed research, writing, and rewriting with building and selling a house, rehabilitating another, writing another book and articles, and finding spare hours here and there to work on chapters during our family-raising years. Nevertheless, with the encouragement of family and mentors, the study gradually drew to a conclusion.

In recognizing the many debts gathered in completing the book, I wish to express particular gratitude to Professor Robert R. Dykstra, under whose direction the original work was completed at the University of Iowa. His advice, sound criticism, editing and stylistic skill immeasurably improved the quality of my work. And to Professor Kenneth Acrea I am indebted for his encouragement and guidance given while completing the Otter Tail portion of the study under his direction at St. Cloud State College. To them I owe much of what I learned in training to become a practicing historian and I hope that this book meets with their expectations. I also benefited from Professor Robert Swierenga's thoughtful criticisms and suggestions which caused me to rethink certain ideas at an important point in my subsequent writing.

I remember with gratitude the assistance and courtesies extended to me by librarians and staff at the Main reference library at the University of Iowa, the manuscript and newpaper collections at the State Historical Society of Wisconsin, the Minnesota Historical Society, and the State Historical Society of Iowa. Special thanks also go to the generous interlibrary loan assistance provided by Dennis Studer at the State Library in Des Moines, Iowa. I am also grateful to the Rev. Donald L. Berg of Kenyon, Minnesota, for providing translations of items from *Rodhuggeren*.

Much credit for virtues that the book may contain springs from the careful editing of Odd S. Lovoll, publications editor for the Norwegian-American Historical Association, and his assistant, Mary R. Hove. Their editorial guidance and considerate exchanges of views and suggestions greatly eased the burdens of bringing the book to completion. Of course, I alone am to blame for any errors of fact or interpretation.

Of all the patience and assistance given, none is more appreciated than that of my wife, Karen M. Soike, who for twenty-three years generously took care of so many things as she watched and helped the study grow through its versions from a dream to a final draft.

Lowell J. Soike

Contents

List of Tables

List of Figures

The Politics of Dissent

Touchstones of Norwegian Politics

Charles Francis Adams, Jr., once mused in an address before members of the State Historical Society of Wisconsin that the Norwegian immigrants' move into the Republican parties of Wisconsin, Iowa, and Minnesota was what tipped the scales and gained Lincoln his 1860 electoral college victory.[1] Other observers over the years, each with his own contemporary angle on Norwegian-American voting, variously described the immigrants' political influence as "rock-ribbed Republican," "hidebound and clannish," "unswervingly pietistic," "deeply conservative," or "unrelentingly progressive." Such varied descriptions would seem to document one truth: Norwegian-American politics were indeed complicated enough to permit a number of seemingly contradictory views, each of which is in some measure true.

Scratch a political historian nowadays and you will likely hear a version of late nineteenth-century politics quite different from that given thirty years ago.[2] Whereas to an earlier generation of "progressive" historians such as Charles Beard the sources of past political struggle seemed centered around socioeconomic conflict, today the thrust of explanation has changed.[3] Socioeconomic divisions, it is now argued, either carried less weight or were more complex than had been supposed; that, except in times of great economic stress, citizens and groups were not politically preoccupied with measures to protect, defend, or enhance their economic self-interest; that voters' religious values explained much of their loyalty to the Republican or

3

Democratic parties; that men tended "to retain and be more influenced by their ethnic group membership than by their membership in economic classes or groups."[4] The historians have done their work well— pursuing innovative investigative techniques, contributing valuable new insights, and producing significant studies of high quality, several of which deal with the Midwest.[5] The prevailing view seems now to be close to what Lee Benson first suggested in 1961, that "ethnic and religious differences have tended to be *relatively* the most important sources of political differences."[6]

This book, intended as a contribution to that body of scholarship, is about the political life of Norwegian Americans with an emphasis on their patterns of voting and the sources of their political dissent. Studies to date have mainly compared the central voting tendencies of one nationality or religious group with those of other groups in particular locales or situations. This study strikes a different direction. It concentrates instead on studying in greater detail differences over time *within* a single group across three states. Proceeding from the large scale to the small, the book begins with an overview of nineteenth-century Norway and the immigrants' entry into American political life. Then their voting behavior at regional, state, and county levels of political involvement is considered. The study is based on votes cast in elections for governor and president from 189 predominantly Norwegian townships and small towns of three states, Wisconsin, Minnesota, and Iowa. These have been examined against the background of a variety of social and economic characteristics of these settlements, supplemented by information gleaned from newspapers and other narrative sources.

The analytical approach of this study is also different in certain respects. Ethnic identity and class consciousness are often seen as being antithetical and separate—the more of one, the less of the other— but in this study they are not so viewed. While, conceptually, religious, ethnic, and economic forces might be treated as independent influences, in practice they are often joined or in constant dialogue with each other.[7] Election studies reveal more of the past when they explore how ethnic, religious, and socioeconomic influences merged, mingled, and became entwined together to shape events.

The politics of Norwegian-American settlements suggest, for example, that the immigrants' national and religious background was culturally infused with a "class heritage."[8] This aspect, as the sociologist Peter A. Munch writes, "has been neglected, in fact, studiously avoided by Norwegian-American historians, I suspect because just to raise the question was seen as a denial of the 'classless' American society."[9] Social class, depending on the proclivities of each Norwegian immigrant generation and the circumstances of their lives, worked to activate or attenuate, strengthen or weaken, what might seem to be ethnic- or religious-based voting. The influence of class on voting involved more than an automatic response to a group's current "objective" economic position. For immigrants, past and present economic circumstances commingled in their social and political points of reference, drawn as they were from experiences in their homeland and from their economic position in America.

To understand immigrants in politics then is to not ignore their memories. And whether the memories proved conservative or radical depended greatly on the particular agrarian backgrounds of European peasants. Such differences had been little appreciated by historians caught up in studying the epic nineteenth-century migrations from the standpoint less of the sending than the receiving countries. This understandable emphasis had occurred as European historians took little interest in writing of those who were leaving their homelands; consequently, research questions had focused on one step of the migration process—immigration. The resulting American-centered approach preoccupied scholars with the aftermath of migration and adjustment to American circumstances rather than with who from among the different peoples had emigrated, where they had left from, and what had distinguished their agrarian outlooks. In this atmosphere, scholars such as Marcus Lee Hansen and Oscar Handlin—major interpreters of the overall immigrant experience and the immigrants' absorption into American society—portrayed the arrivals largely as undifferentiated throngs of peasants who were dislocated, alienated, and conservative, who had lived by the peasants' rule of tradition and deference to authority, and were now looking forward to becoming property owners. Accordingly, dissent and radicalism found little place in their writings about the foreign-born in America.[10]

By the mid-1960s, however, scholarly interest was turning to explore in more detail the distinctive qualities of immigrant groups. Rudolph Vecoli's 1964 critique of Oscar Handlin's The Uprooted (1951) brought these issues to the fore when he showed that, peasant origins notwithstanding, Italian peasants varied greatly, both in their Old World circumstances and in their degree of assimilation and alienation. Soon also the ethnocultural approach to America's electoral past—led by Lee Benson, Ronald Formisano, Paul Kleppner, and Richard Jensen—opened to view the diverse cultural- and religious-based party alignments of nationality groups while other studies uncovered a range of political differences within single groups, as did Frederick

Luebke's of German-American settlements in Nebraska. Recently scholars have explored further variety among immigrants by connecting the lives of people migrating from a region of their old country to their lives in America. Such studies, including those of emigration from Balestrand, Norway, Rättvik parish in Sweden, and Westphalia, Germany, enrich our sense not simply of how their old and new life circumstances changed, but of how things varied among the multitudes of regions, villages, and towns that resisted, remained indifferent, or succumbed to the pull of migration. One effect of all this is that, as differences within and between nationality group migrations are better appreciated, reasons behind the party affiliations of some and the radicalism of others become clearer.[11]

Al Gedicks, for example, found in his review of emigrant streams from Finland that small farmers who emigrated earlier to America from rural northwestern Finland engaged in radical politics far less than did those coming later from elsewhere in Finland where industrialization and socialist politics had taken hold. Walter Galenson found that differences within Scandinavian radicalism resulted from varying social backgrounds of the original generation of industrial workers. Thus workers who had been drawn from the world of independent farming (mainly from Norway and Sweden) supported radical movements more than did agricultural laborers and smallholders (mainly from Denmark) who were conditioned to economic hardship and used to having little say over the rhythms of their work life.[12]

Among Norwegian Americans, immigrant memories that had political impact drew from the character of their religious background, the dynamics of home valley loyalty, and the weight of remembered class feeling from Norway. These invigorated, and sometimes skewed, political life in ways not suggested by the immigrants' immediate economic and social condition. It would seem that immigrant voters acted politically not simply out of the unthinking impulses of raw hunger or in direct proportion to the pinch of business cycles, but also from ideas of what was right in light of attitudes which had been shaped through custom, past social experience, and relations between rulers and the ruled.[13]

When class feeling is seen to animate Norwegian-American politics and is discussed as arising from current economic conditions converging with the immigrants' matured attitudes, perceptions, and predispositions, it resembles the view which has been persuasively argued in the works of Edward P. Thompson. "Class happens," writes Thompson in his often quoted passage from *The Making of the English Working Class* (1963), "when some men, as a result of common experiences (inherited or shared), feel and articulate the identity of their interests as between themselves, and as against other men whose interests are different from (and usually opposed to) theirs. The class experience is largely determined by the productive relations into which men are born–or enter involuntarily. Class consciousness is the way in which these experiences are handled in cultural terms: embodied in traditions, value-systems, ideas, and institutional forms."[14] Such a cultural formulation of class, some dispute, is too one-sided–losing sight of the anchorage of class in objective relations of production and overemphasizing class as happening from people's consciously shared experience with one another while ignoring that classes existed historically, whether or not their members recognized the fact. Nevertheless, Thompson focuses rightly on the importance of shared values and recalled traditions that helped shape, or failed to shape, class identity.[15] Old World recollections helped sharpen, reinforce, or obscure immigrant voter interest toward some issues while sensitizing them to, or exacerbating, others. Rural Norwegian immigrants carried to America local district *bygd* (rural community) prejudices, religious values, anticlerical feelings, remembered Norwegian class rights, discontents, and hostilities, along with notions of equality, decency, obligation, and the promise of America. These helped them to encounter the political present and locate themselves in the sweep of events, to gauge their achieved self-respect and success and yes, to hone their sense of moral outrage.[16]

These influences, being so often intertwined, were difficult to measure with precision, and, of course, quantitative data penetrate some significant relations better than others. There is always a danger of overemphasizing things that can be measured; an attempt has been made here to explain how quantitative and non-quantitative information are related. Simply to know, in the case of religion, the trend of votes cast from precincts well populated by members of one or another Norwegian Lutheran synod is insufficient, for one must understand that it was more than doctrine that divided these groups.

What the Norwegian past gave the departing emigrant was a few attitudes highly susceptible to being politically roused by certain American issues. These they shared to varying degrees depending on which part of Norway they came from and when they landed in America. Those elements of the Norwegian immigrants' cultural baggage that survived in America were ones that had found reinforcement in American political issues and social conditions, and in the institutional arrangements they fashioned. This study, apart from describing something of the political dynamics of Norwegian-American settlements, also attempts to explore their party affiliations in relation to the politics and attitudes prevalent in Norway at the time of their departure. How these fit or matched up with the thrust of American political issues current during the years of their initial settlement and with the personalities who espoused them helps to shed light on corners of their political past. The themes that dominate these pages – quests for political recognition, different political generations, rural-urban conflict, remembered agrarian antagonisms, religious faith and indifference, anti-clericalism and anti-Catholicism – underscore what emerged from coinciding circumstances.

The result is a story of an immigrant people, carrying various predispositions, who fashioned allegiances out of the specific political situations faced – the mix of leaders, issues, groups, and economic and social forces pressing at different political levels. Norwegian-American political behavior – varied or unified – depended greatly on this concert of time, place, opportunity, and the juncture of events.

I

The Norwegian-American
Political World

CHAPTER 1

From Norway to America

"The feeling of unity is so very weak with us." So lamented a Norwegian-American writer in a 1906 political circular as he urged that one of their nationality be elected governor of Wisconsin.[1] Such expressions were not unusual. Many efforts by the press and ambitious Norwegian immigrant politicians to arouse a more clannish regard for political recognition had yielded stories of mixed success. When they succeeded, they typically touched chords of feeling rooted less in national pride than in the togetherness they experienced upon being thrown with unfamiliar immigrant or unfriendly native groups. Sometimes the voter saw "no choice but to be clannish," wrote one Norwegian immigrant, "unless he chooses to associate with those who look down upon him."[2] Nevertheless, Norwegian Americans generally had to work at pulling together – at moving beyond a defensive-minded sort of clannishness – to unify politically on behalf of a cause or a reach for political recognition.

At bottom, what seemed to matter more than feelings of national unity was the identity Norwegian Americans felt as natives of Trondheim, Hardanger, Valdres, or whatever province and parish was their home. Arthur C. Paulson stated it well when he wrote that "customs, jealousies, and ideals which had been implanted in the lives of the inhabitants of a *bygd* by several hundred years of isolation within a narrow mountain valley were retained with almost religious fervor in America. Back of much of the controversial spirit of the Norwegian Americans was the fact that members from one *bygd* felt themselves

11

superior to the inhabitants from other" communities.[3] The character of Norway and its history had focused immigrant loyalties in ways that made their attachments to home tend to work against strong nationalistic feelings. One American historian of Norwegian immigration even concluded half-facetiously that had war occurred in 1905, when Norway separated herself from union with Sweden, "all the recruits from America could probably have been shipped across the Atlantic in one voyage of a small steamship."[4]

Provincial loyalties bedeviled Norwegian unity. Before the coming of modern transportation and communications in the middle of the nineteenth century, ages of geographic isolation had produced sparse rural populations clustered into closely knit, self-supporting small neighborhoods. With outside contact and trade interrupted by mountainous terrain, forest cover, lakes, rivers, and difficult roads, local people had developed, in varying degrees of isolation, distinguishable differences in dialect, religious inclinations, and social class. Until large-scale emigration to America began in the 1860s, the typical rural dweller drew his first breath and lived out his days in the familiar patterns of parish life that knew few attachments to distant towns, cities, or the national metropolis.[5] "The Norwegian farmer's mind is accustomed to move in a narrow circle," observed an immigrant countryman. And because the rural Norwegian's interests "rarely stray beyond his farm, his parish, or his district," he added, "it is very difficult for him to drop his little local scheme for the benefit of the larger commonwealth."[6] Consequently, "patriotism with them in the Old World," writes one historian, became "quite as much a sentiment or love for the parish or the homestead" as it did "a fierce and militant passion for the power and leadership of the nation."[7]

Of course life in Norway did in many ways make a lasting impression on the immigrant. Countless personal, family, social, and other experiences and attachments wove themselves into his outlook and memories, adjusting his horizons, shaping his inclinations. But as Norwegians what did they have in common, the poor fisherman in a northern port and the thriving farmer of Vestfold, or the timber worker of the Trøndelag and the smallholder farmer of Sogn, or the crofter from Hedmark and the seaman from Stavanger, or the parish pastor of Romsdal and the merchant of Christiania? Being a people that in Norway had been territorially dispersed, economically mixed, and for the most part politically inexperienced, immigrants seemingly shared little in common that could be transplanted to the American political scene.

I

Two central facts governed life in nineteenth-century Norway: its severe, inhospitable geography and its legacy of political dominance by
others. Situated on the northern rim of Europe, Norway's long ragged
coastline stretches far beyond the Arctic Circle. Only in the south and
southeast is gentler topography to be found. In sharp contrast to Denmark, where three-fourths of the land is tillable, very little of Norway
is capable of cultivation, comprising bare rock, glaciers, snow cover,
bogs, and land suitable only for grazing. The country's rugged central
mountain system divides eastern and western Norway in twain, while
deep trough-like fjords slice for miles into the interior from the
seacoast.

With most of the rest occupied by forest during the nineteenth century, Norway continued to be the least populated of European king-
doms. Farms were small, with nine out of ten separately registered
holdings even in 1926 having less than twenty-five acres of cultivated
land. And, as might be expected, habitable areas of Norway remained
few and scattered. Small farmsteads and settlements dotted the interior lakeshores and river inlets. Others lay along tillable strips at the
valley bottoms, while fishing communities hugged the islands and narrow rocky coasts.[8]

Norway's climate brought further variety. Although Norway is a
far northern country of long summer days and long winter nights, the
warm Gulf Stream currents moderate the long winters and leave its
many coastal inlets and fjords navigable all year round. In the interior,
however, residents face long and severe winters that, during the nineteenth century, compelled farmers to stall-feed their livestock from
September or October to June.[9]

Climate and the dictates of geography consequently dispersed occupations unequally throughout the country. Most visibly, the east,
with its large numbers of people occupied in summer farming and winter forestry pursuits, differed from the west and north where many
searched seasonally for cod and the capricious herring along the broad
belt of relatively shallow fishing banks just offshore. And the farther
one traveled toward the economically disadvantaged north the more
frequently one found a sparsely settled, poor, debt-ridden people rely-
ing solely on the harvest of the sea for life.[10]

Within agriculture itself, large farms covered the broad expansive
valleys of southeastern Norway where arable tracts made possible
larger fields and more efficient modern farm practices. In the steep-
sloped uplands and mountain areas of central Norway, where the thin

stone-filled soil offered only occasional meadowlands and pasture, farmers relied on the bright summer sun to mature enough vegetation for grazing goats, horses, sheep, and cattle in order to produce such items as meat, hides, and butter. South and east of the central mountains, many smaller farmers worked in the winter cutting timber in the pine forests that extended upward from the cultivated fields and bottom pastures until they were replaced by forests of birch. In the west and north country, however, timber claimed hardly one in ten acres (compared to four of ten acres in eastern parts), so people there divided their time between the seasonal uncertainties of fishing and eking out spare livings from small patches of soil between rocks.

As for the towns, where one-tenth of the people lived in 1801 and roughly one-fourth at the close of the century, visible differences also prevailed among them. Manufacturing industries were most advanced in the counties near Oslo, shipping assumed strength in towns all along the southern coast, and, as one might expect, fishery-related enterprises predominated in towns to the north.

The country's political history before 1815 is largely a story of foreign domination.[11] Norway had first achieved political unification during the Viking era and, though civil wars and border wars recurred in the country, medieval Norway enjoyed general prosperity. But when the great plague known as the Black Death spread across northern Europe in the fourteenth century, Norway's fortunes declined. With her brief centuries of military power, economic growth, and cultural richness in eclipse, the country entered a time of drift as its line of rulers died out and important families went under. By intermarriage, Norway around 1400 slipped gradually under the dominance of Denmark – a relationship that in time reduced her to semi-colonial status.

Not until 1814 – four hundred years later – did the Napoleonic wars give Norway's Danish-Norwegian leadership a chance to assert claims to independence from Denmark. But despite their best efforts to this end, the victorious postwar powers soon compelled Norway to accept a union with Sweden. This, however, Norway's upper classes accomplished on the basis of two equal peoples federally united under a single monarch with their own right of self-government under their own constitution. But such a union, conceived during times quickening with national feeling, would last but ninety years. Increasingly Norwegians became preoccupied with any perceived infringements on their national independence and self-identity by the more numerous and powerful Swedes. Every weak attempt by the sister kingdom to bind the two countries closer together only strengthened Norwegians' conviction that they held an inferior position.[12] Lingering social vestiges of Norway's old colonial status continued for decades to be tender points troubling her political life.

Of the many reminders of Norway's semi-colonial past, the ones imbedded in class relations proved among the most resistant to change. Although Norway's classes were not established in law, a traveler in the 1830s observed that the "different classes are as distinctly separated, and with as little blending together, as in the feudally constituted countries, in which the separation is effected by legal privileges and established ranks."[13] And standing highest on this unyielding social scale were the Danish-oriented *konditionerte* or "people of condition."

Playing the role of an aristocracy in a country without feudal nobility, members of this class were mutually recognizable by their marks of refined civility, professional education, dress of fine texture, and, above all, the stiff formality of the Dano-Norwegian language that drew the curtain of social distance between the upper classes and the less privileged. It was an aristocracy by no means of wealth alone, but one in which professional achievement and family background counted for much. Most typically, "people of condition" included the prestigious but not necessarily affluent *embedsstanden* or professionals – Crown officials, high administrators in municipal and state government, and lawyers, physicians, and civil engineers.[14] Of these, the *embedsmænd* in the Norwegian bureaucracy formed the core, and they comprised the clergy, civil servants, higher court judges, and military officers, whose family members, often of Danish extraction and closely connected by blood and marriage to other Norwegian families of importance, had been emissaries and agents under Danish rule. But notwithstanding the pronounced commitment of this professional leadership to their lives in Norway, based on their own perceived hard-won competence, they found popular support steadily deteriorating throughout the nineteenth century. Their sophisticated, urbane manners and strongly Danish speech and their regard for themselves as a distinct, superior segment of the people left them with few ties to the native Norwegian peasantry once nationalism and egalitarian desires for greater recognition took hold.[15]

In the towns, educated crown officials such as the state-appointed pastor, the magistrate, and the sheriff and their families stood well apart from the ordinary trader, craftsman, and mill operator – and instead linked themselves by manners and contacts to their counterparts in the cities. Out in the rural countryside, it was the parish pastor who stood as the leading state official among the isolated rural district folk. Unlike his poverty-stricken parishioners, he ordinarily lived on a comfortable farm assigned to him. Few country pastors, however, actually soiled their hands with manual labor. Instead tenants and hired men, working under the pastor's supervision, brought forth all that the farm could produce.[16] Meanwhile he tended to his ministerial tasks over what was quite commonly an extensive domain of more than one valley with its isolated hamlets and perhaps three or four churches.

The pastor's Danicized speech and cosmopolitan manners reinforced the social distance between him and his parishioners. And the servile customs of expected courtesy and deference accorded him accentuated it—women politely curtsied upon his arrival and men took off their hats with bowed heads. All those outside the church no doubt had such differences in mind when Erik Foss, in Johan Bojer's novel *The Emigrants*, returned home briefly from America: "He was quite the center of attraction to-day; when the clergyman appeared, the hats did not fly off so quickly as usual. Erik Foss had been saying that there were no class distinctions in America; a laborer or a parson—one was as good as the other. His audience could not believe their ears. . . . Then they saw the colonel from Dyrendal coming; and he was the greatest man of the lot, so they had to make way for him. Hats off, hats off! But strange to say, Erik Foss took no notice of any of these great personages: 'Why don't you take off your hat?' one man asked in a scandalized tone. 'I only take it off to people I know,' answered Erik. Ah, it was all very well for an American to talk like that!"[17]

Class distinctions being what they were, peasants held their own dialect in lower esteem than the preacher's Danish-oriented "book language," which they accepted as "the only speech suited to sacred things."[18]

In this land where Lutheranism was the only officially recognized religion, pastors of the more than 300 rural communities formed a key hierarchy as agents of the state. In addition to keeping vital statistics, they might also serve as schoolteachers, making sure that all members learned how to read their catechism. As educated and dedicated arbiters of higher civilization—morality, cleanliness, and even advanced agricultural practices—and as holders of the power of church discipline and excommunication, the pastors held significant sway over their flocks.

In addition to having what his farm produced, the rural pastor derived income, in the words of an 1841 writer, from "a small assessment of grain in lieu of tithe from each farm, Easter and Christmas offerings, and dues for marriages, christenings, and funerals, which are pretty high."[19] Notwithstanding the generally diligent and conscientious discharge of his duties, the pastor's extra income from dues exposed him to the suspicion, as voiced by one departed emigrant in 1845, that "on several occasions it has seemed to me that religion was not of quite so much importance to them as the emoluments."[20]

Living in a land that was nearly one-hundred-percent Lutheran had its dispiriting aspect for the clergy—religious apathy. Much of the life of the church had become deadened and, as a consequence, beyond partaking of the customary rituals of baptism, annual communion, and weddings and funerals, religious indifference prevailed. In 1805 an English traveler declared in his journal that "the sabbath appears to be very little reverenced in Christiania; the public comptoirs, indeed, are shut up, but generally speaking, all classes follow their various occupations and amusements as on a week day; and in the Cathedral, to which we went for morning service, we found only four or five old women and some charity children."[21] City residents took noticeably less interest in the state church than did their country brethren, although in 1857 a traveler in Norway discerned "little vital religious activity in the whole country."[22] This is not surprising, since levels of religiosity slipped further downward during the third quarter of the century as the numbers of clergymen failed to keep pace with Norway's exploding population and as anticlerical feeling grew against the state clergy's beleaguered defense of the political and social status quo. During the 1880s, therefore, when greater numbers than ever before were emigrating to America, fewer than ever were partaking of the communion sacraments.[23]

Strife between high and low church elements posed yet another problem to the state clergy. Lay church activism had animated Norwegian life ever since Hans Nielsen Hauge (1771-1824) ignited among many peasants the flame of a more inward religion than that offered by the weakly incandescent rationalism of the state church. Especially unsettling to the established clergy were the strong political overtones of agrarian class feeling and anticlericalism that accompanied popular pressures for greater lay control over the state church, much of which emanated from revival-prone western and southern parts of the country.

Many country dwellers, however, either resisted or remained indifferent to the pietists' message. They saw little reason to abandon their drinking, songs, legends, peasant arts and crafts, and old ways that pietists held to be contemptibly worldly. In the novel *Peace* (1892), Arne Garborg depicted the tensions worked by hell-fire pietism in the rural communities. To Enok Haave—Garborg's central character, based on the religious mania of his own father—"everything came back to self-denial." "We should crucify the flesh with its lusts and desires;

keep ourselves from 'gluttony and drunkenness'—cast off all that pertains to the desires of the eyes, the lusts of the flesh, and worldly pride."[24] But Haave's gloomy Haugeanism, being too extreme for most, provoked his older neighbor's stern rebuke: " 'Heh? . . . Do you think that the Lord pays any attention to all that bleating? They say that you lie around and squeal and sing all day Sunday like a she-cat in heat. I think that the Lord would say what I do—that, by God, Enok Haave could find something more worth while to do.'

" 'The natural man receiveth not the things of the Spirit of God. . . . Because they are spiritually discerned.'

" 'Heh? Don't come to me with your texts and your crucifixes. I'm old enough to be your father. I have seen more of the world than you have, and I'd never believe that Our Lord can be the kind of scoundrel that you and the Haugeans think—that I wouldn't. We had a good parson before this one; old Parson Juel was the best one we've had and he didn't talk about hell, except for thieves and rascals, for God's Death, there are some of them that don't deserve anything better. And if He should cast anyone into hell, it would have to be those who think so ill of Him that they believe He should deal that way with people. If you don't get into hell, with all your bleating and whining, then, by God, you won't get into Heaven either—that's what I think.'

"Enok sighed. The poor old man."[25]

As rural religious fervor provoked alarm among the state clergy, another rural issue—the language question—further coalesced anti-urban feeling in the countryside. Although the written Danish-Norwegian language conformed quite closely to the speech of the church, the schools, and the educated urban people, it partook little of rural Norwegian peasant dialects. Nationalistic rural people resented both its close connection with polite Danish urban speech and the class distinctions it implied. When the self-educated son of a peasant, Ivar Aasen, developed a new form of written Norwegian that corresponded more closely to many dialects of the western Norwegian countryside, a large-scale effort commenced to impose it as the national standard. It unleashed a political controversy that lasted for decades—fueling the fires of emerging national pride, sharpening social cleavages between urban and rural and east and west, and prolonging lingering Norwegian antipathies to Denmark.[26]

Through all this the peasantry, divided by their own class distinctions and by regional and cultural differences, rarely acted in unison. These divisions, coupled with their political inexperience and with the time-worn habits of customary deference to their "betters," produced among the peasantry little more than lax political participation.[27] True enough, times had been changing. Attacks during the 1830s against the disproportionate power wielded by state officials in several localities had produced laws on local government. Through elective councils introduced in 1837, popularly elected representatives were able to participate in local affairs formerly controlled by the high officials. But these opportunities for freehold peasant leadership notwithstanding, it took decades for the peasants to coalesce as an opposition party with broad national support in elections.[28] Therefore, it is hardly surprising that a county governor in the western Norwegian district of Sogn reported in 1855 that "people are absolutely naive about politics and never concern themselves with discussing or judging matters which do not directly affect their daily affairs."[29]

Voting requirements also made a difference. At a time when the bulk of Norwegian immigrants were crowding into rural settlements of the Upper Midwest, back in Norway the large landless rural proletariat of cotters and farm laborers still remained unrepresented in the country's political system. But even among those peasants over age twenty-five who met the qualification for property ownership, widespread political apathy prevailed: only thirty percent commonly voted between 1850 and 1880. The size of the Norwegian electorate had declined between 1815 and the 1870s to the point where only one-third of the men age twenty-five and older qualified to vote and only one-fifth had registered to vote.[30] Moreover, only one-tenth of those over the standard voting age actually voted. Not until the fiercely partisan period of 1879 to 1884, when parliament asserted its supremacy over the king and his ministry, did increased numbers of voters (about 47 percent of those who were qualified) begin to cast their ballots in elections. Rural participation never matched that of the cities, however. Even when the franchise criteria expanded beyond property ownership to include men over twenty-five who met minimum income standards, low levels of rural involvement persisted. Indeed, after universal male suffrage came with the 1900 elections, rural voters lagged far behind in entering the electorate.[31]

Political apathy could generally be expected where pronounced class distinctions and limited land and opportunity gave little hope of rising higher than from servant to cotter. Most ended their lives as they began: the best of limited opportunities still went to the culturally advantaged and well born – the unequal results of one generation generally became the unequal advantages of the next. Living in a country where land was both the main source of wealth and an important sign of prestige and where an increasing proportion of their family and neighbors were living in landless status, most tended to cling to their positions on the social ladder, protecting existing arrangements and distinctions, shrinking from protesting their equality to their betters. Ultimately, faraway America would give multitudes of such "land-hungry" emigrants an option to resolve their fears of sinking into lower social status and to end "uncertainties" about "their ultimate place" back home in Norway.[32]

Although landowning farmers, the *bønder*, might face the patronizing aloofness of parish pastors, magistrates, sheriffs, and officialdom with a considerable pride in their own station and family past, others yet lower on the social scale endured the disdain of the *bønder* as well. A traveler remarked of such caste feeling that "If the child of a *gaardemann* (rich farmer) should insist on marrying into the family of a *husmann* (small tenant farmer), the family of the rich farmer will refuse to have anything to do with the young people, or even to see their child again."[33] A wide social gulf separated those who owned land from those who did not—the tenant farmers or cotters, who lived in huts on patches of land granted to them by farm owners in exchange for their labor.[34] Additionally, tens of thousands of laborers and servants, equally underprivileged, filled shabby living quarters in both town and country. No servant, laborer, or cotter had much hope of ever rising to become a *bonde*. In fact, with a fast-rising population and increasing land prices, the children of many landowners were helping to fill the rising pool of the landless.[35]

The social distance separating each rank of peasantry varied from region to region. Social stratification became steepest in eastern Norway where the wealthier landholding *bønder* employed many agricultural laborers and servants on their larger acreages. Likewise, these landholding farmers had little to do with the typical smallholder *bønder* of western Norway. There, where the small farmer himself stood but a step above poverty, social divisions and visible social contrasts narrowed between cotter and farmer.[36]

Fragmented as they were, the heretofore inarticulate Norwegian peasantry only slowly awakened to their strength. During the initial decades after Norway's separation from Denmark in 1814, traditional deference toward the existing body of civil servants and professional upper classes enabled them to continue in control of government and perpetuate their influence over the electoral process. With the election of 1832 the landholding peasantry coalesced sufficiently to elect for the first time more peasants than officials to the Storting (parliament). And yet, still unsure of themselves and working in an atmosphere of condescension, peasant representatives "often found it difficult to take part in the parliamentary debates, and they had to suffer irony and sarcasm for clumsily phrased speeches."[37]

Nevertheless, if self-satisfied officials did not sense the ground shifting, the unsettling Thrane movement of popular protest from 1849-1851 quickly shook their complacency.[38] Aroused by the radical and revolutionary events moving through Europe in 1848, Marcus Thrane, an editor of the *Drammens Adresse*, turned his own radicalism toward organizing the Drammen Workers' Association. Soon workers' associations spread to other towns and then to the countryside, with membership during the 1850-1851 period of from 20,000 to 30,000. The movement's social composition and sources of leadership varied greatly from one area to the next, embracing in fact several movements – some on behalf of farmers, others championing concerns and rights of artisans, cotters, or laborers. The various dissatisfied social elements voiced equality as a central theme and pressed such demands as universal male suffrage, by which the politically excluded rural and urban people might improve their lot through gaining representation in government. In so doing they felt the opposition not only of leading aristocratic officials, but of large farmers and town bourgeois as well, who saw an extended suffrage as a threat to their political power. By mid-1851 the frightened authorities had arrested Thrane and other leaders, which quickly sent the movement into eclipse. The short-lived movement nonetheless helped set the stage for later change, including the eventual political separation of the conservative easterners from the majority of farmers, who would fill the ranks of the Liberal party.

Meanwhile, however, as they continued to be split by regional and local divisions, even the persuasive power of Ole Gabriel Ueland – a principal legislative leader of the farmers' political movement – regularly produced little more than incoherent solidarity and ineffectual accommodation. In their struggles to check the central administration and its threats to traditional rural ways of life, the peasants approached greatest unity when minimizing state expenditures and voting to curb the rights and privileges enjoyed by civil servants.

By the mid-1860s, however, times were changing. Attitudes less respectful and less obsequious toward the professional class were stirring among rural people in the wake of economic prosperity and emigration overseas. More were feeling no doubt like Torkjell Tualand – a cotter in Arne Garborg's novel *Peace* – that they would be less impoverished if they would "throw out all those strutting officials and these pot-bellied clerics and the military jingoists."[39] Anticlerical and lay religious adherents (especially in the west and southwest) in-

veighed against the high-church official clergy and the degraded secularism of urban centers, while resentment smoldered among the native
peasantry against the king's "Europeanized" and "urbane" civil officials
whom they identified with the capital and other large administrative
centers.[40] All these factors together were leading toward a rejection
of all-important central authority.

Expressive of such strains was the effort made by Søren Jaabæck
in the early 1870s to cut public support for the state church. To
Jaabæck, a longtime champion of the rural poor in the Storting, if the
work of the clergy was no more important than "tilling the soil, tending
the cattle, fishing for herring, or spreading manure," then why "should
the clergy be paid far more than the common people?"[41] The controversy, though inconclusive, stirred anticlerical sentiment and
sparked letters of support from like-minded farmers, while, on the
other side, outraged pastors spewed forth denunciations.

As peasant and upper-class relations grew ever more tense, the
leading officials and patrician families tended to draw further away—
many leaving active politics to the skilled bureaucrats who, in strate-
gic miscalculation, increasingly sought refuge from Storting actions in
the Swedish monarch's use of the royal veto. Also, with prices rising
in the advancing economy, the professional class found itself trading
away much of its social prestige and moral authority in the process of
surmounting peasant resistance in the Storting to their salary in-
creases and pensions.

Ultimately, in the 1870s, the peasantry joined together with the
rising commercial and middle classes of the cities in a protracted constitutional struggle. They emerged victorious in 1884 when the king's
executive branch reluctantly accepted a parliamentary system of
government.[42]

These developments were not without influence on the departing
emigrant. The transformations left later generations of Norwegian
migrants with a viewpoint different from that of their predecessors.
While earlier arrivals were disinclined to trifle with the reverence a
citizen should feel for constituted authority, later waves of immigrants
after the Civil War were more politicized in agrarian feeling, more
secularized, more overtly anticlerical in outlook, and less accepting of
the religious and social status quo. In short, as one writer put it, "those
coming after the war in 1865 came from a different Norway to a different America."[43]

Despite the inapplicability of Norway's political and social past to
many circumstances in America, immigrants still shared a few important attitudes that could be politically roused by American issues.

Three were rooted in Norway's agrarian society: a sense of peasant class consciousness, a dislike of government officialdom, and a suspicion of towns and cities. These attitudes were potentially very important, since over 70 percent of the immigrants in the period 1865–1915 hailed from rural districts of Norway.[44] Three other common factors came from the Norwegians' religious background: their near-homogeneous Lutheranism (impregnated with latent anti-Catholicism), a tension between high-church and low-church orientations, and a legacy of religious indifference and anticlericalism.

It did not take much provocation for many a Norwegian American to recall and retain these attitudes. The businesslike abruptness of a Minnesota townsman might do it, or the slightly contemptuous attitude of a Yankee-born census marshal, or the overbearing ecclesiastical authority of some transplanted Norwegian-American minister. These and other reminders of his lowly origins stirred old feelings, transferring to the midwestern small town, for example, ancient animosities against Norway's urban classes. "At the county seat," one of them later recalled, the Norwegian-American farmer "saw men and women who lived in houses that looked palatial to his hungering soul. They wore what he regarded as fine clothes and there could be no doubt that they ate good food. They were believed to have an easy time; they held nearly all the public offices, from which they pocketed large salaries; at least, so the alien believed. They controlled the affairs of the country and the alien was sure that through this control they were able to lay exorbitant taxes on the poor farmers' land."[45] Whether or not unpleasant memories of home would importantly shape his political choices in America depended greatly, then, on when a Norwegian emigrated in relation to what was activating American political life at the place of his settlement.

II

Between 1836 and 1848 only a few hundred Norwegians emigrated to America each year. Thereafter, up to the onset of the Civil War, their numbers climbed to several thousand annually. During these years America's westward settlement swept around Lake Michigan and pushed on into Illinois, Wisconsin, Iowa, and Minnesota. Norwegians established substantial settlements in southeastern and southern Wisconsin and northern Illinois, and these became the mother settlements for those that followed. Soon Scandinavian newcomers clustered in the northeastern and north-central regions of Wisconsin while other such settlements dotted Iowa's central and northeastern counties and southeastern parts of Minnesota. This modest immigration then declined with the darkest years of the Civil War. By war's end, however, news reports and immigrant letters to land-poor neighbors and kin back home now urged them to emigrate, and thus began an unprecedented era of mass migration.

Departures swelled into three great waves between 1865 and 1915. A major exodus to America erupted in 1866 and lasted until the Panic of 1873. Corresponding in length to America's business cycles and in magnitude to bulges of young and unestablished adults in Norway's population, the emigration drew upon those who felt uncertain about their future prospects in the home district and who glimpsed opportunity in the news they heard about America. Immigrants during these years filled Wisconsin's western counties and spread across the northernmost counties in Iowa. Even greater numbers, however, rushed northward into the west-central prairies of Minnesota. By the late 1870s, as business conditions improved in the United States and as Norway's economy slipped into a lengthy depression, "America fever" rose once again and erupted into the greatest emigrant tide of all. Tens of thousands, many of them young products of the fertility surge of two decades before, gathered the needed resolve to uproot themselves in order to pursue better lives overseas. A torrent of new arrivals spilled into the Red River Valley of Minnesota and spread across eastern North Dakota before ebbing as the United States plunged into depression in the 1890s. The last wave of emigration, from 1899 to 1915, sent yet thousands more into western Dakota and remaining lands in the mountain states, the Pacific Northwest, Alaska, and western Canada, and thereafter into America's burgeoning cities.[46]

Politically, in the upper midwestern states, Norwegian-American voters became a deciding element in Minnesota, held a balance-of-power position between Germans and native-born Americans in Wisconsin, and exercised a minor but significant influence in Iowa.

III

Only by degrees did Norwegian immigrants undertake to enter the American political system. Being relatively poor upon arrival and dearly anxious to obtain what he could not obtain in Norway – a productive farm of his own – the typical immigrant initially had little interest in political affairs. Finding work in order to feed his family and save money for a down payment on land, later clearing and breaking ground to plant crops, erect buildings, purchase horses and machinery, and learn some English – these came first.

Moreover, it took time for the Norwegian immigrant farmer to change his Old Country habits of political apathy and recognize that "he is no longer in Norway but in a country where each citizen assists in the machinery of government."[47] With rural Norwegian-American communities living largely within themselves during the early years, habits of political noninvolvement persisted. The Norwegian Lutheran pastor, as the leading cultural force, strengthened early tendencies among immigrants to read religious publications and hold political newspapers in lower regard, which also inhibited learning about American politics.[48] Steadily, however, partly by emulating his Protestant, native-born neighbors but mainly by building on his own experience of his adopted home, the Norwegian immigrant farmer began his apprenticeship in self-government.

Involvement in public affairs typically began as rural townships filled up sufficiently to merit local township government. With this, opportunities opened for Norwegians to learn about elections and the machinery of government, and to mingle with non-Norwegians at conventions to familiarize themselves with the American system. Those who first grasped the opportunities then became those who introduced their countrymen to, and urged their interest in, wider political matters.

Still, the Norwegian immigrant's shy deference toward the native-born often persisted for years. As one countryman accurately noted in 1893, "We frequently consider ourselves smaller, and of less importance than we are," especially when facing "aggressive politicians" and those considered to be "genuine Americans," "thinking perhaps—'Yes, you are an "American" superior to me, you can rush ahead, you have a right to; but I—must stand here, at a respectful distance, and look at you; for I am—a "foreigner" or your inferior.' "[49] Throughout the initial decade or two of Americanization, Norwegians consequently confined their politics to holding township offices and voting in elections. Meanwhile a county's public offices usually remained secure in the hands of its native-born element.[50]

Lower rates of turnout at the polls underscored the Norwegian immigrants' initial lack of interest. By the 1890s, however, with township organization complete and the bulk of Norwegian settlement now established in the region, differences between Norwegian areas and the general populace faded. After 1896 voter interest in Norwegian settlements paralleled general turnout patterns, which slipped into a steep decline from 1900 until 1930.[51] But beyond this overall tendency, settlements participated at different turnout levels. Strictly farm areas, for example, differed from small towns and villages. Between 1880 and

1924, the farmer and his neighbors in predominantly Norwegian farm townships cast consistently lighter presidential votes, averaging 4 to 7 percentage points below their small-town counterparts.[52]

As Norwegian apprenticeship in township offices widened, so too did the horizons of their politically ambitious countrymen. County office first attracted their interest, and the aspirants most popular and most conversant in English quickly capitalized on their countrymen's numerical strength and desire for recognition. Their reach extended even further in counties where sizable Norwegian settlements made them a factor that could be safely neither ignored nor antagonized. Here the most active Norwegian-American candidates might gain party preferment for nomination to state legislative offices.

Only a few able immigrants, men with the confidence and aggressiveness needed to overcome deficient language skills in wider dealings with non-Norwegians, ordinarily reached for higher than township office. The adult immigrant rarely could shake his native accent entirely, and, being sensitive to ridicule before non-Norwegians, tended to hold back from other than local political involvements. Haldor E. Boen of Otter Tail county, Minnesota, illustrates the process. Lacking confidence in his command of English, he spoke in a soft and halting fashion and usually avoided public address. But possessed of far more grit and tireless ambition than his shy neighbors, within a decade after arriving he cast his eye beyond farming, teaching school, and holding local office. He tried and failed on two occasions to represent his district on the county board of commissioners. But, undaunted, he aggressively pursued county political office and, after failing once again in an independent bid for election as state representative, won nomination and election as county registrar of deeds. This post Boen held for two terms until the United States Congress beckoned to him in 1892.[53] The path from township to county to state legislative officeholding repeated itself throughout immigrant localities of the rural Upper Midwest.

Four specific county offices most appealed to Norwegian immigrants: treasurer, registrar of deeds, sheriff, and auditor. Occasionally Norwegians sought the offices of county recorder and clerk of court, but rarely did they interest themselves in becoming coroner, surveyor, or superintendent of schools, all of which required at least some professional training. Consequently, at least during the early years, the overall proportion of Norwegian-born officeholders is estimated to have lagged behind the county's percentage of Norwegian-born residents.[54]

Another contemporary historian has gone further, asserting that

Legislative Representation: Regional

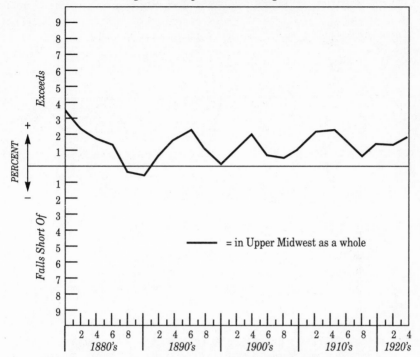

Figure 1. Extent to which the percentage of Norwegian-born state
legislators equals the percentage of Norwegian-born residents in
the Upper Midwest. Nativity of legislators, 1880–1924, derived
from *Iowa Official Register;* Iowa *Journal of the House of
Representatives* (1895); *Wisconsin Blue Book;* and the *Legislative
Manual of the State of Minnesota.* Intercensal estimates of persons
born in Norway are based on population figures in Volume I (Population) of each United States Census published for the years 1880,
1890, 1900, 1910, 1920, 1930. Information proved unavailable on the
nativity of Iowa legislators serving in 1880 and 1882 and for Iowans elected to the senate in 1895.

Norwegians had not secured 'their fair share of public offices, not in
any state or community."[55] But close inspection of state offices throws
this claim into question. True enough, not until after the Civil War did
Norwegians become an influence in state legislatures, but neither had
their population yet reached its greatest voting strength. Throughout
the 1870s, reflecting these changing trends, increasing numbers of
Norwegian-born senators and representatives entered state assem-
blies. And after 1880, no longer could claims be made (if they ever could
have been) that Norwegians lacked equal representation in the Upper
Midwest as a whole (Figure 1). In fact, for all but two legislative ses-

Legislative Representation: State

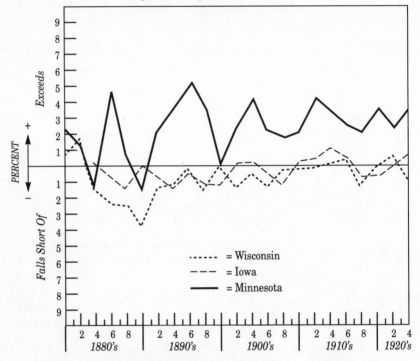

Figure 2. Extent to which the percentage of Norwegian-born state legislators in each state equals its percentage of Norwegian-born residents. Nativity of legislators, 1880–1924, from *Iowa Official Register;* Iowa *Journal of the House of Representatives* (1895); *Wisconsin Blue Book;* and the *Legislative Manual of the State of Minnesota.* Intercensal estimates of persons born in Norway based on population figures in Volume I (Population) of each United States Census for the years 1880, 1890, 1900, 1910, 1920, 1930. Information unavailable on the nativity of Iowa legislators serving in 1880 and 1882 and for Iowans elected to the senate in 1895.

sions, Norwegian-born state legislators exceeded their proportionate share of representation.

Examining these relationships within each state (Figure 2), one notices an under-representation for Norwegian-born legislators in Wisconsin. But the more conspicuous fact is that over-representation in Minnesota buoyed the positive regional trend. What accounts for this? Part of the explanation undoubtedly has something to do with Norwegians comprising a greater percentage of the total population in Minnesota than in Wisconsin or Iowa. But equally important, the Norwegians' "share" of legislative offices depended on how the Norwegian people were concentrated within counties of the state. Norwegian voters could not hope to gain their due representation where they remained too dispersed across county lines or, conversely, where they concentrated themselves too solidly in only a very few counties. These imbalances seem to have characterized Norwegian settlements of Wisconsin and Iowa more than those in Minnesota.

Of course, the relationship of Norwegian officeholders to population cannot be so easily applied to the smaller number of higher elective offices. For years the Republican party reserved token state offices for Norwegians, but it was only a matter of time before one would reach yet higher. Adolph Bierman, the nominee of Minnesota's Democratic party in 1883, became the first Norwegian-born politician to run for a governorship, but not until 1892 did a Norwegian meet with success. This happened, again in Minnesota, when Knute Nelson, a Republican, handily won election over two opponents. Revered by Norwegians as their pioneer politician who had successfully led the first great clash between Norwegian and native leadership for a congressional seat in 1882, he spent the final two decades of his life as the nation's first Norwegian-born United States senator. Not until 1906 did Wisconsin follow suit when it gave two terms as governor to Norwegian-born James Davidson. Iowa's Norwegians, on the other hand, never overcame their numerical weakness to place one of their own in the governor's chair. But with Norwegians concentrated in the Fourth Congressional District, Gilbert N. Haugen successfully elevated himself to Congress in 1899 and achieved re-election repeatedly thereafter. Overall, between 1880 and 1924, the people of Wisconsin, Iowa, and Minnesota sent one senator and fourteen congressmen of Norwegian birth or descent to Washington, twelve of whom served more than one term. Meanwhile, five men of Norwegian birth or parentage gained governorships in the region.[56]

These successes became a source of pride to many Norwegian Americans, instilling in them feelings of close identity with America. But a politician needed more than a Norwegian name. He needed a favorable party affiliation and attractive personal qualities to avoid shattering the Norwegians' fragile political cohesion. The candidate knew that his countrymen thought beyond simply elevating a Norwegian aspirant to office. His fortunes, he realized, were tied inescapably to the tug and pull of issues, Old Country passions and prejudices, other groups and circumstances in the Upper Midwest, its states and localities. It is to these matters that attention now turns.

CHAPTER 2

Unity and Diversity

In the Norwegian settlements of the Upper Midwest political life took form where regional development intersected with important national and local events. Significantly, the three new states of Wisconsin, Iowa, and Minnesota passed through their political youth at the very moment that overwhelming national questions associated with the Civil War came to the fore. Nonlocal politics became ascendant, and state party lines and images congealed around this cluster of issues. Although it can be said that the Republican party became the new political home of earlier Whigs, Know-Nothings, Free Soilers, and other basically Protestant reform groupings, the Civil War essentially moored and secured in place these coalition elements within a single continuing party and made Republicanism synonymous with patriotism, anti-slavery, and high moral ideals. The experience left an indelible imprint on midwestern politics when conventional ethnic, religious, and class politics again resumed center stage.[1]

Although left discredited in this northern region of free-labor states, the Democratic party restlessly unearthed whatever issues it could—for example, black suffrage, nativism, prohibition, monopoly capitalism—in order to score on Republican weaknesses. And backed by most Americans of German and Irish background, Democrats maintained their party strength in the face of slim but consistent Republican pluralities in presidential contests. The Democrats pressed especially hard whenever defections and assorted third-party movements

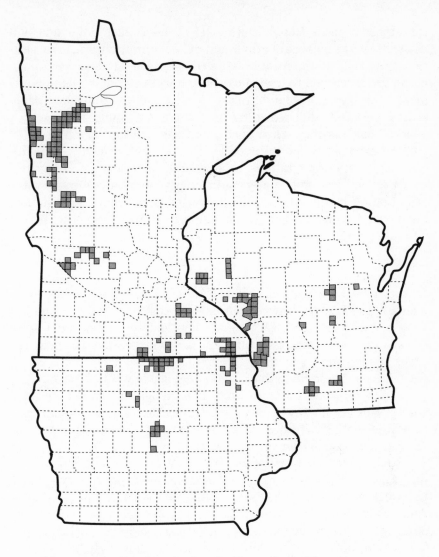

Figure 3. Location of predominantly Norwegian settlements selected for study.

threatened to drain Republican ranks. Economic dislocation and sudden shifts in the balance of ethnic and religious or urban and rural relations stood out as the most volatile threats. Alert to such problems, both parties worked to devise balanced tickets of major coalition elements. But try as they might to avoid truly explosive appeals to deep-seated, politically divisive ethnic and religious prejudices – since such appeals could backfire – their good intentions occasionally fell victim to political expediency and the need to appease coalition elements. Politicians and party organizations, especially at the local level, frequently gave in to political opportunity and attempted to satisfy or divert voter attention by raising the volatile issues of liquor control legislation, Sunday observance laws, nativist slights, or inattention to this or that national group.

I

In the immediate postwar political atmosphere, Norwegian settlements in the Upper Midwest consistently cast their lot with the Republican party. As historical accounts have long suggested, and Figure 4 bears out, most Norwegian townships and villages down through the 1880s and beyond, save in 1924, found Republican presidential candidates more to their liking than did the region as a whole. True enough, paralleling regional trends, down to 1892 Republican impulses waned among Norwegian townships. But thereafter only two temporary reversals – both of which were led by insurgent Republicans – marred their strong Republican voting record.

What prompted Norwegians to embrace Republicanism as they did? An overall answer would be that given the limited party alternatives and the emerging issues which divided these parties, Norwegian Americans saw little choice but to join the Republicans. At first, evidently goaded by Know-Nothing agitation and impressed by the agrarian egalitarianism of the Democratic party, their early settlements voted Democratic in the late 1840s and early 1850s.[2] But then, as the Republican party's appeal took shape by 1856, emphasizing northern resentment over the political power of the South and the danger posed by an aggressive slaveholding society, the stigma of aristocracy, which heretofore had greatly impeded the Whigs, now began to attach itself to the Democratic party. Republicans – as the Whigs' successors – found a powerful new appeal among northern voters in denouncing what they termed the threat of a conspiratorial Slave Power.[3] Once the Republican party emerged to combine as its leading issues an "aristocratic slave power," free-soil fears, and anti-Catholicism, most

Republican Presidential Support

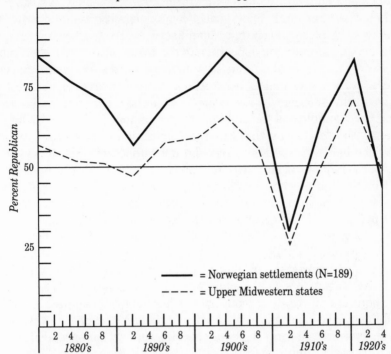

Figure 4. Upper Midwest: Republican share of the total vote for president, 1880–1924, in predominantly Norwegian precincts and in the region as a whole. Precinct returns are less complete before 1890.

heavily Norwegian areas readily abandoned the Democrats and aligned themselves with the new party.

Portrayed as the country's privileged class, slaveholders seemed, in the minds of vigilant defenders of republican traditions, to be an arrogant minority bent on wielding disproportionate power over national affairs. This view gained special credence as events unfolded: the Missouri Compromise was repealed and the Kansas-Nebraska bill passed, while passions climbed with dramatic incidents such as the violence in Kansas and Congressman Preston Brooks's violent assault with a cane on Senator Charles Sumner in the Senate chamber. The Slave Power, seen as an aggressive threat to free men and democratic liberties and as an assault on northern rights, aroused animosity among those in whose hearts beat a democratic prejudice against aristocracy.

To most Norwegian immigrants, sensitized by relations of subservience embedded in Norway's hierarchical society and long-standing colonial status and filled with heady egalitarian rhetoric, the Democratic party–seemingly dominated by an aristocracy of slaveholders and standing in opposition to the Republicans with their motto of liberty and free-labor equality–reminded them of circumstances in Norway. Mons Grinager made the point clear. Writing home from Iowa in late 1856 as witness to the new partisan atmosphere, he stated that the Republicans "resemble the common folk back home" while the Democrats "are somewhat like the Norwegian aristocrats."[4]

The break to the new party did not happen cleanly, however. In 1856, the influential Norwegian Synod leader, A. C. Preus, had written to the leading newspaper *Emigranten* stating that he and his fellow Norwegian pastors shared the anti-slavery principles of the Republican party.[5] And in the same year the Reverend C. L. Clausen of Mitchell county, Iowa, accepted a Republican nomination for the Iowa house of representatives and in a statement to *Emigranten* voiced sentiments about threats to free men by a slaveholding minority that many Norwegian settlers would echo. "My chief consideration," he wrote, "is the hope of uniting all our countrymen here in northern Iowa in the Republican party; for the realization of whose principles I, with God's help, entertain the only hope for checking the further spread of slavery and for preserving our free republican institutions from destruction. Thus far my hope has not been in vain and as far as my election is concerned that seems quite certain, even though I have encountered no little opposition due to local differences of opinion. I also consider it almost certain that the whole Republican ticket will win in this district."[6] Clausen's easy victory in the November election signaled the emerging trend of Norwegian alignments.

But by 1861 Norwegian Synod clergy who had closely associated themselves with Concordia Seminary of the German Missouri Synod took a stand that appeared to condone slavery–one that acknowledged it to be evil but not in itself a sin according to scripture. C. L. Clausen, whose instinct for ethnic leadership had led him first into religious journalism and then into promoting Norwegian immigration, broke with his conservative colleagues. Prominent opponents declared him to be misguided on natural rights and declared that abolitionists had little true regard for the "poor Negroes." But despite the pressure of his fellow Synod pastors to recant, the energetic Clausen adhered to his antislavery views until his resignation from the Synod in 1868.[7]

After the war, issues continued to give order and meaning to the Norwegian immigrant's political world, but how other social, ethnic, and religious groups responded to these issues often determined whether Norwegians also embraced them or suspiciously withheld their support. Their opposition to aristocracy, Catholicism, and the extension of slavery had carried Norwegians into Lincoln's party and the exhilarating prestige that victory brought helped predispose later arrivals to join it. Once in, religious and ethnic struggles helped keep their Republican loyalties alive. Even though Norwegians resented the strain of anti-immigrant and culturally nativist feeling that characterized the elitism of many Republicans, Democratic party features seemed to them more repugnant. In particular, the post-Civil War Democratic party repelled them because they saw it as the political home of most American Catholics, a phenomenon treated in the chapter that follows. Suffice it to say here that the Norwegians' visceral response from ages past found reinforcement in the Protestant moralism and anti-Catholic tendencies of a great many Republicans.[8]

The Republican leanings of Norwegian communities are thus unmistakable, being well known and amply documented. But to stop here is grossly to oversimplify the matter and give the mistaken impression that Norwegians responded in lockstep to the Republican call. The average conceals much variation; local Republican committeemen between 1880 and 1924 could not everywhere report to state headquarters, "Nothing to worry about here." As the distribution and sources of Norwegian departure from their fundamental Republican leanings are understood, one can more fully appreciate the richness of their political experience.

Norwegian disunity rose and fell in three great tides. This is shown in Figure 5. Quite visibly the post-Civil War unanimity had by 1888 lost its coherence. Thereafter only in 1904 and in 1920 did this bastion of Republicanism resume its pre-1890s solidarity. Norwegian turbulence in the region originated not from vigorous two-party competition but from third-party movements splitting off from the Republicans. The People's party in the 1890s, Theodore Roosevelt's "Bull Moose" party effort of 1912, and Robert LaFollette's Progressive party campaign of 1924 amply demonstrated the undependable, loosening grip of Republican party ties on many settlements and the unpredictability of Norwegian popular voting in a regional sense.[9]

II

Some historians point to divergent religious views as having been the driving force for political disunity, arguing that differing doctrinal outlooks figured decisively in the shaping of political alignments and

Presidential Elections: Political Disunity

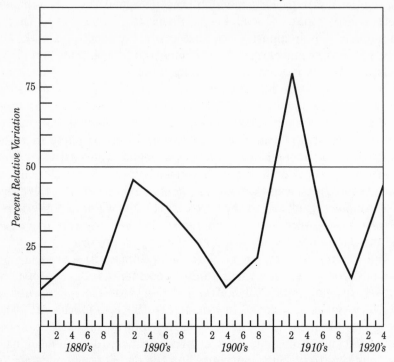

Figure 5. The extent of disagreement in the votes cast from Norwegian settlements for Republican presidential candidates within
the Upper Midwest, 1880–1924. This is expressed as a percentage
that Republican township votes are scattered relative to their origin, the mean, and permits direct comparisons of one year's percentage figures to others. Precinct returns are less complete before
1890.

realignments. According to this view, with the Republicans being the
party of "high moral ideas," party loyalty was to a large degree a matter of "the more pietistic the group's outlook the more intensely Republican its partisan affiliation."[11]

At first glance this would appear to square closely with expectations about Norwegian voters because their settlements so often felt
the bitter strife that rent Norwegian-American synods.[12] Leola N.
Bergmann, in writing of Madison, Minnesota, where she spent her
youthful years, notes that despite the small size of the Norwegian
town, it possessed "two Norwegian Lutheran churches, even though
it was post-1917 and the official merger had already taken place. As far
as cooperation was concerned they might have been a Jewish syna-
gogue and a Roman Catholic church."[13] Another careful observer of

Norwegian communities noted: "It has been said that if you travel through rural Wisconsin and you get to a crossroad with two churches, one on each side of the road, you may be sure that you have entered a Norwegian settlement."[14] More than three of every five townships selected for analysis in the present study contained two or more churches of competing Lutheran synods in 1917.

If differing doctrinal outlooks had expressed themselves politically, the most evangelical "pietist" Norwegian settlements—that is, the predominantly Hauge and United Norwegian Lutheran townships —would have voted more staunchly Republican than the conservative, high-church Norwegian Synod areas. But, interestingly enough, presidential contests yield no such pattern.[15] The slight voting differences shown in Figure 6 give scant support to the importance of religious doctrine in election decisions. Certainly the occasional minor differences of from 5 to 10 percentage points account for little of the 20 to 30 point spread in Republican votes among Norwegian settlements.[16]

So the question persists: Why did contrasting doctrinal orientations leave such a minimal impression on Norwegian immigrant politics while they sowed such discord and bitterness within Norwegian communities?

To find the answer one must look beyond pietist and liturgical religious doctrine and see that what in fact divided the Norwegian-American congregations and synods was, in the words of Peter A. Munch, "a gulf that was as much social and cultural as theological in nature."[17] Congregations often split apart less from strife among those battling for high-church or low-church religious values than from the playing out of deeper social antagonisms between parishioners and pastor, between groups within congregations that hailed from different districts of Norway, or between older and newer generations of immigrants. And if that was not enough, the thriving legacy of religious indifference among the unchurched in the settlements further undercut any likelihood that religious values and pastoral influence would visibly affect vote tallies in elections. Together all dissolved into one another in effectively muting the political voice of pastors in many Norwegian settlements. Each of these factors will be examined in turn.

Lutheran pastors who came from Norway to minister earnestly to the spiritual wants of their emigrant brethren soon faced the rude awakening of anticlericalism, class hatred, and suspicion that many peasants now felt free to voice. The old rituals of deference that had long comforted the ruling professional elite quickly frayed apart in the atmosphere of freedom. No longer did the immigrant have to rise when

Synodal Affiliations and
Republican Presidential Support

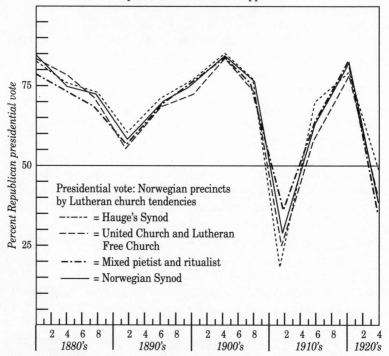

*Figure 6.*Upper Midwest: Republican share of presidential vote in Norwegian settlements according to their predominant Norwegian Lutheran church affiliation as of 1915. The doctrinal orientation of each precinct is classified as to whether an estimated one-half or more of its membership belonged to a single Norwegian synod. Others are included in the "mixed" category. Precinct returns are less complete before 1890.

addressed by his former "better," as he once had had to stand "abjectly humble, eyes downcast, cap in hand, and mumble a reply."[18] From the very outset, constant tension prevailed between the pastor's effort to establish right doctrine and proper church ritual and his immigrant parishioners who, though grateful to have a "real" pastor from Norway, were nonetheless determined to assert their new social equality by curbing and controlling the pastor's authority. The minister saw his influence constantly undermined and his motives suspected by those wishing to confine the pastor strictly to affairs of the church. "Nowhere in Scandinavia," concluded a Norwegian traveler in 1881, "have the ministers been more constrained by the congregations than here."[19]

To his more resentful parishioners, the minister's refined bearing, cassock and clerical garb, fine clothes, and Danicized speech stood out as irritating reminders of their own lowly origins that they hoped to leave behind. Not the least of these was the social separateness, patronizing authority, and ingrained patterns of peasant deference toward one's betters that typified life in Norway's rural parishes. "We do not intend to write for a Norwegian minister," declared one immigrant in a letter to Norway in 1846. "No! there are very few things that we can import from our old Norway which would be of benefit to us, the least of all – Norwegian officials."[20]

Antagonism was not all on one side, for it was hard for the Norwegian pastor and his family to shake attitudes toward the common people as being "sluggish, wholly lacking in ambition and enterprise."[21] Writing back home in early 1856, Caja Munch, wife of a minister serving several Wisconsin congregations, despaired: "Everything considered, we do not really miss anything except the company of cultured people instead of these silly peasants, who for the most part cannot comprehend at all that we are a step above them and have more requirements. No, they regard themselves maybe fully as high and always say [the intimate form] *Du*, and many such things, which sometimes really are highly ridiculous. For example, many will simply call me Caja."[22]

Most often, ambivalence greeted the pastor. Parishioners' attitudes toward the pastor might range all the way from unmixed respect and awe to unmitigated resentment. Some welcomed Norwegian ministers with obsequious deference, many with gratitude and pride in the prestige of having a "properly" trained minister in their midst, and still others with ingrained suspicion or hostility. Conflict reared its head most frequently when there arose questions of church organization, the pastor's ecclesiastical authority in the community, and church discipline – these were the shoals upon which many a congregation foundered and split apart. "The pastor's efforts to establish proper church order on the basis of ministerial authority," writes one historian, "were easily construed to be just another attempt to keep the 'common people' in their place."[23] To immigrants filled with the heady sense of newly won freedom from subservience, "there was an almost adolescent delight in the leveling process" and in rebelling against reminders of oppressive social conventions that had existed in rural Norway.[24]

And yet, commonly, "sufficient awe of the clergy remained to prevent the laity from making their criticisms openly, face to face with the pastors."[25] Instead, a relative calm often overlay life within the established congregation. The church members within whom anticlerical and class resentments smoldered often kept quiet, perhaps in the way observed in 1869 by a Glenwood churchgoer in Winneshiek county, Iowa: "Peace is due to the fact that the congregation member laughs up his sleeve and permits the preacher to rule."[26] Another joked about their church life in Buena Vista county, Iowa: "There is no strife here on the issues of slavery or Sunday observance, on the question of cassock or ruff – all is peaceful, but, it is well to note, for the simple reason that there is neither preacher nor sexton located here yet."[27] Aware of the undercurrents of discontent moving beneath the calm, Norwegian ministers stood powerless – beyond delivering tongue-lashing sermons – to stop what the wife of one recounted in 1858 as "slander and gossip circulating about us and always ill will and opposition and grumbling and an ungodly way of living everywhere."[28]

If class feeling eroded the minister's authority, loyalty to the old country community, or *bygd*, further complicated his fragile political influence. The cement holding congregations together often proved too weak when particular church issues exposed divisions of old home-district feeling.[29] Local patriotism – expressed in the feeling of community shared by immigrants from the same district based on their shared dialect, customs of greeting, courtship, drinking, dancing, marriage, burial, and other social patterns – often got in the way of church harmony and mutual respect when church issues aroused debate. These prejudices reared their head, for example, during the bitter theological struggle over predestination. It swept across Norwegian settlements during the 1880s, and in the end warring factions that split off from the ranks of the Norwegian Synod joined other groups to form a new larger United Lutheran Church. The rancorous theological dispute ruptured many a congregation along *bygd* lines, as occurred in the Crow Wing, Minnesota, congregation when most of the recent immigrants from Gausdal, Norway, seceded.[30] Once the predestination controversy spread beyond the clergy to the laity, prejudices of all sorts came to the surface and pulled apart many such congregations. "All the private feuds which had been simmering for years," writes Arthur Paulson, "found outlet in the strife," and, in addition to local rivalries, "it was in many ways a battle between the older immigration and the new."[31]

"The newcomers were a decidedly disturbing element," stated one historian, "for they refused to accept the aristocratic ideas and the benevolent despotism of the clergy in the same spirit that the earlier immigrants had."[32] Conversely, "the older settlers had less and less sympathy each succeeding year with newcomers whose heads were filled with the recent developments in Norwegian life and politics."[33]

The simmering discord first broke into full view when Bjørnstjerne
Bjørnson, the influential but controversial author, visited America in
1880–1881.

Bjørnson's outspoken attacks against the Norwegian State Church
as being an obstacle to democratic freedom and enlightenment had led
many to brand him an atheist and a heretic. During his first months of
travel—mainly spent in the East—he voiced reluctance, despite their
urgings, to visit the Midwest and speak before his immigrant countrymen: "No. I shall never come to the West to that hive of preachers."
But ultimately Bjørnson consented to take up the battle against what
he termed "the spiritual tyranny of the Norwegian ministers."[34]
Throughout a rigorous speaking schedule during the winter months of
1880, his presence in the Middle West ignited bitter attacks by Norwegian Synod clergy, who pressed their parishioners to boycott
Bjørnson's lectures. Individuals of liberal bent lined up in his defense
while conservatives assailed Bjørnson's beliefs, character, and motives. With many new arrivals being anticlerical or out of sympathy
with the older cultural forces, and with the secular weight of the
Norwegian-American press rising to an influence equaling that once
held by the clergy, the embattled pastors feared Bjørnson and his message. But notwithstanding the effective opposition of many Synod pastors, Norwegian immigrants thronged to hear him speak. Bjørnson believed that this was due to the large number of Norwegian Americans
living outside any church: "The ministers keep their sheep together;
those who come are the unchurched."[35]

These, the numerous "unchurched," constituted a major reason
why the votes cast from Norwegian-American communities seemed
unresponsive to high-church versus low-church differences. Church
membership in name only bespoke a pattern gloomily familiar to pastors in Norway. Pastor Herman Preus wrote in 1863 of the deplorable
condition of his brethren's spiritual lives, based on an acquaintance
with thirty-five immigrant congregations. From his perspective, there
prevailed "neglect of, indifference to, and contempt for the Word of
God." For, apart from the faithful core of parishioners in each congregation, the remainder regarded church attendance as "unnecessary"
except when "they commune or are godparents."[36] Even brief as his
visit was, Bjørnson quickly appreciated the religious indifference of his
emigrated countrymen: "They accept the church as any other business
enterprise: they let themselves be married by it, have their children
baptized and confirmed; they let their dead be buried by the church because it is quite appropriate, and they pay for it; they also contribute
to the demands of the church; but there is no real relationship. In the

cities, many – I dare say in the large cities – most of the Scandinavians have kept apart from any church, and of course do not have a church wedding or have their children baptized."[37]

This view is consistent with the observations of others and with available census information. "It is a notable fact," reports historian Gerhard Lee Belgum, "that virtually all the strength of Norwegian-American Lutheranism came out of the specifically Norwegian-American settlements. When immigrants did not choose to live in those primary centers of Norwegian-American life, they were generally lost to Lutheranism and often to any church at all."[38] That the throngs of unchurched immigrants rose both in urban areas and outside the strongholds of Norwegian settlements is supported by data presented in Table 1. Two-thirds of Norwegian Americans nationwide failed to become baptized members of Norwegian Lutheran churches and nearly eight out of ten in cities swelled the ranks of the unchurched. Even in states heavily settled by Norwegians, a minority of urban and only a bare majority or near majority of rural Norwegian Americans became nominally affiliated with one of the Norwegian Lutheran synods.[39] Proportionately fewer became baptized church members in the newer settlements, evidently reflecting a split between older and newer immigrants. In the newer northwestern counties of Minnesota, for instance, the Norwegian Lutheran churches in 1906 contained 31 percent fewer baptized members than churches in the older Norwegian-settled southeastern counties.[40] Likewise, fewer of the confirmed members in newer settlements partook annually of communion.[41]

Indifference proved endemic within church congregations as well. Most had brought a Christianity in name only from back home, where one minister said that "the Church slumbers sweetly in the arms of the State."[42] Consequently, many failed to understand or accept obligations on their part toward keeping a free congregation alive. Caja Munch wrote back home in 1857 of her and her pastor husband's sad disappointment: "It is not, as we thought before we left Norway, an intense longing to hear the Word of the Lord and a craving to partake of His holy gifts that has moved these people to join together in a Christian congregation, but it was just to get their children baptized, to take Communion once in the fall and once in the spring, like they 'done at home,' as they say, and now and then to go to church and hear a sermon."[43]

Religious apathy, regional antagonism, tension between early and recent immigrants, and memories of social injustice had thus largely neutralized the direct political impact of pietist-liturgical values. Fur-

Table 1 Estimated immigrants baptized in Norwegian-American
Lutheran churches during the 1920s, in the United States and in upper
midwestern states by urban and rural residency[a]

Location	Estimated Norwegian Americans 1920	Number Baptized Members 1926	Estimated Percentage Baptized Members
United States	1,526,324	505,051	33.1
Urban	595,349	124,791	21.0
Rural	930,975	380,260	40.8
Wisconsin	220,261	103,067	46.8
Urban	65,580	26,946	41.1
Rural	154,681	75,422	48.8
Iowa	93,331	48,522	52.0
Urban	20,549	9,009	43.8
Rural	72,782	39,513	54.3
Minnesota	419,135	171,439	40.9
Urban	137,252	37,400	27.2
Rural	281,883	134,039	47.6

[a]Percentages calculated by dividing the number of baptized members of Norwegian Lutheran
churches in 1926 by the number of first, second, and estimated third generation Norwegian
Americans in 1920 within each given geographic area. The number of Norwegian-born and
their children was derived from the 1920 United States Census. For the third-generation
proportion, as of 1920, the factor of 49.168 percent was added based on the calculation established by Norlie, *History of the Norwegian People in America*, 312–313. Urban and rural baptized membership data came from U.S. Bureau of the Census, *Religious Bodies, 1926, Vol. II:
Separate Denominations* (Washington, D.C., 1929), 758–759.

ther complicating things, those strongly committed to low-church
values had expressed a pietism entwined in the larger Old World
liberal reform struggle waged by commoners against officialdom over
questions of traditional values and economic privilege.[44] But in
America the politically untutored pietist newcomer found something
different – a baffling two-party system where evangelical and economic
reform impulses did not unambiguously dwell together in the same
party. He found the Republican party nicely infused with evangelical
reformers but also dominated by old stock "Yankee" upper classes. In
this uncongenial arena of political choices, whatever evangelical ardor
Norwegians felt for the Republican party often came to be neutralized
by remembered class animosities when issues of economic and social
status intruded in elections. The adherence of numerous Norwegians
to the progressive wing of the Republican party in parts of the Midwest probably indicated desires to express jointly these economic and
religious reform impulses.

III

While old-country divisions described above made for Norwegian settlements with internal discord and for pastors with uncertain political clout, other forces were at work creating disagreement among the settlements about Republican party candidates. They developed from how the immigrants' cultural background converged with the political situation that each major wave of Norwegians faced during their initial years after arriving in America. The juncture of these characteristics created different "political generations" among Norwegian Americans as each new wave of citizens entered political life.[45]

The historian Kendric Babcock arrived at the conviction that the party preferences of Scandinavians drew in large measure from "the great questions agitating the country at the time they became citizens."[46] Their initial participation in political affairs became the touchstone for viewing subsequent politics, and it stamped each settlement with a distinctive political identity as it moved through time. As psychological membership in a party lengthened, party identification became a political force in its own right, helping Norwegian-American voters to ward off challenges of new events and new parties with increasing ease. Newcomers and the offspring of earlier arrivals then perpetuated these local voting traditions by being likely to accept the politics of respected Norwegians who had built the settlement.[47]

The circumstances through which Norwegian communities passed were sufficiently distinct to bring about three successive political generations. The first comprised the older cluster of settlements whose members had journeyed from a Norway of weak economic opportunity, moderate religiosity, and lack of political sophistication, only to become immersed in the political life of the nation when issues surrounding the Civil War were defining alternatives and alignments. Up until the mid-1850s, as noted, Norwegian immigrants leaned politically toward the Democratic party, owing largely to the nativism and aristocratic stigma of the Whigs, the third-party weakness of the Free Soil party, and the Democratic party's name and traditional Jacksonian regard for the "common man." But at the same time Norwegian immigrants felt increasingly uneasy about the dominant influence of a southern aristocracy within the party and its acceptance of slavery's permanence, and they disliked associating politically with the Catholic Irish and Germans who crowded into its ranks. So when, after 1854, the largely Protestant Republican party emerged—an apparent bulwark against the threat posed to free men, democratic liberties, and northern rights by a controlling aristocracy of slaveholders—the political situation carried Norwegians into the new party. The ensuing Civil War solidified their votes.[48]

A second political generation took form among the Norwegian settlements that established themselves during the years 1865–1880. Here immigrants were leaving a Norway of uncertain economic prospects where an exploding population was quickly absorbing the opportunities for economic expansion, where landowning peasants were becoming politicized, and where the clergy were growing more separate from and in less contact with an assertive peasantry. These arrivals filled the new immigrant areas of western Wisconsin, north-central Iowa, and west-central Minnesota. Their settlements, baptized in political waters alive with vicarious Civil War memories and moral enthusiasm but darkened by vexing postwar problems climaxed by the Panic of 1873, shared a greater ambivalence towards Republicanism. Norwegian-American editors continued to equate Republicanism with patriotism and keep anti-Democratic feeling alive by publicizing the menace of Catholicism and Irish Catholic victories at the polls.[49] They had not yet begun to capitalize politically on the drinking propensities of the Germans and Irish because temperance sentiment still left Norwegian settlements unaffected.[50] But now the confrontation between Republican and Democratic parties no longer seemed so clearly a conflict of democracy versus aristocracy or Protestant versus Catholic. Postwar economic problems followed by the Panic of 1873 and its aftermath gave rise to Democrats espousing both anti-monopoly themes and the currency inflation ideas embodied in Greenbackism, for which its congressional candidates won a million votes in 1878. And these economic issues, despite successful preemptive efforts by Republicans to dissipate much discontent, limited Norwegian confidence in Republicanism and brought some falloff in the newer settlements' Republican vote.

The third-generation settlements came into being with the massive wave of immigration that rose about 1880 and ebbed in the later 1890s. Those emigrating at this time had lived among an increasingly politicized citizenry in Norway marked by religious indifference and growing urban secular influences. Among their settlements in northwestern Minnesota and beyond into the Dakotas, farmers heard increasing complaints about high interest rates for scarce farm capital in a time of financial deflation and declining wheat prices. With wheat farmers hit by overproduction and decreasing earnings, by increasing mortgage uncertainty and decreasing hope for profits, farming concerns loomed ever larger within a political atmosphere of growing disenchantment with the Republican party. The Republican party "has

Date of Settlement and
Republican Presidential Support

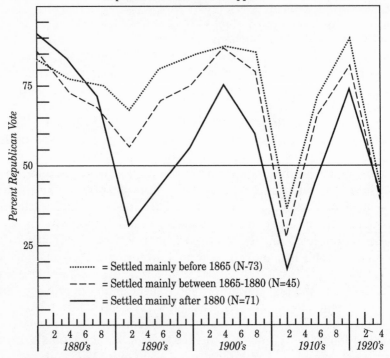

Figure 7. Republican share of presidential vote in Norwegian settlements of the Upper Midwest, grouped according to their estimated period of predominant settlement. Precinct returns are less complete before 1890.

outlived itself," the recent immigrant read more frequently in the Norwegian language press, and "what there is left of it does not bear the shadow of a semblance to what it was in the days of Abraham Lincoln."[51] Anti-Democratic party feelings still held firm among Norwegians, reinforced by an increase in temperance sentiment and stiffened by rising anti-Catholic agitation. But the G.O.P., perhaps feeling safe in the Norwegians' aversion to the Democratic party or thinking the threat of an agrarian third party unlikely, or perhaps believing themselves unable to alleviate the farmers' troubles, pursued an unresponsive course – risking greater discontent and the uncertainties of waning Norwegian confidence.

These three perspectives took on impressive political force, as Figure 7 makes clear. By 1888, a visible change was taking shape in presidential alignments, and by the 1892 election the storm broke. Clusters of like-minded Norwegian settlements brought about a massive and enduring realignment. The oldest settlements held steadfast behind the Republican party while Republicanism weakened among the more vulnerable second-generation settlements. Among the most recent settlements, however, Republicans suffered true disaster; votes for G.O.P. candidates fell 20 to 35 percentage points below those of the other two groups. Consequences of the realignment remained visible all the way into the 1920s. In many areas the Republican party had lost its singular claim to the Norwegian vote.

Economic conditions joined with freshly recalled old-country antagonisms to shape the third political generation and, when it did, the Norwegians' defection far exceeded that of other ethnic groups living nearby. Lower average land values[52] and economically fragile conditions in the recent farming areas existed at the very time when agricultural and class grievances assumed importance. Consequently, these settlements least psychologically wedded to the Republicans expectedly defected to third parties. In this atmosphere of agricultural hard times and anti-monopolist feeling, old-country agrarian animosities made themselves felt in the political sphere.

Conversely, in older Norwegian settlements the shifting political climate only minimally affected party alignment. With their agriculture by 1890 reasonably diversified and financially stable, and their Republican identification firmly rooted in cultural more than economic issues, past agrarian antagonisms from Norway had died out, unnourished as a political force. Compounding the inertia of their longstanding Republican loyalties and the absence of any vital issue in these settlements, there was another reason that few Norwegians felt disposed to turn against their local Republican organizations. "Their leading men," a magazine editor commented, "hold numerous county offices and other positions as members of the Republican party, and do not easily make new connections. . . . Party organizations are the result of time and important events and only time and events can change them."[53]

IV

Even given the influences noted, most differences in voting patterns of Norwegian settlements remain unexplained. The date of a settlement's establishment proved a consistent influence, but even this, when combined with other variables such as percentage of eligible Norwegian voters, percentage of estimated Lutheran pietist church membership, and percentage of small town population, accounts statistically for less than one-half of the total variation in votes. Apparently more elusive factors played significant roles.[54] Not a settlement's percentage of Norwegian-born voters,[55] not its proportion of urban residents,[56] not the predominant Norwegian regional origins (east Norway or west Norway) of its residents[57] corresponds to any but merely ephemeral differences in the Republican presidential votes of the new settlements.

State boundaries, however, do appear to have helped diversify Norwegian voting in the Upper Middle West. Each state expressed a distinctive pattern of political orientation, a framework for raising and resolving issues. In part this was a matter of each state's rules for voting and for operating government or organizing state parties. In part it may have been the ideological tone of state politics, although all three states in the later period under discussion generally were known as "progressive." In great part it was a matter of who rose to leadership and what strength the important voter groups possessed.[58]

In this last respect, it is of special significance that population patterns differed considerably among the three states. Minnesota, being the youngest and a state on the western periphery of the Middle West, received her primary settlement following the Civil War. Consequently, a larger proportion of foreign-born persons lived in Minnesota at a later date than in the two older states. In 1910, immigrants and the native children of immigrants made up 72 percent of Minnesota's residents compared to 67 percent in Wisconsin and 41 percent in Iowa. Of perhaps greater importance, nationalities distributed themselves quite unevenly over the three states. True enough, the same four groups—German, Norwegian, Swedish, and Irish—comprised fully two-thirds of those of foreign birth or parentage in the three states combined. But in Wisconsin 34 percent of the total population was German in background, compared to 19 percent in Minnesota and only 16 percent in Iowa. Conversely, those of Norwegian background made up 13 percent of Minnesota's people, with only 7 percent in Wisconsin and 3 percent in Iowa. Swedes amounted to a far stronger contingent in Minnesota compared to either Iowa or Wisconsin, while proportionately larger numbers of first- or second-generation Irish lived in Iowa. These differences unavoidably shaped the vote-getting strategies of state political parties.[59]

Politically, each state rapidly acquired its own dynamic and it showed in the presidential votes as presented in Figure 8. Iowa's Norwegian precincts led those of the other two states in their Republican loyalty, save in 1912 when they defected to Theodore Roosevelt's Bull Moose candidacy. Wisconsin's settlements proved weaker in their Republicanism except in the elections of 1912 and 1924, when they sup-

Interstate Differences in
Presidential Voting

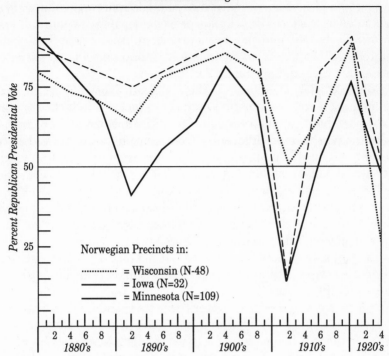

Figure 8. Republican share of presidential vote in Norwegian settlements of three upper midwestern states. Precinct returns are
less complete before 1890.

ported Senator LaFollette in his failed bids for the presidency. By far
the greatest difference, however, showed itself in Minnesota's Norwegian settlements. Their Republican votes slipped fast throughout
the 1880s and fell sharply with the election of 1892. Thereafter,
through World War I, Republican voting in Minnesota's settlements
lagged behind that in the adjoining older states.

Even within the same generation of settlements, state differences
expressed themselves. This can be seen in Norwegian-American townships lying near the point where the borders of Wisconsin, Iowa, and
Minnesota join. Populism's appeal in the 1890s influenced the "three
corners" settlements differently. Even more striking, two Norwegian
favorites, Robert LaFollette and Theodore Roosevelt, failed to attract
voters of the different settlements uniformly. During the 1912 election,
Roosevelt's unchallenged popularity in northeastern Iowa drew large
numbers of votes away from the Republican incumbent, William

Howard Taft. But in southwestern Wisconsin and to a slight degree in southeastern Minnesota, Senator LaFollette apparently reduced Norwegian defections from Taft by his personal campaign against Roosevelt. Similarly, settlements broke ranks in 1924 when LaFollette mounted his third-party compaign, only to find uneven success in organizing his race and appealing for votes.

Gubernatorial elections further shaped Norwegian-American alignments, for the settlements could not escape the influence of state issues, personalities, and prevailing conditions. Norwegian communities thereupon reacted differently from state to state and did so for different reasons.[60] In all three states, for example, the Republican party continued dominant, but each faced particular challenges from disaffected reform elements.[61] Republican candidates won 53 percent or more of the vote in half the sixteen contests in Iowa and Minnesota between 1865 and 1896, while in Wisconsin similar pluralities were achieved only one-third of the time. Republican prospects scarcely improved in fourteen subsequent elections. From 1898 through 1924 party percentages rose in Iowa but declined slightly in Wisconsin and tumbled in Minnesota.[62]

How many of the eligible voters cast their ballots in Norwegian-American settlements also differed from state to state. Take, for example, voter turnout in elections for governor (Figure 9). In Minnesota, voting interest within Norwegian areas remained stronger than the state average until the end of World War I, while in the Norwegian settlements of Wisconsin voter turnout more closely resembled that of the state's entire electorate. Iowa's Norwegian townships, on the other hand, consistently fell behind statewide turnout levels until after 1908.

The lower level of voter interest in Iowa's Norwegian communities likely derived from Norwegians' numerical weakness within the state and from the discouraging effect of election laws. Under the state's franchise requirements, immigrants could vote only after they officially became American citizens. To be eligible in Minnesota or Wisconsin, on the other hand, an immigrant need only to have taken out his first papers, an act that certified his intention to become an American citizen.[63]

Republican loyalty among voters, varying from one state to the next, underscored differences. Norwegian townships gave similar levels of Republican support in the three states during only two periods in the era studied here – in the early 1880s and again in 1916 (Figure 10). The first instance marked the last years of the old post-Civil War coalitions, and the second occurred just before American en-

Interstate Variations in Turnout

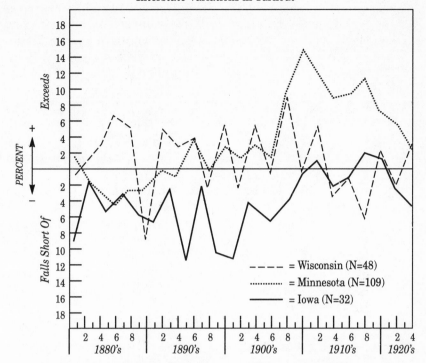

Figure 9. Extent to which voter turnout in Norwegian settlements of each state differed from that of the entire state in elections for governor. Precinct returns are less complete before 1890.

try into World War I, when a respite in Progressive fervor momentarily calmed Republican factionalism. In addition, the direction of their support for political parties moved only twice in unison, once in 1891–1892 when their votes simultaneously pitched downward under the weight of demoralized Republicanism and third-party fervor, and again in 1912 when the Bull Moose candidacy of Theodore Roosevelt attracted widespread Norwegian-American support.

Comparing differences in party preferences to differences in turnout levels reveals deeper contrasts. Voters in the Norwegian settlements of Iowa – a comparative minority within the state – proved to be least interested in voting, although they most strongly supported Republican candidates. Conversely, voters living in Minnesota's Norwegian townships least reliably favored Republican candidates but most regularly showed up at the polls to vote. This would seem to bear out the familiar idea that greater party competition promotes greater voter interest. Evidently, in Minnesota, greater and more turbulent

Republican Gubernatorial Support

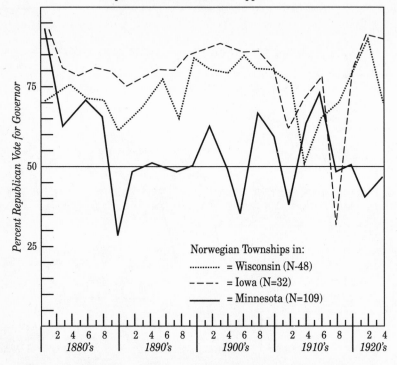

Figure 10. Republican share of vote for governor in Norwegian settlements of three upper midwestern states. Precinct returns are
less complete before 1890.

third-party competition for Norwegian votes enlivened partisan interest.

Even when Republican strength declined in the Upper Midwest,
however, Democrats rarely became the beneficiaries of Norwegian
discontent. Most often the settlements turned instead to various third-
party causes. Only three times, when Minnesota's Democratic party
ran candidates of Scandinavian background for governor, did Norwegian settlements cast large numbers of votes for the Democrats.[64]
Fundamentally, Norwegians could not disassociate the Democratic
party from Roman Catholicism.

CHAPTER 3

Fears, Hopes, New Times

Scandinavians, an observer pointed out in 1892, "are Protestant enough to satisfy the most fastidious Catholic-hater, for a Catholic in Norway or Sweden is a rare, suspicious object."[1] Although dormant in their Lutheran homeland, the immigrants' unyielding Protestantism forced itself to the surface as Norwegians confronted America's pluralist political makeup. "Everywhere and always they are uncompromising enemies of the Roman Catholic Church," wrote historian Kendric Babcock in 1914, adding that "so strong is this feeling that it colors, consciously or unconsciously, their relations in politics and society in the United States."[2] This low tolerance for Catholicism stemmed less from "knowledge or close observation," he noted, than from what amounted to "an instinct, coming down from Reformation times" when the faith was banned from Norway.[3]

Not until 1845 did legal tolerance extend there to Catholics or members of other sects, and for decades Norway denied non-Lutherans the political right to hold office. Feelings ran deep. When, for instance, the Catholics set up a missionary boardinghouse in the northern province of Finnmark, Bayard Taylor, an American traveler in 1857, reported that nearby villagers "regard it with the greatest suspicion and distrust" and "suspect that the ultimate object is the overthrow of their inherited, venerated, and deeply-rooted Lutheran faith."[4] This feeling against the Catholic Church Taylor witnessed personally, for when the boat on which he was a passenger took on board the Catholic bishop in charge of the mission, "loud and angry exclamations" soon broke forth on deck. "Two of our Norwegian *savans* stood before the bishop, and one of them, with a face white with rage, was furiously vociferating: 'It is not true! It is not true! Norway is a free country!' 'In this respect, it is not free,' answered the bishop, with more coolness than I thought he could have shown, under such circumstances: 'You know very well that no one can hold office except those who belong to your State Church – neither a Catholic, nor a Methodist, nor a Quaker: whereas in France, as I have said, a Protestant may even become a minister of the Government.' 'But we do not believe in the Catholic faith: – we will have nothing to do with it!' screamed the Norwegian."[5] The bishop shortly thereupon retreated to his cabin, with the parting comment that Norway "is behind most other countries of Europe" in tolerating other religious beliefs.

I

In the politics of the United States, Scandinavian anti-Catholicism thrived; it expressed itself primarily in a political hatred of the American Irish.[6] "I have heard it cited, not once but a hundred times as a reason for voting the Republican ticket," noted H. H. Boyeson, a Norwegian immigrant literary figure in the 1890s, "that the Irish were all Democrats. It is no use to contradict this assertion, for the sentiment that Democracy and Irish nationality are synonymous terms is so deeply rooted in the Scandinavian agricultural population that it will require . . . a surgical operation to eradicate it."[7] A Scandinavian critic termed as "preposterous" Boyeson's claim that the Scandinavians were Republican because the Irish were Democrats, claiming instead that they had affiliated with Republicans out of kinship with their progressive legislative aims. And yet, the "animosity towards the Irish must be admitted," the critic granted and he found the source of it in the character of the Irish and in their Catholicism. Scandinavians, he stated, found the Irish immigrant "illiterate and indolent, occupying public positions to which neither character nor fitness gave him any particular claim." And on religious grounds, the Scandinavian "fears and denounces" the Catholic religion as a social force that, to him, "means spiritual servility, subordination in matters of conscience to an authority which, with his bold ideas of intellectual liberty, he can never be made to recognize."[8] Most contemporaries, and surely all politicians, agreed that "the whole political organization of the Scandinavians," at bottom, had "chiefly taken place under Republican leadership and in strong opposition to Catholic Irish and South German Democrats."[9]

Ole Rølvaag, in the final two volumes of his immigrant trilogy, explored the veiled hostility corroding relations between Norwegian Lutherans and Irish Catholics living in the Spring Creek settlement. "You will have to find another playmate, Peder," Beret Holm instructs her son.

" 'Why?'

" 'Because you are Norwegian and they are Irish! . . . But likely you don't understand that yet, and I couldn't expect you to.'

" 'They are *people* just the same,' objected Peder sagely, in the utmost candor.

"The mother smiled ever so little.

" 'But they are of another kind. They have another faith. And that is dangerous. For it is with such things as with weeds. The authorities made a terrible mistake when they threw us in with those people. And it is no better for them than it is for us. We should never have had the school together – you can't mix wheat and potatoes in the same bin.' "[10]

As the emotional and imaginative Peder reaches manhood in the 1890s and marries Susie Doheny, an Irish Catholic, his brother cannot contain his bitter embarrassment.

" 'Every place I go people pounce on me, asking me how the Nordlænding is getting along with his Irish wife. They all grin wickedly . . . want to know how it feels to be related to a lot of Catholics . . . how much the pope is taxing you . . . when you're joining in the war on the Protestants –' For a moment Hans could not go on. 'You've disgraced the whole family . . . that's what you've done!' "[11]

These feelings continue to linger beneath the surface of relations in Peder's settlement, eventually erupting again when he explores possibilities in politics as a Republican candidate for county commissioner. His opponent accuses Peder and the Lutheran minister of "scheming to make the whole country Lutheran," while Dennis O'Hara confides to his friend Peder that the "slogan" in his neighborhood is that "no self-respecting Irish Catholic would ever disgrace himself by voting for a Norwegian Lutheran."[12]

The Norwegians in America, therefore, saw no alternative to the Grand Old Party. "The history and record of the Catholic power," wrote one reader to the Chicago *Skandinaven*, "is black, bloodstained and rotten, and cannot bear the light of day. . . . Its sole aim and struggle is to obtain complete power.

"Best to keep politics and religion separate, in general, but as we all know, the Roman Catholic Church is in politics, and on all fours, too;

and whether or not it shall become supreme in this country when it has been repudiated and broken in Europe remains with us to say when we cast our ballots."[13]

Apart from the temperance-minded Archbishop John Ireland of Minnesota, few important American Catholics became involved with the G.O.P. during this era to alter the Norwegian Americans' perception of "Catholic = Democrat." And the Norwegian settlements acted accordingly, allowing little drift toward the political home of most Catholic voters. Between 1880 and 1924, only once—when incumbent Woodrow Wilson ran in 1916—did Democrats successfully attract a sizeable presidential vote—31 percent from midwestern Norwegian settlements. At the opposite extreme, the 1924 Democratic candidate, John Davis, obtained only 3 percent of their vote when many swung behind Robert M. LaFollette's third-party bid for the presidency. Overall, this period of forty-four years witnessed a scant 16 percent of the average Norwegian-American vote going to Democratic presidential candidates.

Because of the uneven presence of Catholic groups across the three states—yet another difference in the states' political cultures—there were political limits on how overt anti-Catholicism might become. Protestant politicians that offended Catholics faced tough sledding in Wisconsin, where Catholics comprised a politically hefty 22 percent of the people. Similarly, Minnesota's 19 percent Catholic residents made them a segment to be treated with care, though Iowa's Catholics, a meager 9 percent of the people, possessed little such retaliatory strength.[14] With the presence of Catholic voters limiting overt anti-Catholicism, the tensions worked their major influence in Democratic-Republican contests when an issue such as prohibition emerged to make clear that Catholic nationalities voted from far different convictions than many Protestant groups.

II

Anti-Catholicism, though perhaps the central coalescing impulse of Norwegian political behavior in America, thrived unevenly among their settlements from one state to another. This can be seen in the region's Norwegian-American encounter with two especially virulent anti-Catholic movements of the period: the American Protective Association and prohibition reform.

Anti-Catholicism in the 1880s, although disorganized and fragmentary, nonetheless grew in strength throughout thickly settled portions of the Midwest. Catholic churches multiplied and the waning force of

Republicanism brought greater power to Irish-American Democratic politicians. Organized anti-Catholic efforts steadily took shape, thriving on local political resentments and anxieties.

In 1887 the most effective of these organizations, the American Protective Association (A.P.A.), drew its first breath in Clinton, Iowa, an urban lumber-processing center on the Mississippi River. Here a city election had turned its incumbent mayor out of office. Convinced that the source of the mayor's defeat lay in Catholic influence over the votes of Irish lumber-mill workers, Henry F. Bowers, a local lawyer, brought the defeated incumbent and several friends together to form a secret political order, the A.P.A. Soon other A.P.A. councils or lodges began to organize in Iowa and surrounding states. Politically the movement's impact proved uncertain, largely as a result of its practice of claiming credit for every Protestant candidate either nominated or elected. But its greater willingness than other anti-Catholic societies to enter politics so publicized and spurred its growth after 1891 as to guarantee that the initials A.P.A. would popularly symbolize all anti-Catholic activities of the era.[15]

By 1893 leaders of the American Protective Association boasted councils in twenty states, and commentators spoke of the "A.P.A. Belt" stretching from Ohio to Nebraska. Although its numerical strength from state to state remains uncertain, indications are that the movement probably flourished most not in Iowa but in Michigan, Ohio, and Minnesota. In its political effects, the A.P.A. pushed the Republican party into a temporizing position, while the Democrats grasped this opportunity to solidify the Catholic vote by lambasting both the secret order and Republican silence on the issue.[16]

Some organizations, such as the Junior Order of United States Mechanics, mixed nativism with their anti-Catholicism by excluding all but native-born Protestants from membership. But in areas with large non-Catholic foreign populations, A.P.A. organizers reacted appropriately. "We cannot see," said the pro-A.P.A. editor of the Loyal American and the North, "why the 'Ole Olesons,' if you please, should be discriminated against, simply because they may not all have been born in the United States."[17] The main deciding principle, such A.P.A. spokesmen insisted, is that Americans owe their allegiance not to "any foreign potentate, i.e. to the pope," but to "the stars and stripes and the institutions over which they wave."[18] The preferred ethnic targets of A.P.A. nativists became strictly the Catholic nationalities—the burgeoning immigrant influx from southern and eastern Europe—"king-ridden, nobility-ridden and priest-ridden"—and most particularly, the visible Irish-American element within the cities.[19]

Scandinavian Americans evidently loomed large within the rank-and-file of the movement. "The Norse or Scandinavian people are hostile to Rome," declared the editor of *Skandinaven*, "because history has taught them to look upon the papacy as the uncompromising enemy of political and religious liberty."[20] "Catholics always co-operate in politics," warned another Norwegian-American editor, for "the chief object of the Catholic church is not the salvation of souls, but the dominion of the world."[21] Frenzied visions of Catholic political conspiracy flourished in the heated atmosphere of the A.P.A. Another Norwegian-American editor exclaimed that "The Church of Rome, that ancient and bitter foe of the [Protestant] church, is plotting and bidding for power in our fair land, [and] is only waiting for the time when she may again manifest the old spirit of the inquisition and the massacre of St. Bartholomew's Eve, and the butchery of the first American Protestant colony in Florida."[22] As for the Irish, perhaps most Norwegian Americans accepted as unimpeachable doctrine the A.P.A. message that responsible Protestants remained opposed–and legitimately so–to "Roman Catholicism in politics and the Irish alone carry it there."[23]

Signs of expanding Irish-Catholic control over municipal governments had multiplied during the 1870s and 1880s. Irish mayors for the first time achieved election in Pittsburgh, Boston, Jersey City, Buffalo, and Chicago. Furthermore, it was claimed, the number of Irish officeholders everywhere far exceeded their proportion of the citizenry.[24] Norwegian Americans felt themselves ethnically superior to Irishmen, whom they looked upon as intemperate, boisterous, and industrious only when seeking political office. "The country would be just as well off," concluded *Skandinaven*'s editor, "if fewer offices were held by Irishmen, and more by Norsemen. The Norsemen know how to make, enforce, and obey laws, and that is the sum and substance of good citizenship, clean politics, true statesmanship, and successful state building."[25]

Accordingly, Norwegian Americans tended to expect only the worst of those they encountered personally. Paul Knaplund, a recent Norwegian arrival at the turn of the century, recalled his first such experience while working as a telephone lineman. "The members of the crew ate their noonday meal at the home of a farmer, referred to by Hans Christ [with whom he had lived as a hired hand] as 'that damn Irishman.' For the first time the newcomer, curious to meet people so unflatteringly described, entered a house where Norwegian was not spoken." A woman of the house noticed that Knaplund "didn't know how to ask for anything," and consequently "waited on him assiduously," a fact that Knaplund mentioned to Hans Christ later that evening. To this Christ "grudgingly" replied that some might not be so bad, "but, of course, they were all Catholics, and that was enough to damn anyone."[26]

A.P.A. organizers recognized, and overtly appealed to, this deep-seated sentiment. A typical broadside claimed that "the Scandinavians in Chicago will, at the next election, unite their voting strength with the loyal Americans. With the aid of Chicago's 85,000 A.P.A. boys, they will crush the political life out of the gang of Irish conspirators who have controlled the city for years."[27] Meanwhile, Norwegian A.P.A. spokesmen such as editor Luth. Jaeger of *The North* reminded readers that "by virtue of their numbers and political activity the Irish Americans have wedged themselves so firmly into our social fabric that they are treated as a privileged class."[28] When a Minneapolis spokesman for Irish Americans retaliated by expressing prejudice of his own against the Norwegians' "ancestry of pirates and free-booters" and "plundering bands," the *Loyal American's* A.P.A. editor tartly replied that "the Scandinavian countries, unlike Ireland, have never been controlled by an Italian clique. Her sons in America can swear allegiance to this country without a mental reservation in favor of the pope. Give us the old Viking blood every time."[29]

Only fragmentary clues remain about specific Norwegian participation from state to state, and what does exist relates mainly to Minnesota's experience.[30] The state's particular Scandinavian strength, one suspects, may well account for the A.P.A.'s more overt emergence in Minnesota than in Iowa or Wisconsin.

In the Twin Cities, A. P.A. organizers concentrated not on St. Paul, where large numbers of Catholics lived, but on Minneapolis, where Scandinavians constituted over half the foreign-born residents. A.P.A. activity began in earnest in late 1892 when one of the American Protective Association's newspapers, the *Loyal American*, began operation in Minneapolis. Under editor Edward J. Doyle, the chief Twin Cities organizer, the small four-page publication swelled beyond a few hundred subscribers to become within a year an eight-page newspaper boasting an average weekly circulation of 17,550.[31] Then, indicating the direction of its political appeals, Doyle in early 1894 merged into his publication an eight-page local Scandinavian newspaper, *The North*. Founded in 1889 and known as the other most fiercely anti-Catholic newspaper in the city, *The North*, according to Doyle, represented a half-million Minnesota Protestants by virtue of its being "the only newspaper in the United States devoted to Scandinavian interests, printed in the English language."[32]

Not surprisingly, it was a Norwegian, Ole Byorum, who joined with Edward Doyle to provide the leadership of A.P.A. efforts in Minneapolis. This "foreigner from the regions of the midnight sun," as the antagonistic *Irish Standard*'s editor labeled him, was "the cockalorum of Apaism and . . . grand master of the Minnesota Orangemen to boot. Ole is an undertaker by profession," sneered the editor, though conceding him to be "an intelligent, wide awake fellow" who "does not come under the category of 'ignorant' Scandinavians."[33]

Efforts by Byorum and others combined with the rising tide of anti-Catholicism to make 1893 the year when the greatest number of new A.P.A. councils formed in Minnesota.[34] Plainly alarmed about the many Scandinavians joining "Know-Nothing secret organizations to keep Irish Catholics from getting any appointive or elective office," the editor of the *Irish Standard* warned of "retaliation by the Irish in other places if the Scandinavians of Minnesota introduce religion into politics, as some of them are doing already."[35] But A.P.A. enthusiasm remained disproportionately high among Norwegian Americans as Minnesota entered the election year of 1894. When editors of the city's leading Republican daily, the Minneapolis *Journal*, sought to plumb A.P.A. strength in Minneapolis and the state, they reported a state A.P.A. organizer to have said that "ninety per cent of the Scandinavian vote is in the order or in active sympathy with it." The article concluded that the A.P.A. numbered among its members "about 11,000 in Minneapolis and 9,000 in St. Paul," and, of these, "all hands admit that its principal strength is in Scandinavian quarters."[36]

Although the St. Paul *Daily Globe*, the *Irish Standard*, and other spokesmen for Democratic and Catholic interests agreed about Scandinavian involvement, they continually discounted the A.P.A. as being neither a large nor a rapidly growing movement. After all, as Archbishop John Ireland noted, Catholics "cannot be expected to take notice of every fleeting wind that passes over the field of American politics."[37]

Simultaneously, in reaction to A.P.A. activity, spokesmen worked to stir indignation and perhaps anti-Scandinavian feeling among Catholics. They printed reports during the summer of 1894 of Scandinavians abandoning the American Protective Association "like rats," and of a "Knute Nelson lodge" disbanding operations in a northern Minnesota town. These the *Loyal American*'s editor chalked up as pure fabrication put out at the "dictation" of the Romish hierarchy, even though indications pointed to the A.P.A. tide as indeed having crested in Minnesota.[38]

In typical fashion, the A.P.A. tried to throw its weight into the

1894 election campaign by publicizing each candidate's religious affiliation. An "RC" printed behind a person's name identified the opposition, while a "P" signified an approved "Protestant." When the voting results showed large Republican gains, the editor of the *Loyal American and the North* exulted over the number of Protestant victories it had supposedly engineered. Ultimately, when it turned out that Republican candidates had won all state offices and swept the entire slate of Minneapolis city offices, the editor praised the Mill City as one of the few undominated by Catholics and congratulated the Scandinavian population as a "Minneapolis safeguard against the encroachments of Romanism."[39]

Despite the bluster, the movement had by 1894 spent itself. Noise and controversy notwithstanding, A.P.A. leaders had little to show for their efforts. Within three months of the close of the campaign, the editor of the *Loyal American and the North* gave up and moved out of state. The newspaper ceased publication a few weeks later.[40]

The A.P.A. movement no doubt had drawn into its ranks disproportionate numbers of Norwegians and other Scandinavians. But apart from helping solidify Norwegian-American animus against the Democratic party, the movement's impact must be considered negligible.

Anti-Catholicism constituted only one influence on the Norwegian-American vote, albeit a major one that cannot easily be distinguished from one such as loyalty to the Republican party. When Knute Nelson ran for governor of Minnesota in 1892, who can say whether Norwegian voters took cues primarily from Nelson's support by anti-Catholic organizations, his Republican label, his backing by the powerful Grand Army of the Republic, the Irish Catholicism of his Democratic opponent, or the fact that he was himself of Norwegian birth? Complicating things further, even A.P.A. spokesmen could do little to hold within Republican ranks Norwegian-American farmers caught up in the politics of hard times. In northwestern Minnesota, Scandinavian Populists even sometimes joined Catholic Democrats to overthrow Republican rule. As will be seen, this happened time and again throughout the 1890s in Otter Tail county, the banner county of the farmers' movement.

The A.P.A. had revealed itself as unable to become a real power in a heavily Scandinavian state such as Minnesota; it made no apparent headway at all in the political life of Wisconsin and Iowa. Still, anti-Catholicism remained alive among Norwegian Americans as they faced another issue – prohibition reform. After all, Norwegian Americans and other foreign- and native-born Protestants shared the widely held opinion that most of America's saloonkeepers were Catholics.

III

"One of the most serious errors of the Republican party," complained an Iowa Republican editor in 1867, is "the party's exercise of its immense power to maintain and carry the legion of social and moral 'isms' that have not wherewith to maintain themselves at present."[41] The most powerful of all came to be temperance. Espoused by the young pre-Civil War Republican party, it revived with even greater vigor at the war's end. Although it became an embarrassment to many and weakened party strength, influential Republican elements succeeded in keeping the issue alive and in the forefront of reform causes.

Norwegians have often been numbered among the strongest supporters of prohibition. The principal reason for this attraction may be open to question, but one might cite the influence of Protestant "evangelical" attempts to "improve" the social environment and strains of anti-urban and anti-Catholic feeling brought over from the old country. These ordinarily overrode whatever irritation Norwegians felt toward the doses of nativism that Yankee leaders injected into anti-liquor crusades.

"In all matters relating to temperance and temperance legislation," wrote an observer of the political scene in 1914, "the Scandinavian voters have almost invariably been on the side of restriction of the saloon and the liquor traffic."[42] Although this exaggerates the point, even casual reading in the midwestern history of the movement reveals a lengthy list of well-known Norwegian anti-saloon leaders. It seems no coincidence that in 1919 Andrew Volstead, the Norwegian-American congressman from western Minnesota, sponsored the National Prohibition Enforcement Act to implement the Eighteenth Amendment.[43] When Prohibitionist party candidates occasionally won legislative office, they often were Norwegian Americans. Furthermore, Knute Nelson, the first Norwegian-born governor of Minnesota and the first Norwegian-born United States senator, was a leader of the dry forces in the Senate.[44] Hundreds of temperance societies formed within Norwegian church congregations to stamp out the evil of alcohol and the institutional means that supported it. At the same time, temperance organizations unconnected with the church (the Good Templars and the Women's Christian Temperance Union, for example) attracted numerous Norwegians.[45]

Temperance sentiment had not always ranked high among Norwegian Americans. Until the early 1870s, the Norwegian-American press largely regarded "the temperance agitation," in the words of historian Arlow Andersen, as "a minor movement aiming at an impossible solution."[46] *Skandinaven* gave little attention to the issue, for, while lamenting the "results of drunkenness," its editors viewed it as a moral rather than a legal question.[47] Perhaps reflecting the prevailing Lutheran Church idea that man's depravity left little hope for movements promising greater perfectibility of society, it took a while for most Norwegians to regard temperance as something other than a personal moral and social problem.

"A dozen years ago," wrote one observer of Minneapolis' Scandinavian temperance organizations in 1892, "there was no temperance movement worthy of the name." But now he could report that "although a large proportion of the liquor sold in this city is retailed by Scandinavian hands and poured down Scandinavian throats, still a decided and ever growing current has been running in the opposite direction over the last ten years."[48] Once feeling shifted, Norwegian abstinence organizations rapidly proliferated and many voters backed local option, county option, and state prohibition measures. Of the major statewide referenda submitted to midwestern voters on prohibition or its enforcement (Iowa, 1882 and 1917; Minnesota, 1918; and Wisconsin, 1920), the returns from Norwegian localities repeatedly displayed clear majorities in their favor.

This expressed enthusiasm can easily be exaggerated, however. Temperance thinking did not perfectly correlate with being Norwegian, and interest in such matters by Norwegians varied from one state to the next. Prohibition party candidates attracted few votes in Norwegian settlements. Prohibition referenda fared better but did not escape opposition. Fully 80 percent of the ballots cast in Iowa's heavily Norwegian townships favored an 1882 prohibition referendum, but by the time of the 1917 referendum this majority had slipped to 63 percent. In Minnesota, Norwegian settlements gave 67 percent of their votes for a similar measure in 1918 while Norwegian areas of Wisconsin mustered but 61 percent in favor of the state's Prohibition Enforcement Act of 1920. A few individual townships, in fact, cast majorities in the opposite direction. In two of Iowa's twenty-four Norwegian-American townships most voters opposed the referendum in 1882, but by 1917 this had grown to six out of twenty-six townships. The 1918 prohibition referendum in Minnesota found majority votes cast against it in only five of 109 Norwegian precincts, while in Wisconsin eight of the forty-eight Norwegian precincts opposed prohibition enforcement. This occurred often enough to make the relationship worth looking at.

At least two sources contributed when Norwegian Americans divided on the prohibition issue. First, ambivalence in old country viewpoints toward drinking revealed Norwegian attitudes to be not fixed but evolving. Second, anti-liquor issues stirred statewide politics in Iowa more than in Minnesota and Wisconsin and consequently sharpened divisions among Iowa's Norwegian settlements along these lines.

Enthusiasm in Norway for temperance had developed slowly. Despite widely reported public drunkenness that followed removal in 1816 of restrictions on the private right to distill liquor, rural farmers for some time greeted temperance agitation with indifference. In part this derived from their lingering resentment against the towns, which had for so long held exclusive distilling privileges.[49] Even as the per capita consumption of alcohol soared to its peak in 1833, farmer legislators continued to guard jealously the farmer's right to distill his strong potato spirits. But by 1845 a growing temperance movement pressed by evangelical believers among the professional upper classes convinced enough legislators that the alarming use of alcohol should be arrested.[50] The parliament outlawed small stills and required distillers to sell either to authorized inns or directly to the customer. Within a decade, brandy consumption had been cut in half and fewer than fifty of the more than 1,300 earlier distilleries remained in business.[51] Yet alcohol use persisted in Norway. Among many rural dwellers, traditional social drinking continued to be an accepted part of wedding and baptism celebrations and, occasionally, of funerals.[52]

Weaker temperance feeling among townsmen further divided Norwegian opinion. As in urban areas of the United States, temperance advocates in Norway had to concede in 1891 that the liquor traffic "is entrenched in the cities, from which, apparently, it cannot be dislodged without making a much harder battle than any yet waged. At present only one city, Haugesund (population 5,000), absolutely prohibits all intoxicants."[53] In Christiania, only with the cholera scare of 1892 did greater numbers of people evidently abandon "the usual Sunday drinking and cardplaying" for church.[54] Even by 1911, an American traveler who examined Scandinavia's handling of the liquor traffic reported that "never in her whole life . . . had she seen such steady-going hard drinking as in a steamer that plies between two prohibition towns." "I saw so much drunkenness, indeed, while in urban Norway and rural Sweden, that I was tempted sometimes to doubt the evidence of my own eyes and ears, and to think that those who seemed to me drunk were in reality sober."[55]

A third influence – one that paralleled urban-rural differences – had to do with the weakness of temperance sentiment within the official clergy. Cultured and academically educated, the government-appointed clergy persisted in their acceptance of convivial drinking despite the challenge from evangelical and "Free Church" temperance elements.[56] Even when prohibition sentiment advanced to a point at which a 1919 referendum made permanent the temporary wartime ban on alcohol, national prohibition did not last long in Norway. Outright public evasion, lax enforcement, and fear for the country's fish markets in the wine lands of southern Europe led to the experiment's abandonment in 1926 by an unenthusiastic parliament.[57]

Neither did prohibitionism in America entirely captivate the Norwegian personality. As Theodore Blegen expresses the ambivalence, "a protest against the use of liquor took form and grew in volume" but "on the part of many there appears to have been a friendly tolerance of liquors."[58] Throughout Ole Rølvaag's novels there are Norwegian Americans who, with scant censure, drink, wrestle, dance, and smoke. Rølvaag, who only weakly shared, though he felt sympathy toward, the somber pietism embraced by numerous countrymen, saw excessive drinking as being less an indictment of liquor *per se* than a symptom of strain in the disillusioned Norwegian immigrant.[59] He, as well as most other Norwegian immigrants before temperance feeling began to take hold in the 1890s, evidently approved of the use of liquor for special occasions. In his trilogy, a trip by menfolk to a distant town for supplies brings numerous orders for "Sunday bottles" to be filled; the city visit is then celebrated with several "rounds of treats." And when the barn is built on Beret Holm's farm, few evade the Norwegian custom of making the barn "leakproof" by giving the ridgepole "a little soaking during the shingling."[60] This tolerance of drinking apparently extended more to Norwegian-American farming areas than to small towns.[61] When the legislatures of Iowa, Minnesota, and Wisconsin proposed anti-liquor referenda for the people to approve or reject, all attracted less support from the most rural Norwegian townships.

But apart from an old-country ambivalence toward liquor and the tendency for rural Norwegian Americans to differ from their small-town brethren, political conditions specific to each state could amplify temperance divisiveness among Norwegians. Theoretically the predominant pietist or liturgical orientation of a Norwegian-American locality might incline its voters for or against prohibition. But voters evidently balanced feelings on this issue against those on other issues and on their past party loyalties rooted in yet other issues. Even within liturgical Norwegian Synod settlements, where pastors might oppose state restrictions on convivial drinking as being hopeless attempts to perfect society and contrary to practices familiar in Norway, they still might be apt to suppress their opinions out of traditional deference to official authority and continue to urge a solid Republican vote as akin to religious duty.[62] Therefore, for solid Republican majorities to be disrupted by differing pietist and liturgical views rather than by something such as agrarian class discontent, an issue such as the prohibition question had to so absorb state politics that pastors and parishioners focused on this issue over others.

The Republican party's less daring promotion of prohibition in states such as Wisconsin and Minnesota where its opponents were strong weakened the issue's capacity to divide Norwegian Americans there. In these states, American Protection Association anti-Catholicism might array Protestants against Catholics, but prohibitionism placed Protestants against both Catholics and German Lutherans, who together were numerically strong.[63] Consequently, of four statewide prohibition referenda conducted in the three states between 1880 and 1924, it is not surprising that only in Iowa, which adopted restrictive forms of liquor legislation at various moments throughout the entire era, did the issue split Norwegian settlements of pietist and liturgical Lutheran bent.[64]

In fact, Iowa proved to be the only state of the three where differing Lutheran affiliations seem to have loosened the Republican grip on Norwegian settlements (Figure 11).[65] As the Republican party moved toward the dry camp from the 1870s into the 1890s, it steadily lost favor in the less evangelical communities.

The sequence of political events in Iowa began when the Republicans endorsed local option laws in the late 1870s and shortly thereafter (1882–1885) openly advocated prohibition legislation. But when Governor William Larrabee began vigorously to enforce these laws (1886–1889), mounting opposition combined with waning dry enthusiasm to help elect Democrat Horace Boise to the statehouse. After Boise secured re-election in 1891, the Republican party professionals decided they had had enough. Declaring that prohibition would be no test of Republicanism, they successfully purged the drys from the party machinery and regained control over state offices in 1893, partly through advocating a return to a local option form of liquor legislation.[66]

In this circumstance, Norwegian areas with predominantly pietist congregations—that is, those of the Hauge Synod and the United Church—generally advocated prohibition while less evangelical Norwegian Synod townships accepted the legislation with greater reluctance. Winneshiek county, a center of conservative Norwegian Synod

Synodal Affiliations and Intra-State Vote

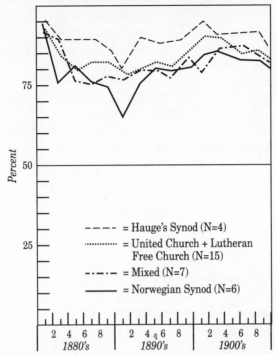

Figure 11. Republican share of votes for governor in Iowa's Norwegian settlements according to their predominant Norwegian Lutheran church affiliations as of 1915. The doctrinal orientation of each precinct is classfied as to whether an estimated one-half or more of its church members belonged to a single Norwegian synod. Others are included in the "mixed" category. Precinct returns are less complete before 1890.

influence, illustrates these conflicting views. When prohibition came up for a vote in 1882, Republican party support and voter turnout dwindled in three Norwegian Synod townships compared to their 1881 vote for governor.[67] Madison, Glenwood, and Pleasant townships all reacted adversely to prohibition agitation while only one liturgical precinct, Highland township, showed increased turnout and the strong support for the amendment that characterized most pietist townships.[68]

The slumping Republican vote extended to other Norwegian Synod areas. It can be seen in Eden and Logan townships of Winnebago county, which were organized in the mid 1880s; their Republican percentages declined for the next several elections. Pietist townships, on the other hand, adhered strongly to Republican candidates, although occasionally they, too, displayed some inconsistency. Linden township in Winnebago county is a case in point. Laurence M. Larson, writing of his early life in Linden, recalled that his father spoke out vigorously for prohibition in 1882 and "it was a matter of real gratification to him that every vote in our township was cast for the amendment."[69] Nevertheless, Linden subsequently dropped steadily in its Republicanism until, by 1891, the past decade had seen a 43 percentage point decline. Yet, despite some disunity within pietist and liturgical camps, the influence in Iowa of Norwegian-American synodal affiliations must be acknowledged.[70]

Earlier it has been seen how national and regional aspects of the political situation had governed party preferences, resulting in a broad Norwegian-American commitment to the Republican party throughout the Upper Midwest and in its erosion among succeeding generations of settlers. Also, a good share of the varied Norwegian-American vote may be seen as stemming from different issues, personalities, and social and economic circumstances within each particular state. These channeled, undercut, or heightened various affinities shared by Norwegians, resulting in different political actions among the settlements. Although regional and state political conditions accounted for differences, many if not most of these differences stemmed rather from local influences. The chapters that follow attempt to grasp this dimension, with special attention to how instances of dissent played themselves out at county and township levels.

II

Populism and Alliance Politics

CHAPTER 4

Agrarian Dissent

"When it dawned on the Norwegians that Republicanism had abandoned its humane mission of protecting the oppressed; that it stands for classes and against the masses; that Republicanism had on the ruins of black slavery built up a system of national slavery of all the producing classes regardless of color or previous conditions; then the intelligent part of them, except such as who were receiving or expected to receive favors from the Republican party, left that party and allied themselves with the new party of financial and industrial emancipation, the People's party."[1]

This forceful statement from a Norwegian politician in Minnesota voiced the feelings of countless Norwegian Americans in 1896. Agrarian radicalism came easier to Norwegian than to non-Norwegian settlements in areas where politics were thick with farmer dissatisfaction. But elsewhere, the overwhelming majority of Norwegian townships joined others to eschew Populism and cling to the Republican party. What explains these remarkable differences?

I

Broadly speaking, Wisconsin, Minnesota, and Iowa resembled one another. All were prairie states that had reached statehood before the Civil War, all were roughly similar in social and cultural composition, and each rested on an economic base of commercial agriculture and its related industries. But beyond that, the differences among them compel attention.

In their agricultural development, all began as wheat-growing states, but soon matured along separate lines. Topography, soil, and climatic conditions combined with where particular markets favored raising particular crops or livestock to bring about regional specialties.[2] Iowa's gently rolling prairies, excepting its rougher northeast counties, became the heart of the Corn Belt with its accompanying beef-cattle and swine industry. In the cooler hilly areas of Wisconsin where much land was unfit for row crops, hay and forage took the place of corn and, increasingly, dairying superseded beef-cattle and hog production as the principal livestock enterprise. A mixed three-region situation emerged in Minnesota: hay and dairying in the southeast, corn and hog raising in the southwest, and spring wheat and small grains in the western and northwestern counties. Also, unlike Iowa, large tracts of rough and swampy timberland unsuitable for commercial agriculture covered northern Wisconsin and northeastern Minnesota.

As for profitability, spring wheat ranked behind dairying or corn and livestock. Located mainly in western Minnesota and in lands to the west and north, wheat cash-crop farming required comparatively little capital outlay in buildings, livestock, and year-round labor needs. But the wheat farmer on the plains faced unfavorable moisture and temperature conditions and long distances to markets – all of which made profit margins unpredictable, and overproduction reduced prices. Minneapolis, situated on the eastern fringe of the spring wheat region, became the leading wheat-milling center as farmers came to depend on it as the nearest place to convert their bulky raw grain into flour for further shipment east.[3]

The wheat-growing areas felt the accelerating and uneven pace of agricultural change most acutely. Over-expansion had occurred, in no small part a result of railroads opening vast new lands to commercial production. Further complicating problems of overproduction, the farmer faced rising costs (labor, interest, transport, taxes, fertilizer), diminished foreign markets, high tariffs, and staggering competition, and the amount of currency in circulation had not expanded accordingly. This intensified the strain on debtor farmers – especially in developing areas where settlers' high demand for capital boosted mortgage interest rates. As a consequence, Farmers' Alliance and Populist party movements flourished during the eighties and nineties in the most distressed areas.[4]

Iowa in the 1870s had led all others as the banner state of the

Granger movement.[5] But the state's shift toward diversified farming in the 1880s absorbed most Populist militancy that might have developed. Generally prospering under these arrangements, farmers saw little reason to vote for Populist candidates, despite Iowa's association with the national Populist movement through the leadership of James B. Weaver of Bloomfield, who stood as the party's presidential candidate in 1892. The People's party in Iowa, having fewer grievances to push, dwelled on broad issues such as monetary reform. Anti-railroad agitation, the most pressing immediate question at the root of much agrarian discontent, had in Iowa largely dissipated after 1888 when Governor William Larrabee and a reform-minded legislature passed Iowa's equivalent of the federal Interstate Commerce Act.[6]

In the heavily Norwegian areas of Iowa, what remained of wheat raising in 1895 confined itself to the most recently settled north-central counties—Winnebago, Emmet, and Humboldt. Here Populist agitation ignited some enthusiasm; Winnebago county's Norwegian townships gave one-fourth to one-half of their votes to the Populist candidate for governor.[7] Conversely, the older Norwegian settlements in corn-producing central Iowa (Story, Hamilton, and Hardin counties) succumbed hardly at all to Populist appeals.[8]

The Populist party also proved weak both in Wisconsin as a whole and among its many Norwegian townships. In 1892 the Populist candidate for governor won but 3 percent of the statewide vote and only 4 percent from Norwegian settlements. Two years later, the average Populist vote of these settlements declined further, trailing 3 percentage points behind that of the state at large. The 1892 vote showed that only five of forty-seven heavily Norwegian townships and villages cast 20 percent or more of their votes for the Populist gubernatorial candidate and, by 1894, the number of such settlements had declined to three.[9]

These few Wisconsin townships shared certain features. As in Iowa, they remained among the most recently settled areas, where adherence to Republicanism had not yet matured.[10] Also, the Populist vote escalated in the poorest Norwegian areas, where lower average land values persisted and potatoes were the main cash crop, grown on the poorer, thinner soils to the north.[11] Together, the circumstances of being freshly settled and in poorer sections of Wisconsin evidently attracted some movement toward Populism. But Wisconsin Populism held little to excite Norwegian involvement. Largely a creation of Robert Schilling, a labor union organizer, the Wisconsin People's party advocated programs more attuned to the interests of industrial workers than of farmers, despite the party's attempts to court farm groups. Under this kind of Populist leadership, the grievances they pushed in Wisconsin left Norwegian farmers largely unimpressed.[12]

Moreover, few Norwegian leaders in the state sympathized with Populism, which further dampened its appeal among their countrymen. Congressman Nils P. Haugen, Wisconsin's Norwegian-American politician of prominence during this time, remained a dedicated Republican. Haugen's important ethnic contacts and his popularity among Norwegian voters undoubtedly helped to minimize defections to Populism. Also, the distraction of a more compelling controversy – the Bennett Law issue – diverted the political interests of many Norwegian Americans.[13] This legislation of 1890, supported by Republicans, threatened foreign-language parochial schools by requiring that certain subjects be taught in English. The conservative Norwegian Synod vehemently opposed the law and labored to swing Norwegian Lutheran elements behind a political effort to punish the Republican incumbent in the gubernatorial election. But although their efforts brought about some defection, Norwegian Synod settlements nonetheless cast 57 percent of their vote for the Republican governor.[14]

II

Because the agricultural politics of the nineties stirred only minimal Norwegian involvement in Iowa and Wisconsin, one might be tempted to conclude a general absence of radicalism among Norwegians. But given the proper mix of conditions, latent Norwegian agrarianism could and did burst forth. These favorable conditions presented themselves in Minnesota.

Each of the three successive waves of Norwegian immigrants to Minnesota settled primarily in a farming region distinguishable from the others. The Norwegian townships that took shape between 1850 and 1865 helped fill in the southeastern triangle of the state, a section that by 1890 had shifted from wheat to diversified dairy farming. The second wave of immigration, which lasted from the late 1860s to the mid-1870s, spread across the prairies of the state's west-central counties that formed a transitional zone between the corn and wheat belts, where Norwegian settlements pursued mixed grain farming. A third phase of heavy immigration, which accompanied an upturn in business activity after the Panic of 1873, spilled into the Red River Valley and helped to make it the heart of the spring wheat cash-crop region. On these cool, less humid prairies, farmers met difficulty in expanding beyond small-grain farming; they found that the short growing season limited corn yields that might otherwise have stimulated stock raising and dairying. And when economic conditions worsened, agricultural discontent multiplied in the freshly settled spring wheat belt.[15]

The Norwegian-American farmer responded to these developments in light of his own recalled experience in Norway, his own economic prospects, what he heard from neighbors and local politicians, and what he read in the newspapers. In the southeastern part of the state, this earlier generation of Norwegian farmers had long enjoyed association with Republicans, and their leading men had for years identified themselves as Republican members and officials. Additionally, because rail connections and the market for their dairy and meat products tied them more to Chicago and Milwaukee than to the Twin Cities, Norwegian-American farmers tended to rely on news published in the staunchly Republican Chicago *Skandinaven*.[16] These fundamental factors stunted Populism in this part of the state, incapacitating the movement's ability to dominate issues and persuade Norwegian-American farmers to sever their Republican party connections.

Farther to the northwest, however, Norwegian settlers faced far different circumstances. There, local political organizations—depending on voter loyalties rooted in time and important events—had yet to mature because turbulence marked the political scene. Agrarian and economic questions, growing increasingly prominent in these counties, forced the Republicans into a defensive posture. Here the politically immature Norwegian settlers heard fewer recollections of a Republican party formed out of the slavery question and listened to more talk of a party rooted in protectionism and balking at tariff reform. And finally, here politically ambitious countrymen lived who recognized the Norwegian farmers' traditional distrust of official ruling groups and stood willing to press these issues and use their ethnic and Farmers' Alliance ties to reach higher political office. In short, here economic issues came to frame the farmers' political outlook and stir Norwegian-American antipathies toward complacent officials and economic interests. If possible, given their anti-Catholicism, they preferred to see economic reform come from the Republican rather than the Democratic party. But when this failed to materialize, large numbers opened themselves to third-party appeals. Consequently, Norwegian settlements of each region of Minnesota agriculture went their own way.

For voters in the older southeastern communities, it might be argued, as does Samuel Hays, that "ethno-cultural issues were far more important to voters than were tariffs, trusts, and railroads" because "they touched lives directly and moved people deeply."[17] In the absence of economic turbulence, ethnic and religious feelings indeed likely carried considerable political weight when aroused. But to the northwest the issues touching farmers' cultural or religious convictions were indeed the tariff, trusts, and railroads that many saw as impinging directly and deeply on their lives. These issues ignited the cultural feelings of agrarian distrust and moral indignation that framed the political rhetoric of agricultural discontent.

Construction of the Northern Pacific and St. Paul, Minneapolis, and Manitoba railroads had opened up the area producing hard spring wheat—the wheat in greatest demand—and stimulated construction of immense flour mills in Minneapolis. But the farmers that flocked into the Red River Valley had soon felt dependency to be their lot.[18] Increasingly, northwestern Minnesota farmers believed that the Millers Association of Minneapolis controlled "railways and elevator systems to an extent that no wheat could leave the country without passing through its hands, and it practically controlled the sale of wheat in the only section of the United States where hard wheat can be grown."[19] Many Norman county farmers stood convinced that the line elevators —mill-owned elevator chains—were running competing firms out of business. "Look at the opposition elevators in Ada," wrote a local editor, "the millers of Minneapolis have long ago put a quietus on them. They would not dare to raise the price of wheat a cent over the millers' quotations for fear of being swooped upon and annihilated."[20] And when farmers heard that buyers at one station avoided bids against one another or those at nearby stations, many concluded that when it came to influencing the price of wheat in Chicago the Minneapolis millers "have at least as much to do with it as Liverpool or London."[21]

Through the later eighties, with prices falling, publicity focused on abuses in the market and resentment hardened in the northwestern counties. Norwegian immigrants who had once felt themselves powerless before their own upper classes in Norway found similar public sentiment rising in their new home. Seeing acts of "the miller ring in company with the railroad ring," many felt as did Ada's town editor who concluded that "the settlers in the Red River Valley are as helpless and servile as were the Negro race in the sunny South thirty years ago."[22]

Unable to cope with agricultural grievances, the Republican party leadership came to be seen as callous and insensitive. Real or supposed marketing abuses primarily bound the farmers' movement together, although many agrarians also embraced low tariff views, believing that protectionism only closed markets for their produce abroad and raised costs for what they had to buy at home.

When in 1890 passage of the McKinley Tariff coincided with the

Regional Differences in Minnesota's
Gubernatorial Voting

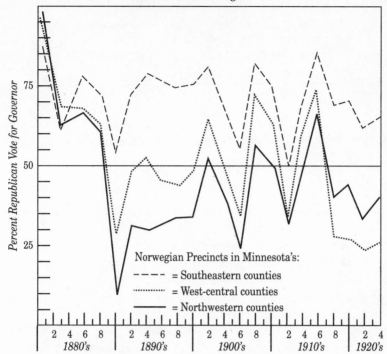

Figure 12. Republican share of vote for governor in Norwegian set-
tlements of three Minnesota regions. Counties of each region were
as follows: Southeastern (Dodge, Faribault, Fillmore, Freeborn,
Goodhue, Houston); West-central (Chippewa, Kandiyohi,, Meeker,
Swift); Northwestern (Becker, Clay, Clearwater, Norman, Otter
Tail, Polk, Wilkin).

formation of a separate political party by the Minnesota Farmers Alliance, the storm broke and Republicans could do little more than seek
shelter.[23] In northwestern Minnesota, the Republican gubernatorial
vote from Norwegian settlements plunged to 10 percent–a nearly 25
percent greater drop than in the region as a whole. Republicans did
scarcely better from Norwegian townships in the west-central counties, where they captured less than one-third of the vote. But in the
Norwegian areas of southeastern Minnesota the Republican candidate
still brought in firm majorities.

The consequences for Minnesota Republicans remained visible for
a generation. A major realignment in a major region had occurred (Figure 12). The party had lost the allegiance of Minnesota's most recent,
most economically vulnerable Norwegian settlements.

Table 2 Extent to which votes by Minnesota's Norwegian settlements for agrarian gubernatorial candidates exceeded or fell short of those given by the region as a whole[a]

Region	1890	1892	1894	1896
Southeast Counties	7.6%	-0.8%	-6.7%	-11.9%
West Central Counties	21.9%	8.9%	0.6%	-0.7%
Northwest Counties	25.9%	18.2%	12.2%	5.3%

[a]Includes Farmers' Alliance, People's Party, and Democratic-Populist candidates. The counties are those listed for Figure 12.

The influence of regional distinctions within the state is striking. Table 2 compares by region the mean average vote given to agrarian party candidates for governor during the nineties. Curiously, Norwegian settlements in southeastern Minnesota proved even more conservative than the surrounding counties within which they were located. But in northwestern Minnesota precisely the opposite occurred; Norwegian communities crowded into the front ranks of Populist insurgency.

Not unexpectedly, the source of the divided Norwegian-American vote can be traced to economic circumstances.[24] Percentage of wheat acreage and average farm values closely paralleled the vote, while no connection existed between Populism and the pietist or liturgical Lutheran orientation of Norwegian settlements.[25] Neither did the vote relate to whether people in the settlements originated principally from eastern or western Norway. But there is some indication that other conditions played a role. Less advantageously situated Norwegian townships—those relatively far from the the county seat with lower land values and without an incorporated town or village—voted less Republican.[26] Perhaps this reflected a sense of being peripheral to, or isolated from, centers of power that controlled the farmers' lives. Also, greater support for the embattled Republican party came from predominantly Norwegian small towns and villages of northwestern Minnesota than from the surrounding rural townships.[27] Although Norwegian communities often favored fellow Norwegian candidates during these years, it did not happen automatically. Also, while some evidence surfaced of Norwegian bloc voting for one or another party, township votes neither consistently nor strongly corresponded to percentages of Norwegian residents.[28]

Knute Nelson when governor of Minnesota. He served as Minnesota's first Norwegian-born Republican congressman (1883–1889), governor (1892–1895), and United States senator (1895–1922). Photo courtesy of Minnesota Historical Society.

III

The 1890 disaster left Minnesota's Republican party thoroughly shaken. To halt the advancing prairie fire and turn it if possible, they desperately turned to ex-congressman Knute Nelson. This Norwegian-born lawyer from Douglas county, in whom the G.O.P. wheelhorses now sought the party's salvation, had in years past hardly enjoyed their undivided good will. Nelson had struggled against the G.O.P.'s native-born leadership to become the first Scandinavian elected to the United States House of Representatives, a position he held from 1883 to 1889. And while there he had voted for tariff reform, against his party's wishes, not once but on two occasions.[29] Although his independent spirit endeared him to his low-tariff countrymen in northwestern Minnesota's Fifth District, in the higher circles of the state's Republican party Nelson was viewed as a troublesome maverick.

But in this demoralized Republican year of 1892, the party powers showed themselves more than happy to forgive and forget. To them, Nelson had already lightened the burden of his political sins by his eleventh-hour endorsement of the McKinley Tariff in 1890. This act helped save Governor William Merriam's election. In so doing, however, it injured Nelson among his low-tariff constituents in a manner akin to the public's estimate of an accused person who turns state's evidence—many accepted the testimony while losing their respect for the man.[30]

Be that as it may, Knute Nelson later recalled with pride how the Republican party leaders, "especially the Americans," came to him "and insisted that I must become our candidate for Governor on the regular Republican ticket."[31] Native-born leaders expected by this move to see Norwegian farmers, who made up the core of the People's party support, abandon their agrarian fervor in the interests of seeing one of their own attain the governorship. In this way, Republicans hoped to start a fire in the Populist stubble.[32]

Following his nomination, Nelson traveled throughout the state appearing at political rallies, sometimes two or three a day. He straddled the tariff question by arguing that "the issue was no longer between high tariff and low tariff, but between protection and free trade." And so, under these circumstances, he claimed to be "a protectionist."[33]

What the party leaders had failed to foresee, however, was that elevating a Norwegian American to nomination angered many Republican Swedes, who had stood more loyally by the party and received little for it. "The American party manager," wrote one Norwegian contemporary, "is not given to making nice distinctions; and it has been found impossible to impress him with the fact that Norwegians and Swedes are separate nationalities."[34] The gubernatorial issue quickly revealed the extent of their mutual suspicion and jealousy. "Two Norwegians on the state ticket and no Swede—" exclaimed the editor of *Svenska Fria Pressen*, "—that is something wrong in the eyes of the Swedes." Another urged that "If the Swedes in Minnesota stay at home at the election or vote for men who are not on the Republican ticket Knute Nelson will go where the mushrooms grow and not into the governor's chair."[35] The growing outrage drew the attention of a Swedish editor in Minneapolis: "The Swedish press," he wrote, "has at last found out its mistake in always praising the Republican party. *Amerikanaren, Kuriren*, the Denver *Korrespondenten*, the Tacoma *Tribunen*, the Duluth *Press* and others have cried against the shameful manner in which the G.O.P. has treated the Swedes in Minnesota and Nebraska. That's right! If we help each other it will not take long before the different political parties will think at least as much of the Swedes as they do of the negroes—if not as much as they do of the Norwegians."[36]

Norwegian-language newspapers had tried in the past to play down Norwegian-Swedish rivalry or the fact that Norwegians had held more offices than Swedes. But while they now scolded newspapers for exposing these "phantoms . . . in broad daylight," they were unprepared to deal with a circular letter written in the Swedish language and sent to all Swedish pastors in the state during the final weeks of the 1892 campaign.[37]

It said, in part: "We take the liberty to address your reverence on a subject of the greatest importance to every Swede who is interested in the welfare of his countrymen. You . . . must have noticed how the Norwegians are trying to get hold of all the state offices in Minnesota, giving us Swedes no chance to be represented on the state ticket; and if a Swede ever is nominated for any office . . . Norwegians and Danes conspire to defeat him, employing every means to accomplish this purpose.

"If we let Knute Nelson . . . be elected, . . . the natural result will be the formation of the Norwegians into a solid league against us Swedes. That will put an end to all our hopes of political advancement in this state. Everywhere Norwegians, but no Swedes. And it has come to such a pass that if we are not to be entirely ignored, and despised by the Americans as 'voting cattle,' there must be an awakening among us, and things must not be allowed to run their own course as heretofore. It is our duty as Swedes to insist on our rights and on political equality with the Norwegians. We would, therefore, urge upon your reverence, and upon every good Swede to do your very best to defeat every Norwegian candidate upon this year's state ticket."[38]

The Norwegian editor of *The North*, Luth. Jaeger, lamented the circular's appearance at a time when "relations are considerably strained already" and acknowledged that placing two Norwegians and no Swedes on the state's Republican ticket gave it "an ultra-Norwegian complexion" that "would particularly tend to alienate the Swedes." Nevertheless, he claimed, "on the whole the history of Minnesota state politics will not uphold the assertion about the Norwegians having antagonized the Swedes. To be sure, citizens of the former nationality have held more offices than have the latter, but this is due to conditions in which the alleged Norwegian selfishness cuts no figure at all. Among these must be counted the fact that the political unrest peculiar to the last few years has taken a firm hold upon the 'Norwegians' of the state, while as yet the 'Swedes' hardly have been touched by it. This again has resulted in the election to office of more of the former class."[39]

If this circumstance frightened the Republican party helmsmen, their fears soon included as well possible retaliation by native-born voters. For when the Democrats cunningly began to publicize the nomination of Knute Nelson as a desperate Republican effort to "fish

Norwegian votes," the strategy stirred the ethnic prejudices of the American born. "It is well known," wrote editor Jaeger, "that quite a few citizens of American ancestry propose to cut Knute Nelson. To them he is not enough of an American." In reply, stirring the pot of prejudice once again, Jaeger warned Democrats that "If Knute Nelson is to be slaughtered because he was born in Norway, then Mr. [Daniel W.] Lawler [the Democrats' candidate for governor] should be opposed because though born in this country he is closely and intimately identified with the Irish element of our population, and with the Roman Catholic church."[40]

While ultimately Knute Nelson won the ensuing political battle, he failed to bring Norwegian dissidents back to the Republican fold. In the southeastern Minnesota precincts, Norwegian settlements gave Nelson strong majorities—nearly three-fourths of their vote. But he got less than one-third of the vote from their counterparts in northwestern Minnesota. In four townships of Otter Tail county having the highest percentages of Norwegian immigrants, for instance, Nelson received only 15 percent of the votes cast, up a scant 9 percentage points from 1890.[41] Ethnic pride in 1892 definitely cut little into their agricultural discontent.

In the state at large, nationality feelings had contributed something, although it is difficult to say exactly how much. Republican votes from non-Norwegian areas had risen 5 percentage points over 1890, while they increased an average 19 percentage points in Norwegian-American townships and villages. This would perhaps indicate that 14 percentage points might be due to Nelson's nationality. Of course, as already noted, at least two other influences likely contributed to this increase. First is that Nelson, in 1892, faced a less popular farm protest candidate than had his Republican predecessor in 1890. The plainspoken Knute Nelson stood in striking contrast to his opponent—the flamboyant, mercurial Ingatius Donnelly—whose controversial leadership of the forces of agricultural discontent strained Norwegian-American third-party enthusiasm. The second new source of Nelson's support stemmed from the rapidly expanding American Protective Association, which encouraged Norwegian anti-Catholics to vote for Nelson by publicizing the Irish-Catholic backgrounds of his Democratic and People's party opponents. "I do not believe you have much to fear" from "Knownothingism," a political confidant assured Nelson, for "you have on your side two elements that will neutralize any work that may be attempted on this line—the Grand Army and the anti-Catholics."[42] The truth of this became visible during the campaign. "Scandinavian pastors," charged the editor of the *Irish Stan-*

dard, had "appealed to the religious prejudice which was lying dormant in the breasts of their countrymen," and consequently the key 1892 issue had become "Lutheranism versus Catholicism."[43] Notwithstanding the marginal gains among Norwegian settlements, however, Knute Nelson later conceded that one-half of the Populist leader's votes persisted in coming from "Norwegians who had got badly infected by the new party."[44]

The view from the northwestern counties had been so colored by the issues of agricultural discontent that ethnic and religious feeling had lost its ability to focus voter sentiment. Otter Tail county politics well illustrates the dynamics of Norwegian-American dissent that made their traditional agrarianism the touchstone for these settlers' political allegiance.

CHAPTER 5

Otter Tail County, Minnesota

"The Fergus Falls people in general, and the politicians in particular, have about the same interest in the farmer that the wolf has in the lamb. They need him to live off of."[1]

Such words, voiced in 1896 by Norwegian leader Haldor E. Boen, touched agrarian feelings beating deep in the hearts of his countrymen, sentiments they heard time and again in political discussions during their settlement years in northwestern Minnesota. Townsmen resented losing their traditional control over political affairs and threw cold water on the Farmers' Alliance and its candidates; farmers saw these condescending middlemen as owing their existence to the farmers' lack of organization, while an alarmed Fergus Falls editor attempted to mediate, urging fellow business and professional interests not to cut the farmers' candidates: "Take my warning; be a hog and take the consequences."[2] Main Street versus the countryside loomed early – accompanying the 1884 entrance of the County Alliance on the political scene – and became an oft-repeated theme throughout the farmers' movement. Together with other agrarian issues, when stirred by politically ambitious Norwegian spokesmen and mixed with Alliance factionalism, it soon took on an irresistible appeal that drew disproportionate numbers of Norwegian immigrants into the movement.

Haldor E. Boen, ca. 1885, a Norwegian-born leader in Minnesota's Farmers' Alliance and Populist politics and spokesman for his agrarian-minded countrymen in Otter Tail county. Photo from O. M. Norlie, *History of the Norwegian-People in America* (Minneapolis, 1925), 331.

I

During 1884 the Farmers' Alliance expanded its organizing efforts both in the county and in the state at large before it turned its energies to achieving reforms through the control of Republican party politics.[3] Otter Tail county farmers held an "anti-monopoly" mass meeting at Battle Lake on March 7 that attracted a large crowd of participants from nearly half of the county's sixty-two townships. A young Norwegian American, Haldor Boen, became one of ten delegates representing the county at the larger mass meeting of farmers in St. Paul later that month. Minnesota's state Alliance leadership soon included two Otter Tail farmers. By 1888 John B. Hompe held the position of state representative to the legislature and president of the Otter Tail Alliance before winning election to the state senate in 1890. Haldor Boen, by contrast, gained influence less through holding prestigious offices than through working within the Alliance organization.

The effectiveness of such local leaders decided to a great extent how closely various Norwegian-American settlements adhered to the general political pattern. Here favorable or unfavorable circumstance set limits to their control. The strength of one's opponents, the clashing goals of one's friends, the timing of political events, the degree of political organization—all these, depending on how they came together, strengthened or weakened agrarian feelings among Norwegian-American farmers where they could make their political weight felt.

Boen and Hompe, like many Alliance farmers, had been part of the major influx of settlers filling Otter Tail county during the late 1860s and 1870s. Settlement proceeded rapidly across the county's numerous prairie belts and out onto the open grasslands of Otter Tail's southwestern townships. But elsewhere, unyielding landscape features—ubiquitous lakes and marshlands, hilly central townships, hardwood forests in the eastern two-thirds of the county—interrupted orderly occupation of the land. Still, the laying of track across the county by two leading railroads spurred a sharp rise in the number of inhabitants, from under 2,000 in 1870 to over 45,000 in 1905. These railroad lines tended to dictate the social and economic orientation of the villages, with those along the Great Northern line having close relations with Fergus Falls while ones served by the Northern Pacific line more closely associated themselves with Perham (see Figure 13). Fergus Falls, the county seat after 1872, became the largest and most important city in Otter Tail county.[4]

Immigrants from four European countries comprised most of the county's residents. Norwegians clearly predominated, followed in descending order by Germans, Swedes, and Finns.[5] The Norwegians took up land in the less timbered southwestern half of Otter Tail county and soon constituted more than half the total voters in thirteen townships.[6] Germans were concentrated in the northeastern half of the county: German Catholics clustered around Perham while German Lutherans predominated in Corliss and Gorman townships just to the north.[7] Swedes, quite numerous but more dispersed in their settlement, constituted majorities in only Eastern and Amor townships while Finns lived mainly in the northeastern townships. All four European groups initially settled the countryside while native-born settlers and those of English, Scottish, and Irish birth more frequently lived in the villages.[8]

Although the 160-acre farms of Otter Tail county did not match in size those farther north in the Red River Valley region, farmers shared with their northern neighbors spring wheat raising as the dominant agricultural pursuit. Of course, some farmers tried planting corn while others in the timbered parts of the county saw opportunities in

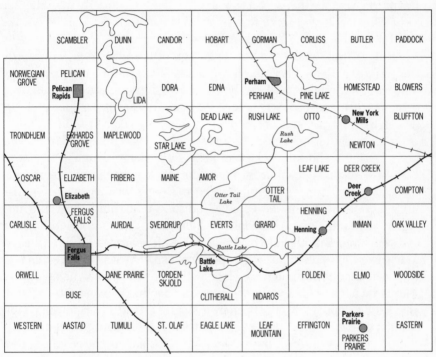

Figure 13. Otter Tail county, Minnesota, 1895. Includes major towns, lakes, and railroads.

raising livestock on their marsh hay and timber pasture acreage, but they were a minority. Wheat was king in Otter Tail county during these years.[9]

II

After his army service in the Civil War, John Hompe had come west from New York in the 1870s. Ambitious and well-liked, the thirty-eight-year-old farmer took the lead in April of 1884 to organize a Farmers' Alliance in his own township of Deer Creek. By mid-May his local Alliance issued a call for sister Alliances to meet at Battle Lake and form a Farmers' County Alliance.[10]

But if Hompe sparked the formation of the new county organization, Haldor Boen became the flywheel maintaining its balance of power. Norwegians filled the largest township alliances and, as their principal organizer, Boen before long wielded a major share of the power within the county organization. Boen had come to Minnesota in 1868 at age seventeen, when he and two brothers emigrated from Norway. Within a short time he had mastered enough English to attend the state normal school at St. Cloud briefly before moving on in 1870 to settle in Otter Tail county. There Boen's facility with English brought him work in the county auditor's office until he could buy eighty acres nearby in Aurdal township in order to take up farming and teaching. But already by the time of his marriage at age twenty-four the quiet-spoken but eager political aspirant was making his way into local Republican politics. His election to various township offices, coupled with a term as county commissioner in 1880 and intermittent service as deputy sheriff, prepared Boen to lead in organizing Norwegian wheat farmers in 1884.[11] When the local Alliances met in Battle Lake at the behest of Hompe's Deer Creek Alliance, the resulting new County Alliance selected Haldor Boen as secretary.[12]

At the Republican county convention in September the new County Alliance made its first attempt to influence nominations. On the evening before the convention a number of farmers met and endorsed as candidates for the legislature their native-born chairman, Washington Muzzy, and, to Haldor Boen's disappointment, a Norwegian American named Hans P. Bjorge, based upon the two men's commitment to Alliance reforms and to Muzzy's ability to "intelligently and forcibly" express his views in public. The next day's Republican convention endorsed both Alliance choices, partly to please the Alliancemen and partly to preempt any Democratic attempts to court the Alliance candidates.[13] The Alliancemen did not press at this time for any other offices, but internal disharmony showed itself in Haldor Boen's later canvass of the county to see if he could muster enough strength to run as an independent legislative candidate. Untimately, though, he decided not to challenge the Alliance/Republican selection.[14]

The modest strategy of 1884 gave way in 1886 to an unsuccessful attempt by the County Farmers' Alliance to expand control over county Republican nominations. Having doubled the membership of the local Alliances over the past year, Alliancemen's appetite for controlling offices had likewise increased. Those who attended the County Alliance meeting in Battle Lake decided to press ahead and endorse candidates for both county and state legislative offices. John Hompe obtained the nomination for state senator and Haldor Boen received the nod for county registrar of deeds.[15] The next issue of the *Ugeblad* – the local Norwegian-language weekly – carried the editor's favorable comments, but elsewhere some Republican leaders balked.[16] When Republican county delegates convened in July, Alliancemen gained no more than they had two years before.[17]

Stung by their rejection, Boen and Hompe mounted independent candidacies based on their Alliance endorsement.[18] Hompe tried and failed to win the Democrats' endorsement, but he did secure that of the Prohibitionists. Boen had heightened his prestige within the farmers' movement through service on the executive committee of the state Alliance, but neither he nor Hompe could overcome the lost Republican party nomination. In their respective races, Boen and Hompe drew their vote from different constituencies. Boen outperformed Hompe in the thirteen principal Norwegian townships – winning 72 percent compared to Hompe's 59 percent – while Hompe drew more votes from eastern townships surrounding his home in Deer Creek. But despite each winning pluralities in twenty-six townships, the gains failed to offset losses elsewhere, especially in Fergus Falls. Only those Alliance candidates nominated by the Republicans made it into office.[19]

As the 1888 election campaign neared, an air of personal acrimony began to seep into the County Alliance as the number of local alliances here and elsewhere in Minnesota declined.[20] Submerged personal hostility erupted in attacks on Haldor Boen because of actions taken by the executive committee of the state Alliance, a body for which Boen was corresponding secretary. When only one gubernatorial candidate – a St. Paul banker named Albert Scheffer – showed up at a state executive committee meeting to announce his support for the Alliance platform, this apparent endorsement brought down a storm of criticism on the committee by those who favored the Republican candidacy of A. R. McGill or suspected that Scheffer still remained a Democrat.[21] In Otter Tail county, Alliancemen unfriendly to Haldor Boen or fearful of his growing power seized the occasion to cut their local secretary down to size.

A leading county Allianceman, State Representative Henry Plowman, fired the first shot. He wrote to the Fergus Falls *Journal* complaining that the move by the state executive committee had been "a bad mistake" that should not be considered binding. Boen replied at length, noting that it "evidently makes some difference whose ox is gored," because Plowman favored A. R. McGill over Scheffer. But Boen was unwilling to let the matter rest there. Anxious to vindicate himself, Boen two weeks later had his supporters introduce a resolution near the end of the annual Alliance meeting to endorse Scheffer for governor. And after a heated exchange of words, the final vote upheld Boen, sustaining the resolution by a margin of nearly three to one.[22]

The appearance of success proved deceptive, however. Haldor Boen held lesser offices – secretary of the local and state alliances – and aimed in 1888 to run simply as a candidate for county registrar of deeds. For a politician Boen demonstrated little skill as a public speaker. His voice lacked volume, his words hardly varied in emphasis or pitch, he shyly adhered self-consciously to his text. Boen's public diffidence notwithstanding, however, he was a true leader of men. He antagonized many by his ambitious, headstrong disposition and unwillingness either to brook opposition or readily take advice. But despite his faults, other qualities marked him for leadership among Norwegian-American agrarians. A farmer himself, he knew how to handle his countrymen, performing at his best in private conversations, where he persuaded in an offhand homespun fashion. And many countrymen, respecting Boen's courage, vigor, and uncommonly correct English with but a trace of Norwegian accent, looked to him to voice their aspirations to non-Norwegians. A man of rangy handsome appearance with dark brown hair and mustache, he apparently lived to exhaust himself every day, fueling a tireless ambition with stamina, grit, and resolve – a man constantly on the move. Republican editor Elmer Adams, even when attempting to break Boen and the Populist-Alliance movement, acknowledged the Norwegian-American leader to be "possessed of both shrewdness and courage," a man who "does not usually pick a quarrel, but once in one is ready to fight."[23]

The 1888 meeting amounted to an opening skirmish in the battles to come. The first sign of trouble appeared one week later when a local newspaper printed a bitter letter signed by "Spectator." The writer sought to deny Boen the Republican nomination for county registrar of deeds by impugning the hard work and honest performance Boen had supposedly given to the Alliance. Boen, the writer accused, had undercut past Alliance candidates and made suspicious fence-wire and twine deals for the Alliance during the previous season. To these statements, Boen promptly replied, saying he would be happy to furnish information about his twine and wire deals if the writer would reveal his name so that people might "understand the motive" of the writer's "spirited attack,"[24]

Despite Boen's foes, the 1888 Republican county convention found Boen to be "so strong that the opposition against him [for registrar of deeds] amounted to but little."[25] Other Alliance candidates also received their Republican nomination. Although there had been a decline in the number of alliances, the many that remained were especially strong among the politically important Norwegian townships, which made the movement a force to be reckoned with. The critical moment for a clash would not occur for two years.

III

The year 1890 set the Otter Tail Farmers' Alliance movement on a new course. Alliancemen formed a separate political party, the county Republican party closed the door to any cooperation with it, and local Alliance, Democratic, and Prohibition forces united to effectively challenge Republican supremacy.

Throughout 1889 Minnesota alliances had argued about what future direction the organization ought to take. But by the spring of 1890 the answer was clear—a consensus favored establishing a new political party to field its own candidates and press a wide range of farm-oriented issues.[26]

Back in Otter Tail county, all wondered what action the County Alliance would take. Republican newspapers, especially the Fergus Falls *Weekly Journal*, worked hard to talk the Alliance out of forming a new party.[27] Elmer Adams, the *Journal's* editor, marshalled effective arguments, mixing anger, coaxing, Republican pride, and efforts to foment division within the Alliance leadership. "If there are any," an exasperated Adams told nervous Republican candidates, "who prefer an alliance, prohibition, or democratic nomination to that of the Republican party, let them take it, but don't let a few malcontents of all parties wipe the Republican party around as if it were a dishrag." If the Alliance decides to field its own ticket, Adams declared, "it will not be forestalled by the Republican party prostrating itself before it"; in other words, the G.O.P. would not beg.[28]

The Fergus Falls *Ugeblad,* on the other hand, turned its back on what it termed "the Republican god." To teach Republican party leaders that the people's will was not to be ignored, the Norwegian newspaper advised the Alliance to nominate its own ticket for county offices and the state legislature. In reply, editor Adams of the *Journal* accused the *Ugeblad* of being "domineered by a few radical alliance-men" who are deaf to the fact that "there are other interests in Otter Tail County besides farming interests."[29] Then Adams pressed his attack along ethnic lines: "The *Ugeblad* also raises and discusses the nationality question and says that as blood is thicker than water countrymen will vote for countrymen. The Norwegians and Swedes have always had their full quota of county offices and when there were two representatives [in the state legislature] they had one. Now when there are four they are fairly entitled to two. This does not seem to suit the *Ugeblad.* It seems to want four. It disposes of or ignores every one of the American candidates."[30]

Editor Anfin Solem of the *Ugeblad* replied that he meant neither to complain about the Scandinavians' share of offices nor to ignore native-born candidates. "When we do not mention other American candidates," he said, "it is because we do not know of any, as we seldom have a chance to meet with Americans."[31]

Haldor Boen, concerned lest envious Alliance leaders might later say that "Boss Boen forced the Alliance to commit suicide," surveyed local alliances in advance of the forthcoming meeting. Of the thirty which responded, all but three favored independent political action. Knowing the outcome thus enabled Boen to avoid accusations that he had tricked the Alliance into a mistake and also, by announcing the forthcoming move a day ahead of the meeting, helped disarm Republican opposition.[32]

When County Alliance members gathered on the morning of June 10, they had therefore resolved, albeit with some uncertainty, to put forth their own slate of candidates. John Hompe's right-hand man, Swedish-born Charles Brandborg, became the unanimous choice for president and the large number of Norwegian delegates easily elected Haldor Boen secretary over two other candidates. Then attention turned to assembling a balanced slate of candidates who would attract votes from several ethnic and political interests.[33] Norwegian Americans received their due in nominations for state representative: delegates renominated an incumbent from the north-central Norwegian settlements of the county and selected a young schoolteacher from the Norwegian settlements to the northwest. As for the county Alliance leaders, John Hompe won the nomination for state senator by acclamation and Haldor Boen easily secured renomination for registrar of deeds.[34]

Although the Alliance had now gone ahead with its own slate of candidates, its leaders worried about the movement's prospects for victory. Reportedly Boen and Hompe, two 1888 Republican incumbents, had fretted about putting forward a separate ticket, fearing that Republicans might oppose their new party rather than try to arrange some accommodation to it.

Their fears proved well founded. The next issue of Elmer Adams' *Weekly Journal* flatly rejected accommodation: "No man should be placed upon the Republican ticket who is not a Republican and will not support the Republican ticket. Close up the ranks that we may know who is for us and who is against us."[35] Within a few days, four Republicans who had received Alliance nominations for county office wrote letters refusing the honor.[36]

Indecision now visited Alliance leaders. What arrangements should now be made for the four positions? Though it was distasteful to some such as president Charles Brandborg, Haldor Boen now believed their only choice lay in combining with other parties.[37] So, over the succeeding days, Boen quietly negotiated a new coalition ticket with the Democratic and Prohibition forces.[38] When it was completed, three Democrats and one Prohibitionist had replaced the four Republicans nominated earlier.[39]

The Republicans, their bluff called, immediately set about ridiculing the "combination" ticket for de-emphasizing principles in order to gain office and keep their coalition together. The Democratic county platform "is strangely silent on the liquor question," chided a typical *Journal* editorial, "to enable the prohibitionists to stand on it."[40]

Local Republicans nevertheless could feel the tide of opinion running strongly against them and serious losses seemed imminent. Compounding their troubles, in October the Republican Congress passed the McKinley Tariff. This act touched a raw nerve among spring wheat farmers trying to sell their produce in an unprotected world market while paying for goods and supplies priced at protected rates. Word of the new measure quickly spread. "As soon as the McKinley bill was passed," observed the editor of the Battle Lake *Review*, "some merchants seized upon it as a handle for advertising purposes. Newspaper columns bristled . . . with . . . 'Prices going up on account of the increase in Tariff. Buy now before the rise.' "[41]

In his final pre-election issue of the *Weekly Journal*, Elmer Adams pleaded to voters to "think a second time before you leave the Republican party to which you have always belonged."[42] But Norwegian-

Table 3 Republican share of vote for governor by rural ethnic sources of previous party support, 1888–1896, in Otter Tail county[a]

Predominant ethnicity of townships	1888 %	1890 %	1892 %	1894 %	1896 %
Norwegian	59.5	8.5	29.5	21.2	21.5
Swedish	67.4	22.1	43.9	46.7	36.8
Native-born	61.7	46.5	50.8	40.8	48.1
Finnish	55.4	42.6	39.8	48.3	63.4

[a]The thirteen predominantly Norwegian townships used for this tabulation include: Oscar, Trondhjem, Norwegian Grove, Aastad, Aurdal, Dane Prairie, Tumuli, Sverdrup, Tordenskjold, St. Olaf, Everts, Nidaros, and Folden. Swedish townships were Amor and Eastern. Native-born precincts were Inman, Maine, and Ottertail townships. Finnish precincts included Blowers, Deer Creek, Newton, and Paddock townships.

American and other farmers had already made up their minds. "Good News!!!" rejoiced a candidate in his letter to the County Alliance president a full week before the election, "Our ticket is solid in Blowers and Bluffton, Finlanders, Norwegians, Germans, Americans and everything."[43]

The entire coalition ticket swept to victory, thus ending fifteen years of uninterrupted Republican rule in the county. Norwegian precincts reversed their voting patterns—shifting from the Republican to the Alliance party (see Table 3). They did not, moreover, vote simply for Alliance regulars while crossing out Catholic Democrats and Prohibition candidates on the "combination" ticket. Rather, they gave almost identical majorities to all. The same held true for heavily German and Irish precincts, which supported the coalition county ticket down the line while voting Democratic for the state candidates.

Now it was the Republicans' turn to complain about the evils of voting by nationality, as the *Journal* did in its post-election review:

"The Scandinavian towns [townships] have voted solidly for the alliance ticket, as the returns from such towns as Trondhjem and Sverdrup show. In this contest voters have not stopped to consider the merits of the candidates, so that good men have run no better than poor ones."[44]

A county realignment had resulted. But although traditionally Republican farm precincts all registered declines, the Republican vote especially plummeted in Norwegian strongholds, followed by losses in townships of predominantly Swedish, native-born, and Finnish populations.[45]

Rural Norwegian townships, the 1890s would show, provided the

Table 4 Agricultural Protest Parties' Share of the Vote for Governor By
Various Units of Otter Tail County, 1890–1896[a]

	1890 Farmers' Alliance Percent	1892 Populist Percent	1894 Populist Percent	1896 Populist/ Democrat Percent	Average 1890– 1896 Percent
Norwegian	89.0	55.7	68.9	73.2	72.3
Swedish	75.2	45.6	50.7	63.2	58.5
Native-born	42.7	25.7	53.5	50.5	45.0
Finnish	40.5	21.4	39.8	33.9	33.4
German	13.4	8.5	30.3	62.4	30.1
City of Fergus Falls	28.6	16.4	40.7	52.2	36.7
Entire county	54.4	33.1	49.1	58.7	49.9

[a]The thirteen predominantly Norwegian precincts used for this tabulation are identified in note 6; Swedish precincts were Amor and Eastern townships; native-born precincts were Inman, Maine, and Ottertail townships; Finnish precincts included Blowers, Deer Creek, Newton, and Paddock townships; and German precincts were Corliss, Edna, Effington, and Perham township and village plus Dead Lake township. The 1895 Minnesota state census schedules provided the data to locate ethnic concentrations and the *Legislative Manual of the State of Minnesota* provided the election results.

core of support for Alliance and subsequent Populist party candidates in Otter Tail county. Being the largest single ethnic group, the Norwegians with their consistent agrarian militancy determined the course of farmer insurgency in the county. As Table 4 suggests, Swedish townships also gave majorities, but proved less willing to abandon the Republican party. Weaker agrarian party support came from areas with predominantly native-born farmers. Instead they vacillated, responding somewhat to Alliance/Populist candidates on the state ticket while giving less support to local candidates of the Norwegian-dominated Alliance party. Finnish precincts consistently gave more votes to Republican than Alliance/Populist candidates, but tended generally to scatter their votes among the major parties more than other groups. As for Germans and Irish, hardly a Catholic or Lutheran farmer joined and participated in the Farmers' Alliance or People's party organizations, but instead remained loyal to the Democrats. Only when local Democrats negotiated a coalition county ticket did the Alliance/Populist parties make gains in the traditionally Democratic German and Irish precincts. Surprisingly, between 1890 and 1896, voters in the city of Fergus Falls cast an average one-third of their ballots for Alliance and Populist gubernatorial candidates. Upon closer inspection, however, it seems that once again Norwegians contributed most to this county-seat trend. The combined votes of the first and fourth wards, where the most Norwegians lived, averaged nearly 12 percentage points higher than did those of the second and third wards.[46]

IV

Although Norwegian-American voting strength moved solidly behind the new party, state and county events after 1890 suggested a more melancholy fate for Alliance politics generally. At the state level, internal upheavals had by 1890 shifted control to Alliancemen antagonistic to Ignatius Donnelly and his influence. Leaders of the anti-Donnelly faction had managed the gubernatorial campaign of Sidney M. Owen in 1890. But after Owen's defeat, Donnelly seized the initiative and, within two months, overwhelmingly won the presidency of the party's parent organization, the Farmers' Alliance. The state central committee still held tight rein over the political arm of the movement – the Alliance party – but Donnelly deftly neutralized its power over the next few months. This he accomplished when the national People's party drew its first breath in Cincinnati and invested Donnelly's delegates instead of his rivals with the honor of organizing the new party in Minnesota. With this advantage in hand, he stood well positioned to merge the Farmers' Alliance into the new People's party, leaving Minnesota's Alliance party isolated and ineffectual.[47] Donnelly's opponents resolved not to take this challenge lying down but, recognizing their severely weakened position, tried all measures short of a formal break to hold onto some independence and some future voice in People's party affairs.

Otter Tail's Alliance state senator, John B. Hompe, had emerged as a leader of those opposing Donnelly after becoming disgusted with Donnelly's legislative machinations during the 1891 session. Hardly had Ignatius Donnelly returned from the Cincinnati convention when Hompe succeeded in getting the Fifth Congressional District convention of the Alliance to resolve that it would only "cooperate with the People's party through the state central committee of the Alliance Party."[48] But the assumption of equal standing between the Alliance and People's parties no longer carried force. By May of 1892, with the adroit Donnelly having sidestepped all confrontations, the Alliance party lay in an advanced state of decay and most of its members were ready to join the new People's party. Only the Otter Tail Alliance organization, or what little remained of it, tried to put forth candidates in 1892, but they attracted embarrassingly few votes.[49]

Given Hompe's opposition, prospects for Donnelly's new party in Otter Tail county seemed dim. But then a single event opened the way:

the climactic resolution of a bitter personal struggle in 1891 between Hompe's ally, Charles Brandborg, and Haldor Boen that drove Boen and his Norwegian followers from the county Alliance.

The 1891 meeting of the County Alliance broke apart in conflict as its proceedings brought about Boen's resignation and publicized the factional battle. Hompe nominated his loyal friend, Charles Brandborg, to remain as president of the County Alliance and the motion carried unanimously. Boen, however, found challengers for his position as secretary. G. O. Greeley, a Brandborg and Hompe man, and another candidate were placed against him. Although Boen led Greeley by eleven of the seventy-three ballots cast, no candidate received a majority. But when the third candidate then withdrew in favor of Boen, Greeley lost by twelve votes. Brandborg waited until all quieted down and then stood to announce:

"A year ago you elected Mr. Boen and myself to serve as your secretary and president for the next year. Now there is no secret about the fact that good feeling does not exist between Mr. Boen and myself; we have not been in harmony for some time past. When we were elected last year the time was an important and critical one for the Alliance, and for the good of the cause . . . I did not feel justified in handing in my resignation. I suppressed my personal feelings for the sake of the Alliance . . . but now there is no fight on hand, and I will not do it again. I will not – I cannot – serve by the side of Mr. Boen again. For these reasons I now tender my preemptory resignation from the office of president."

Momentary silence filled the hall as members looked toward Boen to see his reaction. A conciliator then insisted that both men honor the vote of the majority and remain in their elected offices, and he mildly reprimanded Brandborg for bringing such disputes into the meeting. Hompe also urged Brandborg and Boen to work together despite their differences. But "we can't let Boen have everything," exclaimed the defeated candidate G. O. Greeley; "we have got to fight him a little, you know, though we can't do nothing."

Somewhat embarrassed, Brandborg reiterated his feelings, but by that point Boen had heard enough. Quickly standing, he expressed amazement at this turn of events. Pointing out that the secretary amounted to a dray horse that did all the work and insisting that he had not been a burden on the organization, Boen showed growing anger: "Why then am I attacked? It may be for private reasons, for personal reasons that I do not care to discuss now; it may be partly for nationality reasons [Brandborg was of Swedish birth and Boen, Norwegian]. I am a very independent man; a privileged American citizen, and I do not bow the head to any man, however dictatorial he may be; perhaps this is my offense. At any rate I shall not now resign, as I thought I might do when I rose to my feet."

A brief burst of applause greeted Boen as he sat down. To give the atmosphere a chance to cool, members called a fifteen-minute recess, which was then extended further while a conciliation committee worked to resolve the matter. At the end, Boen played the martyr's role, making a falsely humble, sarcastic speech of resignation in the interests of harmony and keeping such an "invaluable" man as Brandborg in the president's chair.[50]

Unknowingly, the temporary advantage gained by the Brandborg-Hompe group sowed the seeds of their eventual defeat. Ignatius Donnelly's Populist party needed popular local leaders unaligned with his opponents in order to capture both Otter Tail county and the rest of the congressional district—the citadel of farmers' movement strength. And in a disaffected Boen Donnelly found the most aggressive leader possible to fashion a new Populist structure.

But this is to get ahead of the story. A good deal of resentment lingered among Boen's supporters during the weeks following the convention clash. It contributed to an unfortunate incident during the Fourth of July celebration at Henning. Before the day ended, Ole Anderson, a twenty-five-year-old Swede, lay dead—accidently killed by the president of the County Alliance, Charles Brandborg. Too much beer and whiskey, the editor of the Fergus Falls *Journal* concluded, had been at the bottom of it all.[51]

As part of its festivities, the Alliance had erected a stage from which various addresses were being given. A drunken Boen supporter, embittered about his leader's ouster, persistently harassed one of the speakers and, at Brandborg's insistence, the heckler was arrested and jailed.[52] A crowd gathered outside the jail and, when Brandborg happened to pass by, they surged toward him urging the man's release. Brandborg refused and, becoming alarmed by the rather unruly crowd, warned them to stand back. When one man moved toward him, the powerfully built, two-hundred-pound Brandborg knocked him out with a blow from his fist. As all waited for the man to revive, the crowd turned ugly. Brandborg started for home but many followed and several began to throw stones at him. Brandborg seized a rail to protect himself. Swinging it once, he narrowly missed one man. But swinging it again he caught a young Swede squarely on the side of the head and he crumpled to the ground. As Brandborg hurried home, men in the crowd carried the unconscious man back to town, where he died shortly thereafter.[53]

Controversy ensued. Brandborg's enemies claimed that the whole thing would not have taken place had not the Alliance president angered people by his offensive, dictatorial, and tactless manner.[54] Defenders stoutly insisted that Brandborg was being unjustly maligned, with John Hompe reportedly saying that "we must stand by Charlie."[55] Although all charges were dropped after a court hearing, the publicity heightened public emotions. One Brandborg follower particularly aroused ethnic tension when he retaliated in a letter describing the slain Swede as a "poor, ignorant devil" whose life had been taken by a "free American club."[56]

Demoralized, Charles Brandborg withdrew as head of the Hompe faction's newspaper company, the Henning *Alliance Advocate*, and in May, 1892, he refused another term as president of the County Alliance.[57] But John Hompe had no intention of giving up. He enlivened politics during early 1892 in several articles lambasting Ignatius Donnelly's motives and behavior in the 1891 legislature. Not to be outdone, Donnelly counterattacked with several articles of his own.[58] But despite Hompe's attempts to deny further honors to Donnelly's new party, his hopes for Otter Tail county to lead a successful statewide party revolt quickly fizzled.[59]

In January, 1892, Haldor Boen re-emerged – this time as organizer of the Populist party, not only for the county but for the entire Seventh Congressional District as well. The new assignment had come after Boen publicized a recommended plan of campaign for the upcoming year that identified Donnelly as the man who should be the next president of the United States. The political turnabout, as Adams of the *Journal* gleefully phrased it, had lifted Boen "out of the suds where the other fellows thought they had him and put him into the saddle. This knocks the alliance committee, of which Mr. Brandborg is chairman, into the soup, unless an effort is made to keep the Otter Tail alliance out of the People's party."[60]

Boen took steps to prevent that eventuality. As Donnelly would later do, Boen sought not to quash his opponents but to bring the discordant elements together once again, beseeching them "to bury their differences, forget their misunderstandings of the past and stand shoulder to shoulder" under the new banner of Populism. Their subjugation would gain him nothing while conciliation might bring public support both for the new party and for his own effort to win nomination for a seat in Congress. In line with this plan, Boen announced in March the names of those he proposed to include on his Otter Tail county central committee. His list contained representatives of most political groups including the leader of the Alliance opposition, John Hompe.[61]

"We do not recognize that Mr. Boen had any right to act in this matter," said one spokesman upon leaving a hastily called meeting of Hompe's faction, and "we don't propose to have any bosses take our power away from us."[62] Over the next several weeks, however, confidence waned and John Hompe's announced retirement from what he termed "political struggles" further weakened the pro-Alliance faction, despite efforts of the *Ugeblad* and the *Alliance Advocate* to buoy the dying Alliance cause.[63]

By May 19, when the County Alliance met, nearly all stood ready to accept Boen's People's party as the legitimate heir to the Alliance party. Some disgruntled Alliancemen wanted to try to discredit Boen's past handling of County Alliance treasury funds, but Brandborg ended that—reminding them that a previous investigation had satisfactorily settled the matter. John Hompe delivered a final plea deploring the impending merger and the desire of a few to be bosses, but resignedly told Alliancemen that he would go along with their decision. By early afternoon delegates formally gave their party over to the new People's party and unanimously elected Boen's new executive committee to represent them.

Charles Brandborg took the whole matter well, joking that all those who had predicted a big fight ought "to give up the role of political prophets." But John Hompe accepted things in a less forgiving spirit. The new county central committee met in Haldor Boen's office following the Alliance meeting, and they had just fixed the date of the upcoming county People's party convention and the form of delegate representation when Hompe interrupted. Referring to Boen's description of their new body as the county committee of the People's party, he asked if this committee in any way recognized the state Farmers' Alliance party central committee—the anti-Donnelly campaign committee. When told that of course it did not and could not, Hompe said, "Then, I must decline to serve as one of its members," and got up and walked out of the room, disregarding a colleague's protest about quibbling over words.[64]

Delegates to the People's party county convention met three weeks later. Most were farmers from the Norwegian townships with scarcely any Germans, Irish, or native-born Americans present.[65] With but two exceptions, nominations went to the incumbents who had been elected by the county Alliance party in 1890. Members also unanimously approved a delegation to the Seventh District Congressional convention pledged to Haldor Boen for Congress.[66]

One week later, when convention delegates met at Moorhead, Minnesota, most expected that the candidate would come from either Otter Tail or Polk county–the two largest in the district. State Senator Edwin E. Lommen fought Boen for the nomination but lost when his divided following failed to coalesce behind his candidacy.[67]

Haldor Boen now stood as head of the county and district central committees of the People's party and his political fortunes had never looked brighter. Success had not come easy to him. In fact, disappointment and even personal disaster had darkened nearly every achievement. Political prospects that seemed bright back in 1884 when he helped organize the Otter Tail County Alliance dimmed when the death of two sons tragically cut short his effort to canvass the county for support. The children had walked out on thin ice to pick rushes and had fallen through, drowning in only a few feet of water. Six years later, tragedy struck again just after he had negotiated the 1890 "combination" ticket with Democrats and Prohibitionists. His fourteen-year-old son, driving to town with a load of hay, fell beneath the wheels of the wagon, which passed over his neck and killed him. This second loss to his family of nine children reportedly left Haldor "nearly wild with grief."[68]

Politically, Boen had lost the Alliance endorsement for state representative in 1884, been denied a Republican nomination for registrar of deeds in 1886, and met subsequent defeat as an independent candidate. And, of course, he had felt the bitterness of forced resignation in 1891 from his long-held post as secretary of the County Alliance. Although he was persistent indeed, other qualities handicapped his career. "No one regrets more than I do," said Boen, "my lack of ability as a public speaker. It is unfortunate for myself and often very embarrassing to my friends."[69] Although he excelled in private conversation, large groups seemed to erode Boen's self-confidence and reduce him to speaking in a way that reminded one man of a youthful clergyman offering prayer.[70]

But now, in the 1892 campaign, immediate problems beset Boen. Boen and Donnelly's victorious struggle for leadership had demoralized and divided the forces of reform. The local Democratic party organization lay ruptured, split in two over fusion with the People's party, and debilitating infighting between Farmers' Alliance and People's party forces had left many farmers bewildered and dispirited. While concerned that all this might erode Populist pluralities at the polls, Boen hoped that his core of Norwegian voting strength would see him through. But here, the editor of the Fergus Falls *Ugeblad* threatened these chances by rejecting Boen's People's party. Whether or not this would destroy Boen's prospects for victory remained a major question.

Anfin Solem's *Ugeblad* circulated fifteen hundred issues weekly to Norwegian readers throughout Otter Tail and adjoining counties. Although he devoted much space to religious and literary matters, Solem also commented on county and state politics, which made *Ugeblad* a considerable political force. Solem had advocated a separate Alliance party back in 1888 and when it finally happened in 1890 the Fergus Falls *Journal* described the "normally conservative paper" as having become "fairly frenzied" over the reform movement.[71] But when the Alliance split apart, the *Ugeblad's* editor vigorously took up the defense of Hompe and Brandborg's pro-Alliance cause against Boen and Donnelly. To editor Solem, Ignatius Donnelly seemed unreliable, a leader unworthy of public confidence. As for Boen, the highly principled Solem found him to be "a politician from the top of his head to the tip of his toes, and like almost all such, he is not altogether too particular about the principle if only his plans can be carried out." Though respecting his courage and perseverance, Solem believed that it was "against the reform party's first principles to promote such a man" as Boen, who "has always been an office seeker."[72]

Elmer Adams of the *Journal* thought the disagreement went far deeper, however: "What the starting point was which led Mr. Boen and the editor of the *Ugeblad* in different directions is not known, but if we were to make a guess, it would be their differences on religious questions. The editor of the *Ugeblad*, trained as he has been from childhood in certain beliefs, is orthodox to the core. Mr. Boen is an extremist in the opposite direction . . . . To Mr. Solem's mind, Mr. Boen's views are extremely harmful and it is but natural to expect that they should wind their way in different directions."[73]

Whatever the reasons, by late July the *Ugeblad's* anti-Boen and anti-Donnelly campaign had surfaced.[74] Although Boen knew that the *Ugeblad's* opposition to him would also cost the newspaper some influence, he could not be sure how much damage Solem might do.[75] When he wrote to Donnelly the last week of July, Boen seemed preoccupied with the newspaper. After stating that he did not know how much truth there was to reports that farmers were going back on them, Boen continued:

"The truth is that this is not a 'Donnelly County,' whatever that means, and the chief opposition to myself according to Mr. Solem is that I am 'too much of a Donnelly man.'

"So I think both of us will have a harder struggle and perhaps fare worse in this county, than anywhere else in this district.

"Mr. [Hans P.] Bjorge the president of the County Alliance informs me that the *Ugeblad* will support the legislative and county ticket of the People's party but that it will pound 'Donnelly and Boen.'

"I expected that he would support the whole ticket or nothing with the exception of myself."[76]

As Boen feared, editor Solem announced in early August his backing of Norwegian-born Knute Nelson for governor against Ignatius Donnelly. Likewise the editor declared his support for Republican Henry Feig, of German parentage, for Congress against Haldor Boen.[77]

By mid-September Boen's mounting concern about inadequate newspaper support led him to sound out other People's party/Democratic/Prohibition county candidates about whether to start a newspaper on their behalf. A new propaganda sheet never materialized, however, since most of the candidates indicated that the *Ugeblad* had treated them fairly and only reacted unfavorably to Boen.[78]

In hopes of further obstructing and killing off Populist candidates at the polls, John Hompe in late September called a mass County Alliance meeting at Henning, which mainly selected candidates already nominated by the other major parties. Against Boen, for instance, those who attended endorsed the Republican candidate for Congress, Henry Feig.[79]

Owing to Otter Tail's unsettled politics, Boen rarely got out to campaign in those parts of the district where few knew him. Consumed with trying to protect earlier won gains at home, no sooner did he seem to carefully construct one political fence before opponents tore another down.[80] But despite his inattention to other parts of the congressional district, Boen's effort to prevent large anticipated losses in Otter Tail county paid off.

Notwithstanding opposition from the *Ugeblad*, the Republicans, and John Hompe's pro-Alliance party endorsements, Boen nearly obtained a plurality in the county, being only 112 votes shy of those received by Henry Feig, the Republican candidate. And majorities elsewhere made Haldor Boen the next congressman from the Seventh District. Polk, Marshall, and Kittson counties provided the key pluralities that brought him a narrow victory of 165 votes.[81] "I pulled through—through a small knothole," Boen wrote to Donnelly. "It was a tight squeeze but I am mighty glad it was not tighter."[82]

The *Ugeblad*'s political influence turned out to be limited. In the race for Congress, the strongly Norwegian precincts gave an average of only 19 percent of their votes to the candidate endorsed by editor Solem compared to 62 percent for Boen. Evidently local leadership, loyalties, and prejudices counted for more than the *Ugeblad*'s influence. Five of thirteen Norwegian precincts denied Boen a majority of their votes while five others gave two-thirds of theirs to him. At one extreme, Boen attracted only 25 percent of the votes cast in Dane Prairie township while 92 percent of the voters favored him in Folden and Trondhjem townships. Nevertheless, one would still have expected the *Ugeblad*'s endorsement of the popular Republican Knute Nelson for governor to have easily swung the Norwegian precincts into line. Even here, however, seven of the thirteen precincts cast majorities not for their Norwegian countryman but for the Irish-Catholic Donnelly. Although the *Ugeblad* worried Boen, the strength of Boen's political organization and personal following apparently assured him of victory in Norwegian strongholds.

Winning the congressional seat marked a high point in Haldor Boen's public career. By shrewdly manipulating the authority of Donnelly's new party, Boen had absorbed the Farmers' Alliance party into his new Populist organization and led a fully committed following to the district convention. A weak base supported these successes, however, one that demanded Boen's constant attention to keep it from crumbling away. Boen's earlier invitation to the weakly committed, the openly antagonistic, and all other office seekers to join his new party had prevented an open split in the county farmers' movement. But this proved costly as soon as Populism fell on more difficult days.

V

Congressman Haldor Boen served in Washington during a period when the depression of 1893 shook the country, intensifying agricultural and industrial unrest and threatening national turmoil. By midsummer of 1893 some of the nation's largest railroads had fallen into receivership. Banks everywhere fought to stay afloat by calling in their business and individual loans, and banks in rural sections toppled one after another.

In Otter Tail county, relations deteriorated between the county seat banks and the farmers. Editor Frank Hoskins of the Henning *Alliance Advocate* faced trial and commitment to the state mental hospital for a few weeks after being charged with criminal libel against the management of a Fergus Falls bank. He had advised depositor withdrawals after alleging that three Fergus Falls banks were insolvent.[83] But upon his release, Hoskins and former County Alliance president Charles Brandborg went about the townships delivering speeches claiming usurious practices by the banks.[84] They argued or implied, partly by citing Biblical references, that farmers should not have to pay on notes they owed Fergus Falls banks, since the banks charged unjust interest rates.

Their speeches instigated what became known as the "Folden farmers' affair." Fifty members of the Farmers' Alliance in Folden, an almost solidly Norwegian township near Henning, took action in March of 1894. Hoping to see other towns organize whose people had felt the "tiger's claws" of bankers, they signed a paper repudiating their debts and pledging to resist payments on their notes. Three of the farmers even escaped briefly to Canada with some property mortgaged as chattel security on loans. The editor of the Republican Fergus Falls *Journal* quickly seized this opportunity to link the Populist cause with anarchism.[85]

Boen and other Populists tried to disassociate their party from the acts of Hoskins and Brandborg. Fergus Falls' *Rodhuggeren* (The Radical), reputed to be owned substantially by Haldor Boen and now the principal Norwegian-language newspaper in the county, asserted that these two ill-tempered eccentrics could not possibly be Populists because they used their speeches primarily to attack People's party leaders.[86] After hearing one of Hoskins' talks, *Rodhuggeren*'s strongly Populist editor declared:

"It was Boen he was after principally. He also criticized [Populist] County Treasurer Hans Nelson for not withdrawing the county funds out of the Fergus Banks last summer, thereby forcing them to close their doors. He wanted the People's party congressman [Boen] to . . . work wholly and solely for one object only, i.e., 'The subtreasury bill.' If they did not do that they were traitors to their party and should be replaced by men who would do it."[87]

If staunch Republicans became disturbed by the Folden affair or the class strife accompanying the Great Northern Railway strike of 1894, Haldor Boen's controversial record in Congress hardly encouraged their tranquility.[88] In keeping with his radical temperament, Boen proposed drastic political and economic reforms to cope with the troubled depression years.[89] Owing to the shrinking per capita stock of money in circulation, for example, he introduced a bill to expend what the *Weekly Journal* termed a billion dollars of irredeemable currency on public works. Another bill proposed to reduce by 25 percent the pay of government officeholders, on the grounds that those responsible for the ruinous deflationary conditions should not reap the advancing purchasing power that their fixed incomes gave them. Yet another of his bills called for all deposits of public money to be withdrawn from national banks and kept in the national treasury. But Boen's most controversial action came when he introduced a joint resolution directing the War Department to provide tents and provisions to Jacob Coxey's famous "army" of unemployed industrial workers who marched on Washington–making their futile plea for national public works before being arrested for trespassing on the Capitol grounds.

Because of Boen's narrow victory in 1892 and the uncertain politics of the district, the Republican national committee targeted the congressman as being vulnerable to challenge. Accordingly, they devoted considerable attention, financial and otherwise, to defeating him.[90] Frank M. Eddy, Pope county's clerk of district court since 1885, received the Republican nomination and the *Journal's* Elmer Adams– known as "one of the shrewdest political managers and manipulators in the state"–took charge of the campaign.[91]

The residue of past factional bitterness encouraged rumors that Congressman Boen might fail to secure renomination even in his own county. But these subsided after the annual Farmers' Alliance meeting in June endorsed both his course in Congress and his re-election in November. At the People's party convention in mid-July, Boen's friends easily saw to it that an Otter Tail delegation, instructed to support Boen's re-election bid, went to the Seventh District convention, thereby making his renomination certain. The Populist county convention had also decided against coalescing again with the severely weakened local Democratic or Prohibition parties, insisting instead that their candidates pledge to uphold the platform adopted at the Populist party convention at Omaha in 1892 and forsake all other party endorsements. Furthermore, county Populist delegates backed away from their previous leanings toward prohibition and declared instead their willingness to accept a controlled liquor traffic.[92]

But though Boen's men had managed matters, the congressman himself committed a careless political blunder that eventually would be his undoing. Whether from over-confidence or inattention to county matters, he gave to others his chairmanship over both the county party organization and the county central committee, thereby relinquishing personal political control. Chairman Boen appointed Charles F. Hanson, the clerk of court, and Charlie Smith, the candidate for state representative, to serve with eight others on the county central committee.[93] As it happened, the two men would use the power of this committee in 1896 as a wedge to dislodge and topple Boen from leadership.

Boen relied on the vigorous Populist organ *Rodhuggeren* for his main source of Norwegian press support in the district. Meanwhile, his foes in the Norwegian press–not daring to support a Republican candidate openly against Boen and the Populists–turned to another third party to drain off Norwegian votes; *Nye Normanden* (The New Norseman), edited by Hans A. Foss in Moorhead, deserted him to aid the Prohibition candidate and, as expected, so did Anfin Solem's *Ugeblad*. Solem dismissed the People's party county convention as the "Boen convention" and the candidates as the "Boen ticket" while throwing his support to the Prohibitionists even though he favored temperance over prohibition principles.[94]

Throughout the campaign both newspapers fought with Ole Hagen's larger *Rodhuggeren* for the allegiance of Norwegian voters. Hagen charged *Ugeblad* with hypocrisy in supporting a prohibitionist while disclaiming their cause and of being "plutocracy's servant" who "runs the errands of the monopolists and lives by their motto: 'Anything to beat Boen.'" Countercharges came from Solem that *Rodhuggeren* was "opposed to Christ"; Ole Hagen claimed that the editor was trying to get voters "to look at us as frightful people."[95] And through *Nye Normanden* editor Foss lost no opportunity to castigate Boen, alleging, for example, that the congressman had kept a liquor plank out of the congressional district Populist platform, while a correspondent in Hagen's *Rodhuggeren* said of Foss: "We have known him all too well from his vagabond days of drunken sprees, and it is with pleasure that I and many others now observe that he finally has been found out."[96]

Rodhuggeren's editors also could not ignore anti-Catholic activity by the American Protective Association. If, to Republican eyes, the A. P. A. could stir up disunity among Norwegian Populists through publicizing the Catholic backgrounds of, say, statewide leader Ignatius Donnelly or county attorney Mike Daly, so much the better. To counter this, a *Rodhuggeren* editorial warned of how "millionaires and corporations have a hand in this game" of igniting religious passions in order to kill political reform. The editors also accused A. P. A. agitators of wanting to slip religion into the common schools. Nativism, they warned, most threatened Norwegians: "When the mask falls," the A. P. A. "will deprive us—even if we are Protestants—of our civil rights just because we could not ourselves choose our place of birth." And by A. P. A. insistence that only approved Protestant candidates gain office, "It will soon become here as it was in Norway in the old days: people had no rights, either to think, speak, or act without first asking the State Church's advice."[97]

Republicans and Populists alike sensed that this would be a much closer contest than either of the two previous ones. Charles Hanson, whom the *Journal*'s Republican editor termed "the most astute and skillful worker in the People's party in the county," strenuously labored with his protégé Charlie Smith to blunt the Republican offensive. Hanson and Smith were "running the party," noted the *Journal's* editor, and trying hard "to whip the people into line."[98] No wonder. By October the Republicans, noted another editor, were "turning heaven and hades to defeat the ticket."[99]

As the campaign moved into its final days, the *Journal* grew increasingly shrill. "Boen Must Be Defeated" rang one of Editor Adams's headlines, and fresh attacks were launched on Boen, dragging forward the congressman's religious views and assailing his record in Congress.[100] "If Mr. Boen does not believe in a God, personal or otherwise, in a hell or heaven, that is his right," said Adams, for "religious liberty is one of the foundation stones of our federal constitution."[101] As for the Populist leader's achievements, however, Adams declared that "no man ever in congress in one session had introduced more absurd, ridiculous, pernicious measures than he . . . His bill to print $2,000,000,000 irredeemable paper money [Boen's proposal had called for one billion] is sure to scare capital out of the district as long as he sits in congress. It is difficult enough to get an eastern man to loan money on a Park Region and Red River Valley farm."[102]

Rodhuggeren fought back. The *Journal* "shudders," they said, when Congressman Boen has the nerve to propose measures which, if enacted into law, "would destroy both the transportation and the banking monopolies of which it is the chief spokesman and defender."[103] To topple Boen, it was charged, the *Journal* had lied and distorted his record. "Doubly false," wrote Boen's secretary, Syver Vinje, had been Adams's allegations that Boen wanted the government to print two billion dollars of "irredeemable' paper money, because the money would in fact be both "full legal tender for all debts" and "receivable for taxes." And it was "inexcusable ignorance" or "dishonesty," said Vinje, to say that Boen had proposed to give "rations" to Coxey's army in Washington, D.C., for the bill had never even mentioned "government rations." As for the *Journal* striving to "belittle and ridicule" Boen's bill for improvements to the Red River of the North, Vinje reminded readers that the measure had been introduced earlier by the Republican congressman, that it was in accord with the resolution passed by the Republican state legislature and signed by Governor Knute Nelson, and that Boen's congressional opponent was promising to take up and continue this work if elected: "Honesty, cover they face."[104] And *Rodhuggeren's* editors lambasted the *Journal* as the organ of railroad and banking corporations, identifying its owners as two leading men of the Great Northern Railway, the president of the First National Bank of Fergus Falls, another "very wealthy" property owner, and Elmer E. Adams himself, described as "presumably also very wealthy, as he occupies the most aristocratic residence in the city."[105]

In the last moments of the contest, when it would have been difficult to answer charges, the *Ugeblad* accused Boen of, among other things, threatening bodily injury to two Norwegian Republicans and traveling with a free railroad pass to and from Congress. All this *Rodhuggeren* labeled as a "last minute falsehood," a "laughable" collection of "Republican fictions" reprinted from the Fergus Falls *Journal*, the Great Northern's own newspaper.[106]

Despite the drama of attacks and counterattacks, voters seemed less influenced than before by agrarian agitation. Election returns showed that Otter Tail Republicans had checked the momentum of the People's party. Several offices went to Republicans and those Populists who succeeded in the county races won by margins far thinner than in earlier elections.[107]

Even more significantly, Haldor Boen lost his bid for Congress. He carried his own county as well as the six Red River Valley counties that had given him majorities in 1892. But this time, instead of repeating another narrow victory, he suffered a narrow defeat by 800 votes out of nearly 42,000 cast. The Otter Tail county vote for Boen, whether out of respect for his radical independence or in reaction to harsh Republican tactics, increased to 39 percent compared to 33 percent in 1892. In Norwegian precincts, the congressman's vote declined slightly. A strong majority of 57 percent stood behind him, but this had dropped 4 percentage points since 1892. Once again, there was considerable variety — six of thirteen heavily Norwegian precincts withheld majorities from Boen while five others mustered two-thirds or more of their votes on his behalf. Perhaps reflecting the influence of the *Ugeblad*, whose editor favored a prohibition candidate over Boen, Norwegian precincts increased their prohibitionist vote by an average 9 percentage points from that of two years before.

His hopes for victory shattered, Boen played the martyr in an address published in *Rodhuggeren*:

"Election is over and I lost. The people lost. But since I . . . received at least 4,000 votes more this time than at the last election I regard it as approval of my work in congress. The monied men in general did not like that I voted for the free coinage of silver and against the Sherman law; nor did they like that I proposed that the government should issue one billion dollars, full legal tender treasury notes, and put them in circulation by building railways, erecting needed public buildings and improving rivers and harbors.

"But Foss [of *Nye Normanden*], Solem [of the *Ugeblad* and

others] . . . could not defeat the Populist candidate. . . . Other means must be employed. Saloon keepers, lawyers, machine agents, toughs of all kinds took a hand against us."[108]

Opposition newspapers in the region gleefully pounced on his bitter statement, wondering wryly how "monied men" had defeated Boen in an area where farmers constituted over 90 percent of the voters.[109]

VI

The ex-congressman, alone with defeat and heavily in debt, returned from Washington the first week of April. Now divorced – his marriage of eighteen years having fallen victim to congressional success – Haldor found a house in Fergus Falls and attended to his farm at Aurdal.[110]

As Boen sulked, pondering past setbacks and future possibilities, the years 1895 and 1896 brought steady consolidation of local Populist forces under Charles Hanson that slowly shunted Haldor Boen from the inner circles of political planning. By the fall of 1895 Boen realized that his political interests must be revitalized if he was to maintain his standing in the party and so he purchased the poorly performing Fergus *Globe* for $350.[111] This gave him an English language vehicle with which to praise his supporters and castigate those who had fought him in the race for Congress. "He was not able to punish his friends fast enough with his Norwegian paper [*Rodhuggeren*]," jeered Elmer Adams, "so now he will try them with both languages at the same time." He added that "it is understood that a Unitarian monthly will also be started so that advanced religion as well as advanced politics will be disseminated."[112]

Those expecting more editorializing and a more enthusiastic Populist organ were not disappointed. Sparks flew in February when at a banquet Boen made disparaging remarks to a visiting military man about maintaining a standing army. This brought down on Boen's head the wrath of a locally prominent Civil War veteran, who attacked the Norwegian-American politician as "a foreigner who either stole or begged his citizenship in the country of his adoption."[113] And in March, when Boen saw political motives behind railroad magnate James J. Hill's invitation for seventy Otter Tail farmers to visit the State Experimental Farm, editor Adams could not resist noting that "It seems to be the purpose of not only Boen but his ring of office seekers to keep the people as moss-covered as possible so that by appealing to their prejudices they can continue themselves in office."[114]

By the spring of 1896, however, control over the local Populist party began to overshadow other issues. Boen's adversary, Charles Hanson, was a thirty-nine-year-old Norwegian American from Fergus Falls. In 1883, after having received a business education in Norway, Hanson had immigrated to Otter Tail county and worked in the county auditor's office until he joined Boen's new Populist party in 1892. Intense and energetic, Hanson achieved election as clerk of court in 1892 and also in the next two elections. People who knew him described Hanson has an astute, courteous, efficient, and plain man who expressed his opinions in a clear, cordial manner.[115] In due course, however, after they had known one another for a long time, he and Boen split in 1896 – Hanson becoming acknowledged leader of the "fusionist" wing of the party and Boen the defender of "mid-road Populism." Boen commanded a majority of popular support among Norwegian farmers while Hanson controlled the county Populist machinery through the county central committee.

Boen's popularity with the general electorate posed a problem to Hanson for which he had no immediate solution. He recognized the truth of the *Journal*'s statement that Haldor Boen "understands how to handle men, and particularly his countrymen who practically make up the Populist party in this county. He knows the ins and outs of every township; he knows the men who control."[116]

Charles Hanson and his friends concluded that to protect themselves and their present political arrangements they would need to get the jump on Haldor Boen by scheduling the county Populist convention early. But Boen seemed already out in front. Ordinarily the county central committee, which Hanson controlled, called its convention only after members of the Seventh Congressional District committee set the date for the district convention and announced the number of delegates for each county to send. Boen held the advantage here because his friends controlled the Seventh District committee. Of course, he could postpone things only so long, since county conventions had to precede state and national conventions. Still, despite criticism from around the district, Boen managed to hold things off until late May, when he scheduled the Seventh District committee to meet June 3 at Fergus Falls.[117]

This move to buy time exasperated the Hanson forces and they saw their chances for success jeopardized unless they acted at once. Calling together members of the People's party county central committee, they made two shrewd political moves. First, Hanson's committee decided to force Boen's hand by announcing that the date of the county convention would be June 23, 1896, two days before the Republican county convention. Caught off guard, Boen commented that "this is rather hasty action in view of the fact that the district committee meets here on the third day of June."[118] But second, and far more important, they ingeniously reapportioned the delegate representation in a way that broke Boen's Norwegian political power at the county convention. Elmer Adams of the *Journal* explained how it promised effectively to "give Boen a very black eye.

"The ex-congressman is the strongest in the heavy Populist towns [townships] namely, such towns as Norwegian Grove, Trondhjem, Aastad, Sverdrup, Tordenskjold, Nidaros, Folden and a few others. In fact the Populist vote is almost entirely cast in about twenty [strongly Norwegian] towns, these twenty giving twice as many votes as the remaining forty-five precincts. Boen is strong in these towns. In order to weaken his influence in the convention the apportionment was juggled so that these big towns lost their influence. This was done by giving each town one delegate at large."[119]

This bold stroke would insure Hanson's renomination to the clerk of court position and severely undermine Boen's control over the convention proceedings.

Despite this setback, the ex-congressman continued to fight Hanson and his group all the way into the convention. Charles Hanson was no longer a true Populist, Boen charged, since he had willingly placed some non-Populists on the ticket to broaden support and filled subordinate positions in his clerk of court office with non-Populists. Although in 1890 and 1892 Boen had himself broadened support by coalescing with other political parties against the Republicans, this year the Boen forces strongly opposed fusion. Only staunch middle-of-the-road party men should be nominated, they demanded: "nominate only Populists! Fusion ends in confusion."[120]

With the additional at-large delegates from ordinarily non-Populist townships, the People's Party county convention proved large, with over two hundred delegates present. After working out compromise language on the liquor question between wets and drys, they began nominations. All went harmoniously until the time came to consider Hanson for the clerk of court post. After one speech recommended Hanson's nomination, Haldor Boen walked to the platform and, appearing entirely at ease, declared: "I have worked to have harmony in selecting our legislative ticket, but we have now come to a parting of the ways. Mr. [A.T.] Vigen has said that Hanson is a Populist. I say he is not a Populist and that is the reason I am opposed to his election. I know of no better test of a man's beliefs than his acts. He has been willing to place men not Populists upon our ticket. He has given the position of deputy in his office to a rabid Republican, one of the wealthiest in the county, when many deserving and competent Populists would have . . . filled the position. Otto Nilsby, whom I desire to have placed in nomination, is a Populist – is competent and will stand by the Populist party."[121]

Hanson's co-worker, Charlie Smith, then stood on his chair and shouted that when Boen had been registrar of deeds, he too had given a Republican a job. Stepping back to the podium, Boen replied that he had appointed the Republican before 1890, when he himself had been a Republican. As soon as he became a Populist officeholder, Boen said, he notified the Republican that he would have to go and a Populist took his place. Although Boen's rebuttal scored points, Hanson easily achieved nomination by a vote of 141 to 59. On this crucial matter Boen had been soundly beaten.[122]

When the time came for appointing a delegation to the Seventh District congressional convention, the dispirited Boen made little effort to control the matter and so received a delegation only loosely and generally pledged to him. At the Seventh District convention, Boen's competitor, Edwin E. Lommen, won the nomination to Congress. Lommen, who had lost to Boen in 1892, now led from the start and steadily gained votes from Boen's own delegation and others until on the eighth ballot he emerged as victor. Boen had allowed his name to go before the convention to prove that, despite rumors by Hanson's faction that he had lost his following, he still had considerable strength. With mingled bitterness and pride, Boen wrote after the convention:

"When the delegation was made up I paid very little attention to its personnel and wrote down any name suggested whether I knew him to be friend or foe, even insisting that my bitterest political opponent C. Smith [Hanson's protégé] should remain on the delegation. . . .

"I am conceited enough to think that had I asked the county district convention for it, I would have been permitted to select the delegates to the district convention with myself at the head of the list as was done in 1892, and that in the face of the two scamps who, during the last few months, have been maligning me."[123]

Thereafter, Boen traveled to both the state convention and the national meeting at St. Louis, steadfastly opposing the tide of fusion sentiment that swept over the Populist and Democratic parties. At the state convention, Boen stood "on the outside of the breastworks," refusing "to meet with the Otter Tail delegation when it caucused" and staying " 'middle-of-the-road' to the last."[124] At the national convention, he fought against total fusion by advocating the Bryan and Watson combination ticket that was ultimately nominated.[125]

Gradually, however, Boen resigned himself to statewide fusion, and urged "every citizen who favors a cleaning out of the state stable, otherwise known as the State Capitol, to . . . work for the election of [Democrat/Populist] John Lind until the polls close."[126] But in Otter Tail county the struggles between Boen's strictly Populist and Hanson's fusionist forces continued unabated. When Boen's county campaign committee encouraged activities that stressed the separateness of the People's party, Hanson's wing countered by deferring to Democratic candidates and formed a new campaign committee in place of Boen's organization.[127]

As elsewhere through the Prairie and Plains region, Free Silver became the main issue in the campaign.[128] Otter Tail's Republicans predicted that many Norwegian Populists would desert the fusion party, as would the German Democrats around Perham who held decided "sound money" views. But voting returns directly contradicted this forecast. The eight most heavily German settlements increased their Democratic vote by 20 percentage points over their average gubernatorial vote in 1894.[129] Norwegian precincts increased their vote as well, giving the fusion candidate 5 more percentage points than their Populist vote of two years before. Although once again a Republican captured the seat for Congress, in Otter Tail races fusionists gained back – albeit with thin pluralities – several county offices lost in 1894 and all of their seats in the state legislature.[130]

Dissatisfied, editor Elmer Adams grumbled that the Populist victories were "due to the fact that ten or twelve heavy Norwegian towns [townships] in which English papers are not taken, voted solidly for every man on their ticket, regardless of qualifications or record."[131] To this Haldor Boen heatedly replied that "the world knows that you slander them." Norwegian Americans, he said "have been the surest pay and the closest readers of the *Journal* in this county" and "every Norwegian here ought to resent all the insults of the *Journal*" by abandoning it.[132]

From 1896 onward the People's party steadily declined in Otter Tail county as it further traded with other parties and as the state and national party faded away. The Hanson-Boen feud continued past 1898 when the party proved capable of electing but half of their legislative ticket and only a portion of their county slate.[133] Still Charles Hanson's Fergus Falls and Perham Populists remained in control of the party machinery until after 1902, when the People's party lost its identity entirely through amalgamation with the Democratic party. As for Boen, he never again attended a county Populist convention after 1896, but his radicalism increased with time, moving him into socialism and impelling him to publish his sharply outspoken views until his death in 1912.[134]

Otter Tail Populism may have lost its identity, but Norwegian settlements carried the imprint of their political legacy. Republicanism had little appeal for them for the next two decades after the election of 1896. Gradually Ole Sageng, a young rural politician who had joined the Populist organization in its dying years, eased Norwegian voters into independent progressive Republicanism. But such ties remained fragile at best. With the onset of the Nonpartisan League during World War I and the ensuing Farmer-Labor movement, the latent populism of the settlements burst forth again. Norwegian precincts where Populism had most thrived became the strongest adherents of the new agrarian movement, while the weaker Populist precincts continued to find Ole Sageng's progressive Republicanism most attractive.

III

Progressivism and the LaFollette Movement

CHAPTER 6

Progressive Dissent

The Farmers' Alliance and the People's party evaporated from the Upper Middle West, but the agricultural rhetoric of populist times lingered on, attacking railroad abuses and animating the Farmers' Equity movement as it agitated for legislation favorable to cooperative marketing and purchasing arrangements. The umbrella of progressivism, however, soon embraced far more. Strictly agrarian discontent lost its coherence, and reform impulses broadened into middle-class anti-monopolism. Associated movements sprang up aimed against big business corruption and municipal graft, and a host of other movements worked out their programs for efficiency, humanitarian relief, and social uplift. Political reformers divided their energies between expanding popular control over politics by forcing through direct primary legislation and enacting regulatory controls to curb the influence of railroads, public utilities, and other large interests.

I

Republican organizations across the Upper Midwest became fragmented as these issues kindled bitter factionalism between conservative and progressive elements. The discord continued on until World War I. Although roughly similar, the many strains of progressivism worked themselves out in the context of each state's indigenous politics. Under Robert M. LaFollette, Wisconsin's progressives came to dominate the Republican party from 1900 until 1914. During the same period, Albert B. Cummins led active but less coherent progressive agitation in Iowa. In Minnesota, on the other hand, no single individual emerged to lead progressive forces within the Republican party, although the full complement of progressive issues weighted its politics.[1]

The Norwegian vote reflected these differences in political leadership. The more single-minded progressive causes in Wisconsin and Iowa, organized almost as one-man movements, increased Republican support among Norwegian settlements compared to their votes cast in the 1890s. The change proved less great in Iowa than in Wisconsin, however. Three times Iowa progressives brought gubernatorial victory to their magnetic leader, Albert B. Cummins, before senatorial honors sent him on to Washington. Nevertheless, progressive control over Iowa's Republican party only slightly increased the party's share of votes from either Norwegian settlements or the state at large. Cummins's statewide vote (1901–1906) improved by an average 4 percentage points over that of his Republican predecessors in the 1890s while it expanded 7 percentage points in Norwegian settlements. Being a relatively small portion of Iowa's population, Norwegians did not find themselves actively courted as a significant ethnic addition to Iowa's progressive coalition. Accordingly, without local progressive leaders among Norwegian Americans, it evidently mattered little whether the Republican candidate was "progressive" or "conservative," for votes from Iowa's Norwegian settlements only slightly declined when floundering progressive leadership permitted arch-standpat candidate Beryl F. Carroll to become governor in 1908 and 1910. Carroll's vote in these elections slipped an average 3 percentage points statewide from what Cummins had garnered and, similarly, it fell a mere 4 percentage points in Norwegian settlements. Meanwhile in Wisconsin, Republican votes from Norwegian settlements showed stronger progressive loyalties. They rose an average 10 percentage points for progressive candidates (1900–1912) and plummeted 25 percentage points in 1914 when party regular Emanuel Philipp successfully tapped the growing vein of conservative feeling running through the state.

Minnesota's Norwegian settlements responded differently, however, shifting back and forth between parties and candidates. There, progressive forces lacked leadership of equal stature. Two governors held office during most of the progressive years of 1904 to 1914 and neither could be considered a crusader. Of them, the popular John Johnson, a St. Paul editor, came closest to being a reform governor, but he was a Democrat. Voters elected this son of Swedish immigrants to the governorship in 1904 and twice thereafter before he died one year into his third term. Despite the Democratic label, Johnson's personal popularity attracted over 57 percent of the votes in Norwegian settlements in his first bid for re-election. But then in 1908, when the Republicans nominated "Jake" Jacobson, a reform-minded Norwegian from western Minnesota, Johnson won only one-fourth of the votes cast in Norwegian settlements.[2]

With Johnson's death in office, Adolph O. Eberhart, the lieutenant governor, returned control to the Republicans. But in his hands progressive impulses went unnourished. Also of Swedish birth, Eberhart soon gravitated toward the party's conservative wing as he served two additional terms in office. He alienated Republican "drys" in 1910 when he refused to pledge for county option, he backed President Taft in 1912, and, in his own campaign for re-election, he secured quick enactment of a state primary law in 1912 with the intention of splitting and overcoming his progressive political opponents. Clever and affable, though heavily reliant on his political strategist E. E. "Big Ed" Smith, Eberhart remained pallid in his progressivism, his commitment to reform seemingly more expedient than sincere. Still, Norwegian settlements cast most of their votes for him in 1910 although, two years later, many turned to the prohibition candidate, denying the governor their earlier majority support.[3]

II

During the Progressive Era hopeful reformers looked to Wisconsin—the laboratory of political progressivism. And perhaps no one element did more to elect the strong-willed man who made it so than the state's Norwegian settlements. Robert LaFollette's infectious rhetoric captivated Norwegian audiences, and his energetic, daring politics and image as an implacable foe of special interests held their respect, even though his hasty judgment, occasional self-righteous abrasiveness, and what Rasmus B. Anderson termed his "Iago spirit" cost him friends along the way.

Steadily from the mid-nineties, Robert LaFollette put together an insurgent coalition that came to dominate Wisconsin politics during the first fourteen years of the new century. Particular help came from three sources: a discontented younger generation of lawyers within the Republican party who itched for office; William D. Hoard, the former governor and an influential dairy promoter; and, perhaps most important, votes of Norwegian settlements that expressed sensitivity to anti-monopolist and agrarian issues coupled with feelings of past party neglect in matters of political recognition.[4] "Despite defections," writes an historian of Robert LaFollette's rise to prominence, "the Norwegians delivered an almost solid bloc of votes for the progressives in each of their campaigns."[5]

A most potent ally helping LaFollette gain his grip on the Norwegian vote was the Norwegian language newspapers, especially the powerful and widely distributed Chicago *Skandinaven*, published by John Anderson. It was circulated to "well nigh every Norwegian home in Wisconsin," and its highly regarded views found ready acceptance from many countrymen.[6] Finding in LaFollette an able champion against public abuses, John Anderson's *Skandinaven* and many Norwegians, including such ambitious ones as Congressman Nils Haugen, Andrew H. Dahl, and Herman Ekern, campaigned mightily for "Fighting Bob" and other candidates who promised effective reform.

Although LaFollette's close association with *Skandinaven* helped garner the loyalty of most Wisconsin Norwegians it did not win them all. *Amerika*, an influential Norwegian-language newspaper under the editorship of Rasmus B. Anderson in Madison, had little sympathy for the politician whom its editor characterized as "Robert (Iago) LaFollette." While Anderson admired LaFollette's "pluck, his ambition and his great ability as an organizer," the editor had "no faith in his so-called 'reforms,' " and decried Fighting Bob's "lack of loyalty to those who have given him their aid and support." But the firm Republicanism of Rasmus Anderson's *Amerika* stood little chance against John Anderson's *Skandinaven*, which circulated in 1903 five times the 9,000 weekly copies that *Amerika* printed. When it came to molding public sentiment and wielding political clout, Rasmus Anderson himself admitted that *Skandinaven*'s influence was "simply tremendous. . . . All Norwegians in Wisconsins who had any political ambition realized that their only hope of success lay in giving their allegiance to 'Skandinaven' and to Lafollette."[7]

Robert LaFollette had grown up in the predominantly Norwegian township of Primrose in Dane county and he understood the political sentiments that moved Norwegian settlers. Moreover, his deft political sense and natural gregariousness were undoubtedly helped by his rough knowledge of Sogning, a dialect of western Norway. Knowing the Norwegians' sensitivity to hints of patronizing neglect and their agrarian suspicion of elites, LaFollette assiduously courted the Norwegian vote and entwined much of his hopes with theirs.[8]

Norwegian Americans' reputation as the very bone and marrow of the party's progressive wing can easily be misinterpreted, however, as

Robert M. LaFollette Sr. at unidentified speaking engagement. Norwegian-American votes were a mainstay of his reform coalition, helping him attain the governorship (1901–1906) and later gain senatorial honors (1906–1925). Photo courtesy of State Historical Society of Wisconsin.

simply an attachment to the admired Robert LaFollette. Actually, the Norwegian commitment extended fully as much to LaFollette's cause and to their own striving for political recognition as it did to LaFollette himself. Sometimes even LaFollette seemed to believe in the inseparability of himself and his cause that he had so masterfully fused together in the public's thoughts. This made serious trouble for him when his own interests departed from those of his constituents. It happened most strikingly in 1906, when LaFollette's Norwegian-born lieutenant governor, James Davidson, sought the governorship after LaFollette became United States senator. The new senator strenuously opposed Davidson's effort – desiring another man instead – but, nevertheless, Davidson handily beat LaFollette's choice in the primary to win by a larger margin of Norwegian votes than LaFollette himself ever garnered during his years as governor. Even the Milwaukee progressive Francis McGovern won the governorship in 1910 by a plurality from Norwegian settlements that equaled any of LaFollette's past gubernatorial victories.

Nevertheless, although LaFollette's machine did falter, Wisconsin Norwegians' general enthusiasm for progressive Republicans readily showed itself. Compared to the period 1880–1898, when a hefty 71 percent of the votes in Norwegian settlements went to the Republican candidate for governor, their Republican vote swelled by 10 percentage points during the period 1900 through 1912 when progressives controlled the party. Thereafter, from 1914 to 1924, the Norwegian Republican vote receded to an average of 74 percent. Meanwhile, the overall state vote hardly changed. Wisconsin's average vote of one period differed from that of the next by no more than 3 percentage points.[9]

But this is just the average, and it conceals variations. Norwegian settlements responded in different ways to the rise of LaFollette progressivism.[10] And it cannot be said that all Norwegian settlements were equally enthusiastic for the progressives' cause. Compare, for example, the decade when progressives secured their greatest Norwegian vote (1900–1910) to the years before LaFollette's rise to the governorship (1892–1898). The shift in votes from one decade to the next—dramatically sharp in some townships and nearly indiscernible in others—ranged from 1.3 to 39.4 percentage points.[11] The most extreme differences (that is, over 20 percent) came from settlements evidently disillusioned with Republicanism in the 1890s but fairly enthusiastic in their support for progressive gubernatorial candidates after LaFollette's emergence. The votes showed no particular geographic distribution—Norwegian settlements that shifted strongly toward progressivism could be found near or adjacent to those at the other extreme.

But despite considerable variety in the Republican percentages returned from Wisconsin's Norwegian settlements, for any one election these percentages remained closely bunched. In typical contests, 20 percentage points or less ordinarily separated the most from the least Republican Norwegian township. Yet, notwithstanding this political homogeneity, the sources of this modest spread in votes do give added clues to what moved Norwegian settlements to vote as they did.[12]

Two characteristics of Norwegian-American settlements stand out as consistent influences: the extent to which farm renters operated holdings in each settlement, and the extent to which potatoes made up an important part of the total value of harvested crops. Both can be taken as indicators of distinctions between wealthy and marginally prosperous settlements. In general, the more prosperous Norwegian townships proved weaker in their support for both LaFollette and other Republican candidates for governor (Figure 14).[13]

Most of the Norwegian farm renters lived in places such as Dane county where better agricultural lands could support, on a single farmstead, both an owner and a tenant. Here, where sons and sons-in-law

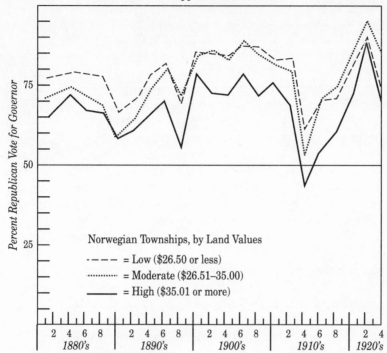

Average Value Per Acre and Republican
Gubernatorial Support in Wisconsin

Norwegian Townships, by Land Values

- - - - = Low ($26.50 or less)
.... = Moderate ($26.51–35.00)
———— = High ($35.01 or more)

Figure 14. Republican share of vote for governor in Wisconsin's
Norwegian settlements classified by average value per acre.

of farm owners usually became tenants or moved as renters onto the
main holdings when the father retired to a town nearby, progressive
Republicans attracted lower than average voter loyalty. Conversely,
Norwegian settlements with greater potato production – the poorer
sections of the state – provided greater than average Republican
strength both before and during the rise of LaFollette's powerful organization. Why before? It is not entirely clear, but the fact does suggest limits to a strictly economic interpretation, as well as a vigorous
support for regular Republicanism regardless of who occupied the
party's ticket.[14]

During the time of Fighting Bob's progressive assault against
privilege, then, poorer potato-growing settlements not surprisingly favored his cause. Agricultural lands in the southern half of Wisconsin
stood apart from these "cutover" settlements to the north, where lum-
bering dominated until the end of the nineteenth century.[15] Farm
productivity held strong in most of the southern portion, but farmers

in the northern cutover needed to carve their holdings from vast stretches of pine, stump, and brush cover and stony, unfavorable soil. Farms occupied only 50 percent of the land in several Norwegian settlements that were situated in the southern portion of the cutover. Here many farmers, in their need to make intensive use of their land, had turned to potatoes, which grew well in the cooler growing season among the stumps and light soils of freshly cleared land. Unfortunately this gave them little more than marginal farm prosperity, for profits remained low because of potato overproduction.[16]

Among Wisconsin's Norwegian settlements, however, their particular economic or cultural makeup seemed to affect voting less than was the case in Iowa and Minnesota. In Wisconsin, perhaps the great political weight of *Skandinaven* throughout the state overwhelmed and subdued the influence of other economic and cultural differences between the state's Norwegian settlements.[17]

Nationality and religion—the great ethnocultural influences in American politics—held Norwegian settlements safe within Wisconsin's Republican party during the progressive years.[18] Socioeconomic distinctions worked their influence by helping set the level of their Republicanism. But while most year-in, year-out voting differences reflected these socioeconomic conditions and differing political circumstances, the most tumultuous contests flared up when nationality or anti-Catholic feelings pitted Norwegians against others in the Republican party.[19]

Thus, while under normal circumstances the Republican party label along with the personal popularity of LaFollette and his anti-trust rhetoric proved irresistible in most Wisconsin Norwegian settlements, progressives needed to avoid the cross-currents of Yankee versus immigrant, rural versus urban, Catholic versus Protestant, and other intensely felt cultural antagonisms. When occasionally one or another of these issues ripped the LaFollette ship loose from its coalition moorings, progressive Republicanism floundered. Just such a time came during the period 1906–1908 when Norwegian Americans became disillusioned with Robert LaFollette; thereafter he could no longer count on their undivided support. An instance of this is found in the story of Republican factionalism and Norwegian dissent in Trempealeau county.

CHAPTER 7

Trempealeau County, Wisconsin

During the period 1906 to 1908, large numbers of Norwegian Americans abandoned LaFollette's leadership and his influence among them waned. Ethnic discontent, political miscalculation, and local political rivalry combined in Trempealeau county to prompt several Norwegian settlements both to turn against LaFollette's choice for governor and to vote out of office his trusted Norwegian assembly leader, Speaker Herman L. Ekern.

Political lines in Trempealeau county conformed to the particular mix of people who settled there.[1] American- and British-born settlers, the earliest arrivals, laid out farms and villages on the fertile Trempealeau and Decorah prairies to the south. In their politics, this section came to lean toward conservative, so-called "stalwart" Republicanism. "The Ridge"–a series of limestone bluffs that ran between this section and the remainder of the county–geographically reinforced the group's sense of political separateness. Local rivalry persisted throughout this time between the citizens of earlier settled townships south of the Ridge and newcomers to the north. This rivalry showed itself particularly during county conventions, as older towns such as Galesville and Trempealeau sought to retain their privileges in selecting candidates. By the sixties, Catholic Bohemians and Poles were also crowding into the Pine Creek and Arcadia area of southwestern Trempealeau county, their greatest concentration being in Dodge township along the Trempealeau River. Here the Democratic party found a reliable base of support.

But by far the largest group in the county, and the major source of Trempealeau Republicanism, was the Norwegians. Filtering into the county's eastern and northern reaches along its timbered valleys and hillsides, they outnumbered all other groups by the late 1870s. Important Norwegian settlements took shape in the Trempealeau Valley near Blair, along the north branch of Beaver Creek in Ettrick township, and in the large fertile Pigeon Creek Valley farther to the north. Norwegian-born settlers also established Eleva and Sumner along the Buffalo River in the far northern townships. Migrants from eastern districts of Norway tended to concentrate in central and northern parts of the county, while along Beaver Creek – in southeastern Trempealeau – a community of settlers originating from Hardanger in western Norway made up much of Ettrick township's population. The heavy Norwegian presence soon gave them a central position in the Republican domination of the county.

Achieving their due share of political recognition came only gradually in Trempealeau county's "democratic" political system, however, For "behind the party conclaves," historian Merle Curti acknowledges, "a small group of county leaders planned strategy" and served as Trempealeau's major multi-term officeholders.[2] But although this inner "cohesive and enduring" group of six or seven prominent farmers, lawyers, and businessmen controlled the county's politics, they could not ignore for long the political realities of new groups rapidly settling their county. The inner circle of party wheelhorses needed at least to admit leaders among the newcomers into "party councils and give them patronage and political favors."[3] By the late 1870s local Republican leaders felt moved to accommodate growing Norwegian strength. Under the guiding hand of such Norwegian immigrant spokesmen as the well-to-do merchant Peter Ekern of Pigeon Falls and the leading merchant and flour mill owner in Ettrick, Iver Pederson, Norwegians by 1880 attained influence proportionate to their numbers in the county's political life.[4] The two immigrant leaders continued throughout the decade to play a strong role in Republican party circles. Thereafter, forceful individual Norwegian leadership in politics ebbed until Herman L. Ekern, Peter's nephew, rose to lead LaFollette's cause in the county beginning in 1898.

I

A new political order arrived when the educated offspring of Trempealeau's early settlers began to enter county politics in the 1890s. Coinciding with the rise of Republican party factionalism in the state,

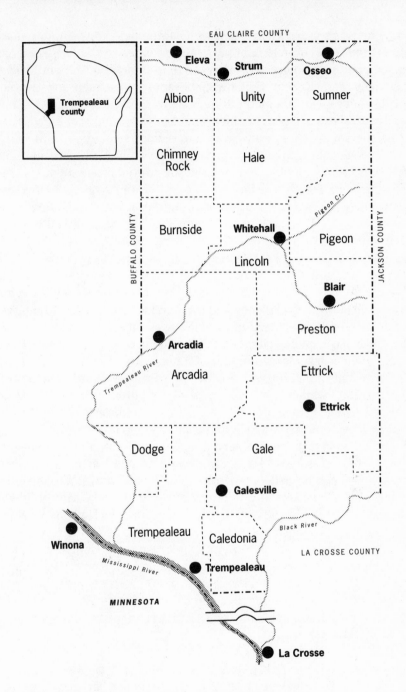

Figure 15. Trempealeau county, Wisconsin.

the emerging generation found an unaccustomed variety of political opportunities. Three men in particular stepped to the forefront, each having recently completed his training in law. Two of them, John C. Gaveney and Robert S. Cowie, became spokesmen for the non-progressives who dominated Republican organizations in the southern and central townships. The third, Herman L. Ekern, proceeded to harness the votes of his Norwegian countrymen.

The eloquent John Gaveney returned from a brief residence at Stevens Point in 1890 to manage the substantial interests of his Irish-born father's estate and begin a law practice in Arcadia.[5] Of course, young Gaveney's marriage in 1890 to the daughter of state Republican "boss" Elisha W. Keyes undoubtedly whetted his political appetite. But the political ambitions of the twenty-seven-year-old lawyer remained dormant until Robert Cowie's arrival in 1894. Cowie, of Scottish ancestry, became Gaveney's law partner upon graduating from law school. Having grown up in nearby Buffalo county, Cowie, through his association with Gaveney and his marriage in 1897 to the daughter of John Melby, a protégé of local Norwegian leader Iver Pederson, soon became a leading citizen of Trempealeau county. Together, Cowie and Gaveney assumed leadership of conservative Republican elements in the county. The energetic Gaveney served as state senator from 1901 to 1905 while Cowie held a variety of public positions, including county district attorney (1898-1902), deputy auditor with the U.S. Naval Department (1903-1905), and county judge (1906-1909).[6]

Meanwhile, Herman Ekern assumed leadership of Trempealeau county's progressives.[7] He became county district attorney in 1894 — the same year he graduated from the University of Wisconsin law school. He also entered law practice in partnership with an earlier schoolteacher of his, the respected Norwegian-born Hans A. Anderson of Whitehall. To most, Herman Ekern might have seemed a quiet and thoughtful, even passive, man, but Anderson saw in him an ambitious, tireless youth who possessed "a remarkable keenness for system and details" that he lacked.[8] Serving as district attorney until 1898, when Cowie moved into the position, Ekern turned to full-time private law practice until his election in 1902 as a progressive Republican member of the State Assembly.[9]

This position he held through 1908; in the last year of his term he served in the capacity of speaker. A devoted lieutenant of Robert M. LaFollette, Ekern played a leading role in guiding "progressive" legislation through the Assembly. During these years he became most widely known for his service as a member and special counsel of the

Herman L. Ekern, ca. 1905, an ardent lieutenant of Robert M. LaFollette first elected by Trempealeau county voters to the state assembly in 1902 and then for two terms thereafter, during the last of which he served as speaker. Photo courtesy of State Historical Society of Wisconsin.

Wisconsin Insurance Investigation Committee, which between 1905 and 1907 delved into insurance company practices in the state.

Before 1902 Robert LaFollette won favor throughout Trempealeau county, with little factional division of the kind taking shape in state politics. Local ambitions and traditional local rivalry predominated. A county delegation might be sent to the state convention in support of LaFollette, while conservatives shared county and legislative offices and participation in party affairs. But it could hardly be said that county politics were the same as five years before.

The strident message of LaFollette progressivism within the party had unsettled local political relations. By 1898, non-LaFollette elements showed signs of coalescing. The same year that Ekern and J. B. Beach, county Republican chairman and editor of the influential Whitehall *Times-Banner*, accompanied a solid Trempealeau delegation for LaFollette to the state convention, the balance of the county slate shifted toward nominees from Arcadia and other townships south of the Ridge. Most prominent among these new faces appeared that of Robert Cowie as Republican nominee for district attorney.[10]

But 1900 proved to be the actual turning point, when the reins of control passed to conservatives. Robert Cowie not only gained renomination as district attorney, he also replaced Beach as chairman of the county central committee, a position the editor had held for fourteen years.[11] Perhaps more importantly, Cowie's partner, John Gaveney, beat Ekern's law partner, Hans A. Anderson, in a heated race for nomination as state senator. Strong feelings lingered from the fight and visibly affected the November election when GOP voters scratched Gaveney's name from their ballots in some of the northern townships, especially Whitehall. From this moment on, statewide politics encouraged a widening of the local rift; contending Republican forces in Madison worked hard to secure local allies as their party split between those for LaFollette—the progressives—and those opposed to him—the stalwarts.[12]

Consequently, Ekern and other LaFollette men soon joined in common cause. With Ekern as their recognized leader, Beach became the chief editorial spokesman of local LaFollette progressivism, while game warden E. L. Immell hustled about the county keeping progressive political fences in order. Like LaFollette in pressing for tight organization as a major way to defeat those who frustrated reform programs, Ekern and his friends quietly fashioned an efficient political organization—one aimed at harnessing the full participation of Norwegian voters.[13]

In 1902 they launched their counterattack. Progressives swept all but two precincts in caucuses to select delegates to the state gubernatorial convention. Conservative resistance stiffened in the fall convention, however, where delegates met to nominate GOP candidates for county offices. Robert Cowie gained re-nomination for district attorney, but was forced to give over his chairmanship of the Republican county committee to a LaFollette man from Arcadia Village. A few Treampealeau stalwarts drew nomination for lesser offices. As one conservative editor put it, "The strife for offices was not of the friendly kind, and only the years to come will heal some of the wounds."[14]

The convention's most bitter contest placed Herman Ekern against the aging but prominent Republican delegate from Galesville, Captain Alex Arnold, for nomination to the assemblyman's seat. Recognizing that the wind was blowing strongly toward LaFollette, the wily Arnold—a perennial officeholder—declared himself for Governor LaFollette on the one hand and, on the other, for the re-election of conservative United States Senator John C. Spooner. Countering Arnold's transparent pseudo-progressivism, Ekern and Beach contended that Ekern's nomination was necessary if the platform's reform pledges were to be effectively carried out. Conservatives denounced such tactics as amounting to an insulting assertion that Captain Arnold's pledge "is not to be relied upon," but to no avail – Ekern's friends had the delegates to win.[15]

The year 1902 marked the high point of LaFollette strength in the county. By the time caucuses convened in the late spring of 1904 to select delegates to the Republican state gubernatorial convention, non-LaFollette forces had successfully captured eleven of the twenty-four townships, compared to only two in 1902. Heavily Norwegian areas all held firm behind Governor LaFollette, although his support slipped elsewhere.[16]

With local prospects brightening, editors of the county's conservative newspapers confidently claimed that the people had had enough. They alleged that only indifference and disgust with politics lay in the wake of "four years of turmoil." The alleged high expenses of LaFollette's administration had "let daylight in and the aroma out," wrote the editor of the Galesville *Republican*, who further remarked that reform in this administration "is not found on the bargain counters."[17]

Despite such bravado, conservatives' leadership in the county was not what it had been. The most energetic and popular of their number, Robert Cowie, had recently resigned as district attorney to accept an appointment arranged by Senator Spooner as deputy auditor with the Navy Department in Washington. And State Senator Gaveney could do little for others, as he was busy defending himself against LaFollette's determined effort to oust him and other major legislative opponents. Trempealeau county conservatism had lost its cutting edge.

Perhaps to compensate for this, anti-LaFollette newspapers pressed their attack in more personal terms. They branded the county's progressive leaders "a blind trio" of shouters for LaFollette. Specifically, so they asserted, Assemblyman Ekern, editor Beach, and game warden Immell had become a "self constituted trio of political dictators," marking non-LaFollette politicians for slaughter. An important local conservative warned: "We have not forgotten, nor neither have the people generally, how the party rose up and dethroned J. B. Beach a few years ago [1900].

"Ekern is a young man of good character and average ability. He has had much of the fruit that has fallen from the party tree and done but little to merit it. We think we can give him some good advice, however, and that is to frankly act the part that he so constantly talks. If he dislikes political machines let him avoid the company of men who have no other occupation than running political machines. Let him treat with consideration men who have been Republicans before he was born."[18]

But the fever of Trempealeau county factionalism changed few minds – the well-organized Norwegian voters saw little in the speeches of Ekern and LaFollette that did not conform to their own views. With Cowie gone and Gaveney thrown on the defensive, the progressive-dominated county convention met without incident.[19] The editor of the Galesville *Republican* was reduced to lamenting how, unlike earlier conventions in which every delegate had a voice, "since we have been reformed" Ekern himself now "selects the candidates and tells the people's representatives that he has orders from Madison to name this particular slate."[20] Progressives easily carried all the Norwegian precincts and most other of the county's rural sections in the November election.

II

Herman L. Ekern's political career never looked brighter as the Assembly convened in 1905. He had swamped his Democratic opponent in the recent election, attracting nearly three-fourths of the county's ballots cast. And his steadfast loyalty found its measure of reward – the thirty-three year old assemblyman was elevated to the chairmanship of the important judiciary committee.

Simultaneously, few Wisconsin voters were surprised when Governor LaFollette was chosen as United States senator to succeed the stalwart faction's candidate, Senator Joseph V. Quarles. Conservatives had fought to prevent it by defeating the governor at the polls in November, but failing in this, they simply awaited his inevitable selection by the 1905 legislature.[21] With LaFollette now senator, voters numbed and weary after seven years of constant political warfare hoped a time of peace now lay at hand. Such hopes soon evaporated.

James O. Davidson, the lieutenant governor, now succeeded LaFollette to the governorship.[22] But before this popular Norwegian American had even assumed office, he could see that his chances for sitting in the executive chair very long were slim. For although LaFollette was now turning his interest to Washington, he and his political intimates were determined to retain their leadership in Wisconsin politics. And in sizing up the prospects for exerting effective control from afar, LaFollette examined "Yim" Davidson and found him an embarrassment. He judged him to be not enough of a militant, too uneducated, too amiable, perhaps, with more than a touch of naiveté.

Governor James O. Davidson, ca. 1907, the Norwegian-born successor to Robert M. LaFollette after a hard-fought primary which disrupted Norwegian political relations with LaFollette's reform coalition. Photo courtesy of State Historical Society of Wisconsin.

Davidson's "shortcomings" as governor, in the view of one Norwegian-American advisor to LaFollette, were painfully obvious: "It pervades the atmosphere about him. You can feel it. It was especially noticeable when the delegations from Rock [county] appeared last week. I just looked in and withdrew, but Jim had sunk back into the chair the very personification of insignificance and nonentity. I felt humiliated at the sight." Consequently, he concluded, "the impression will go out that he is not quite big enough for the position, and . . . that view will increase the longer he remains.[23]

But this rationale simply reinforced a decision already made: Speaker of the House Irvine L. Lenroot, an energetic young lawyer of Swedish background, should be Wisconsin's progressive governor.

A better mix for disaster could have been devised by neither stalwart nor Democrat. To Wisconsin's Norwegians, James Davidson represented not merely a popular reformer, but a symbol of Norwegian aspirations in America. Plain-living, modest, and likable, he had attained the highest political office in Wisconsin yet held by one of their kind. Furthermore, the man selected to challenge Davidson was a Swede—this coming at precisely the moment when relations between

Norway and Sweden had seemed poised on the brink of war owing to Norway's recent declaration of independence from Swedish union. But ignoring the cultural realities that underlay their early victories in the state, LaFollette's inner circle focused on elevating the right kind of leader, a man who would continue to keep Wisconsin reform ideas alive.

Former congressman Nils P. Haugen, a Norwegian-American ally of LaFollette, warned the senator that supporting Lenroot over Davidson was folly and reminded him that it would be "at least unwise, yes, ungrateful, to deny him a reelection, of which he was reasonably assured, if nominated."[24] LaFollette's law partner, Alfred T. Rogers, expressed similar early alarm: "It has always been your mainstay to line up the solid Scandinavian elements and it's like having a broken arm to fight without them."[25]

Nevertheless, signs of Davidson's intended fate were not long in coming, although he himself showed no intention of stepping down. In June of 1905, a short time after Davidson had assumed the governorship, his colleagues in the lower house hailed Speaker Lenroot as the next governor, presenting him with a chair and couch suitable to high office. The following February, in hopes that Davidson might be induced quietly to remove himself, Lenroot vigorously entered the primary contest before Davidson had publicly announced his candidacy.[26] The issue now became joined in the state's Republican primary, with Lenroot and Davidson openly competing for progressive support.

If these developments disturbed some progressives, they positively delighted conservatives. Heretofore resentful and brooding, the conservatives in Trempealeau county grasped this unexpected political opportunity and rushed full tilt to Davidson's defense. The editor of the Galesville *Republican*, relishing the chance to cut Ekern down to size, spewed out facts and rumors to see whom they might splatter. Why, he asked, "does Ekern hasten to climb onto the Lenroot wagon? He knows that Trempealeau County prefers Davidson to Lenroot. If he had any regard for his constituents or for Davidson, he would wait a bit before chasing around in the interests of Lenroot."[27] He repeated rumors that Ekern's efforts to carry the county for Lenroot might endanger the "congressional bee buzzing in the covering of his auburn locks." And chiding Ekern as the administration's pet who had been exceedingly lucky in politics, the newspaper mockingly allowed that "if he can convince the Norwegians of this county that they should support Lenroot in preference to one of their own countrymen, it must be admitted that he is clever rather than lucky."[28]

Publicly, Herman Ekern appeared unruffled. Whether because of personal promises made to Lenroot and LaFollette or a sincere belief that Davidson should be ousted, Ekern expressed himself devoted to supporting the most capable man for the job, Irvine Lenroot.

The sting of reaction from the local conservative press was far from deadly. But Ekern could ill afford to take lightly negative reaction from the leading Norwegian-language newspaper circulated in Wisconsin, Chicago's *Skandinaven*. Always in the thick of political battles, John Anderson's newspaper had as its editor-in-chief the politically astute Republican partisan, Nicolay A. Grevstad, a trusted confidential advisor to Minnesota's Senator Knute Nelson.[29] *Skandinaven* had generously supported LaFollette and his reform administration, which Wisconsin's progressives recognized as a major asset in their favor. But when readers caught a whiff of LaFollette's move to dump Davidson, things began to change.

The machinations of LaFollette's inner circle placed John Anderson in a most awkward and uncomfortable position. In their quest for more decisive reform leadership than Davidson could give, the senator's inner group wanted Anderson to forego helping to realize the gubernatorial aspirations of Wisconsin's leading Norwegian-American politician. If an embarrassed Anderson ever agreed to go along with the idea, as he apparently did initially, he soon had second thoughts. Letters had been trickling in from all parts of the state urging the publisher to advance their Norwegian countryman's candidacy over that of the Swedish Lenroot. The pro-Davidson letters owed themselves in part to the work of one Gryttenholm, a Wisconsin agent and correspondent of *Skandinaven* and a reputed "Swede-eater," who urged subscribers to voice their anti-Lenroot feelings to the newspaper. As pro-Davidson letters came in, so many of Anderson's respected friends also urged Davidson's candidacy upon him. All of this further drew the old publisher away from the LaFollette intimates who had enjoyed his past political benefaction.[30]

Sensing Anderson's wavering support and already feeling the effect of the newspaper's editorial silence toward Lenroot, Herman Ekern stopped by the *Skandinaven* office in Chicago on his return from the East in mid-February. There he had a long talk with the publisher. Ekern reported back to LaFollette John Anderson's view that "the fact that Lenroot's announcement awakened no interest among his readers and that he has been receiving letters friendly to Davidson makes him think that it is going to be impossible to beat Davidson."[31] Nils Haugen put the matter more bluntly to LaFollette: "A[nderson] is very much disposed to come out for D[avidson]. The representations made to him by our very positive friend Bergh to the effect that

John Anderson, publisher of *Skandinaven*, eating the disagreeable crow soup of Irvine Lenroot's candidacy after readers prompted the publisher to abandon Lenroot, Robert LaFollette's choice for governor, in favor of their countryman, James O. Davidson. A delighted rival publisher printed Lars Haukaness's cartoon in *Amerika* (Madison, Wisconsin), August 17, 1906.

D[avidson] is really the father of the reform movement in Wisconsin and that LaFollette and the rest simply got onto his bandwagon and stole his thunder . . . really captured the old fellow."[32]

By March Ekern was wishing that *Skandinaven* would simply remain silent on the gubernatorial campaign, but he found instead the newspaper growing ever cooler toward Lenroot. And ultimately, as the pro-Lenroot campaign got underway, *Skandinaven*'s publisher and editor threw the journal's considerable regional weight behind Davidson and denounced the shabby actions of LaFollette and his lieutenants. Fortunately for Ekern, *Skandinaven*'s editor vented most of his spleen at Lenroot and gubernatorial politics, but Ekern was not altogether spared. His friends in Trempealeau county worried about the Chicago newspaper's position, one candidly informing him that there were "several things that work against you, among which is your *pronounced* stand for Lenroot, and the policy of *Skandinaven*, said paper being largely circulated here and its teachings taken as gospel truth."[33] Ekern privately admitted that "the influence of *Skandinaven* is very hard to overcome." He had recently, indeed, had little success in influencing its publisher's specific political positions, including those concerning himself. Ekern complained to a friend how he had "answered much of their legal correspondence for some time without any pay," and yet "they have ignored even those [newspaper articles submitted] in my behalf."[34]

Notwithstanding *Skandinaven*'s influence, Ekern brought a share of his problems upon himself. Instead of quietly accepting the criticism and waiting for the storm to pass, he added to its fury by openly answering back.[35] In early June, 1906, for instance, he wrote an article for the Milwaukee *Free Press* strongly endorsing Lenroot as the man best able to carry on LaFollette's plans and policies. Stressing that ethnic loyalties should have no place in voters' decisions, he went on to minimize Davidson's reform spirit by suggesting that the governor was conducting "a harmony campaign, a mere struggle for office in which no matter of principle is at stake." When the editor of the Blair *Press* in Trempealeau county attacked Ekern's *Free Press* article and *Skandinaven* reprinted the attack, Ekern wrote complaining of distortions in the Norwegian journal's reprint. This John Anderson and Nicolay Grevstad chose to make the basis for their newspaper's full-fledged entry into the contest on Davidson's behalf.

Seeing Ekern's letter to the *Free Press* as "an attack, by inference, upon the policy" of *Skandinaven*, the Norwegian editor responded with special energy, pointing out that "Mr. Ekern makes a plea for the nomination of Irvine L. Lenroot as the Republican candidate for governor, but Senator LaFollette is the beginning and end of his article. It would seem that . . . the question is not what manner of man the people want or the state needs at the time, but what Senator LaFollette needs and wants.

"The Norwegians did not march into the LaFollette camp; he came into their camp. Effective public control of railroads and other corporations, equal taxation, unhampered popular control of nominations and elections, etc. – these and other reforms were firmly established in the fatherland of the Norwegians long before Mr. LaFollette entered public life. The Norwegians of Wisconsin have fought with LaFollette . . . because they have found him to be a fearless foe of public abuses, an able champion of things that should be done, a fighter of skill and courage, a man to lead a fight in the field and win it. They still expect good work from him, and will stand by him so long as he is true to the people, to himself and the cause of representative government – but no further. His unfortunate interference in the orderly contest for governor the Norwegians of Wisconsin, in common with other self-respecting citizens, regard as impertinent bossism that is not to be tolerated."[36] Newspaper reaction like this hardly helped Ekern's position, but he stuck with Lenroot nonetheless, refusing to bend.

Trempealeau county conservatives quietly organized a campaign to destroy Ekern's local strength. Robert Cowie, now returned from Washington as newly elected county judge, met secretly with John Gaveney and other local conservatives at nearby Winona, Minnesota, to work up an effective opposition to Ekern.[37] They settled on backing for assemblyman Dr. George Hildershide, a known LaFollette supporter but also a Davidson man. Cowie and his friends recognized that if they openly opposed Ekern it would only help redirect the issue away from his unholy alliance with Lenroot against Governor Davidson and toward the familiar political warfare of "progressive-versus-stalwart" where Wisconsin progressives had triumphed. So, assuming a low profile, they worked to feed Norwegian disenchantment over the Davidson-Lenroot primary battle.

This strategy succeeded in frustrating Herman Ekern's desire to see the Norwegian-American governor tarred with the stalwart brush. "Judge Cowie is very quiet about his opposition to me," grumbled Ekern, "and I cannot find that any of the Davidson leaders are [attacking me] openly." Yes, complained Lenroot's campaign manager to Ekern, "I wish we could get some positive proof of the combination between Cowie and the Conner-Davidson headquarters. If we could get it out that they were trying to defeat you it would *just about win this fight*."[38]

Nevertheless, despite Ekern's uneasiness, he still held strong advantages over the opposition. His prestigious membership in LaFollette's circle of close advisors remained fundamental, since many local Norwegians took great pride in the fact that one of their own was so closely associated with Wisconsin's rising national progressive leader. Not only that, Ekern's opponent was neither of Norwegian background nor from the Norwegian part of the county. Moreover, although Governor Davidson twice visited the county, he never directly encouraged Ekern's punishment at the polls. LaFollette, on the contrary, appeared openly on the assemblyman's behalf at Blair, where anti-Ekern sentiment persisted among Norwegians. Finally, the assemblyman himself aggressively canvassed the county and maintained intact his tightly knit organization.[39]

Such advantages enabled Ekern to defeat his opponent in the primary and overcome the Democratic candidate in the general election of 1906. Despite uncertainty, and Governor Davidson's victory over Lenroot at the state level, Ekern managed to retain a comfortable majority. The extra measure of support customarily received from Norwegian townships had evaporated, however, for his 58 percent of the vote averaged no more in these townships than in the county at large. This decline from the "solid" Norwegian Republicanism of previous years showed itself mainly in desertions from Ekern where Norwegian townships contained villages. Voters in Albion township, which included Eleva village, gave Ekern only one-fourth of their ballots and he secured a bare majority in the township surrounding Blair village. Consistently, Norwegian townships supported Ekern less than they did Governor Davidson.[40] Only in Pigeon township, where his locally influential relatives lived, and in adjoining Hale township, did Ekern's efforts successfully mobilize for Irvine Lenroot even a quarter of the Republican vote.

III

Between 1906 and 1908 Herman Ekern, rewarded for his heroic loyalty to LaFollette in the difficult Lenroot-Davidson fight, expanded his role in state politics. The three-term assemblyman succeeded Lenroot to the speakership of the general assembly and figured prominently in legislation enacted to regulate insurance companies—legislation that had grown out of the earlier committee investigations for which he had served as chief counsel. He also became occupied with managing the 1908 presidential bid by Senator LaFollette. These statewide duties, however, left him less and less opportunity to keep his political affairs in order back home where foes stood ready to capitalize on his neglect.

By the spring of 1908, watchful conservatives began to probe Ekern's unattended local defenses. Playing on the theme that Ekern paid little heed to the needs of Trempealeau county, they characterized him as aloof and so preoccupied with larger matters that he no longer listened "to the lesser things to which a member of the country districts is expected at all times to give ear."[41] In a similar vein, the conservative press took Ekern to task for supporting LaFollette's financial backer, Isaac Stephenson, over their popular local congressman, John Esch, to succeed Spooner in the United States Senate. Yet another theme they played upon constantly was that three terms in office was enough—for Ekern to ask for more would be nothing less than insatiable greed in pursuit of office. On occasion they also hinted that Ekern took only lukewarm interest in legislation of interest to farmers in the American Society of Equity, a power in Wisconsin. But most important for Norwegian communities, they took continued delight in reviving memories of Ekern's opposition to Governor Davidson.[42]

Ekern's greatest danger, however, stemmed not from the conservative press, but from a new figure in Trempealeau politics. Albert T. Twesme, the sixth of eight children raised on a farm near Blair in Ettrick township within a settlement of immigrants from western Norway, had worked his way through the University of Wisconsin and now had established a flourishing law practice in Galesville. He had also demonstrated a flair for public speaking and widened his acquaintance in politics as a clerk in the 1907 Assembly.[43] Twesme's political credentials appeared impeccable to Norwegian voters. He had, after all, delivered speeches on Governor Davidson's behalf in several districts during the 1906 campaign. Such qualities soon caught the attention of local conservatives anxious to loosen the grip on Norwegian settlements held by Ekern and his progressive organization.[44]

Twesme announced his decision to run for assemblyman to the Blair *Press* instead of his hometown Galesville *Republican*, probably to forestall accusations that stalwarts were booming his candidacy. Even so, the editor of the progressive Whitehall *Times-Banner* immediately suggested that Twesme might in fact be an unreconstructed stalwart.[45] Twesme aggressively commenced to canvass the county, voicing the theme that Trempealeau county should be represented by a man in touch with the popular Jim Davidson. At the same time he shied away from any association with local stalwarts. The "not too radical ones," wrote an Ekern informant, are being approached by Twesme

Albert T. Twesme, ca. 1917, a young Trempealeau county lawyer who defeated Herman L. Ekern for the state assembly in 1908. Photo from F. Curtiss-Wedge and E. D. Pierce, *History of Trempealeau County, Wisconsin* (Chicago, 1917), 456.

"on the argument that you [Ekern] have had three terms and then you have the gall to ask for more." All of this the conservative editor of the Galesville *Republican* took delight in terming "one of the most interesting political mix-ups in the state today."[46]

Herman Ekern assumed the incumbent's pose that Twesme represented no real competition. But privately he became increasingly concerned as the primary campaign unfolded. The albatross of LaFollette's 1906 effort to dump Davidson continued to drag upon Ekern's prospects, while his forthright but inexpedient support for county option on the liquor question threatened to cost him votes in villages where saloons would close if the entire county went "dry."[47]

He worked hard to shift the ground of the argument to that of the people-versus-the-interests. The "real" behind-the-scenes enemy, said Ekern, were outsiders—the state's liquor interests and the old-line insurance companies still smarting from the regulatory legislation of the previous year. By charging them with interference in local affairs, Ekern hoped to stir public indignation. "It is a question," wrote Ekern, "whether the insurance companies and the brewers shall run this county or whether it shall be run by the folks at home."[48]

Meanwhile, Twesme toured the Norwegian townships, neutraliz-
ing progressive opposition by applauding "the efforts of Senator
LaFollette and Governor Davidson to restore to the people the rights
usurped by the great aggregations of wealth." And conservatives
quietly worked to feed the resentments of those who disliked Ekern's
county option stance and to remind those whose ethnic feelings had
been kindled by the Lenroot-Davidson struggle. Now on the defensive,
Ekern hung onto the fraying conviction that his stalwart friends were
"working the nationality question so hard" that it would produce a
backlash effect.[49]

As if he were not beset by enough difficulties, new events further
confounded Ekern's political fate. Up to this time, both Governor
Davidson and Senator LaFollette had remained on the sidelines. But
during the final week Davidson acted indirectly to tip the political
scales against Ekern. Judge Cowie had invited the governor to attend
an American Society of Equity picnic at Galesville, promising that
"what is done politically or otherwise by reason of your visit will be
done in a diplomatic way and that no one can be offended or object to
it. In fact Mr. Twesme and myself merely expect that your visit to the
county will revive and put new life into the strong Davidson sentiment
here and that without saying a word about Ekern on your behalf, the
effect will be the same."[50]

Davidson instead chose to send his private secretary, Colonel
Oliver G. Munson, to the gathering while he appeared that same day
at the nearby Mondovi Fair, where he privately indicated his opposition to Ekern.[51]

Perhaps of even greater importance in the closing days of the primary campaign, a circular mysteriously appeared and made its way
among Norwegians at the Farmers' Equity picnic and in various townships on election day. Believed by many to have been put out by *Skandinaven* through its agent and correspondent in Wisconsin, Gryttenholm, who had distributed a similarly influential political circular in
1906 in the Davidson-Lenroot primary, its meaning was clear—
Nowegians should defeat Ekern and other leading LaFollette men because their election would be detrimental to the political advancement
of Governor Davidson and Norwegians generally.[52] The important circular stated in part:

"Two years ago for the first time an opportunity arose for one of
the Norwegian nationality to occupy the highest position in the state.

"Then was made a brutal attack upon our faith. And the attack
came from a man whom we Norwegians three times in succession had
made governor of the state and since United States senator. Never has

any man in this state been so enthusiastically supported as LaFollette has been by us Norwegians.

"There is yet considerable left of admiration for the man, but our faith has been wrecked."

It went on to describe the current political situation as one in which LaFollette was concerned to make his senatorial position more secure by preventing Davidson, the only possible strong contender, from challenging his reelection. If LaFollette had his way, the circular warned:

"With Ekern as speaker in the assembly and John Strange as president in the senate [by virtue of being lieutenant governor], LaFollette will control the legislature in such a manner that there will be little honor for Governor Davidson's administration.

"We are so shortsighted in politics, we Norwegians, and besides the feeling of unity is so very weak with us. But we have pledged ourselves to hold up Davidson's arms and we owe it to the state and ourselves to do our duty.

"Through Davidson we have, after a generation or more, reached an influence in the state which our intelligence and our never failing faithfulness to principles and morals entitles us to.

"LaFollette has put everything at stake. He has brought out as his candidates Davidson's bitterest political enemies: Lenroot, Mahoney, Strange and Ekern.

"A vote for Jenkins, Atley Peterson, Trottman and Twesme next Tuesday will grow to thousands of votes in a victory for Davidson two years from now."[53]

The balance of Norwegian public sentiment tipped against Ekern's less well-prepared political effort. Albert Twesme captured 55 percent of the county's Republican primary vote. Ekern still held a slight overall majority in the divided Norwegian townships, but with an average of only 52 percent there his strength proved insufficient to offset losses elsewhere. This represented a further erosion of 5 percentage points from the Norwegian vote he had obtained during the troublesome 1906 primary. Once again enthusiasm for Ekern varied considerably among Norwegian townships. Over two-thirds of the combined vote in the towns and villages of Albion, Ettrick, and Unity went to Twesme while Ekern commanded nearly three-fourths of the combined votes of Pigeon, Hale, and Chimney Rock townships.

Consternation filled the Ekern camp. His personal hurt over the voters' decision mingled with anger against those responsible for his defeat. Only a short time ago the young speaker of the Assembly had led LaFollette's national presidential campaign. Now even his goal of speaking for Trempealeau county eluded him. Having believed that progressive candidates would naturally succeed once a direct primary existed to end the days of intriguing special interests, he now faced the fact that the primary could also be wielded to progressivism's disadvantage. At this moment peevishness outweighed generosity of motive in Ekern's camp. The people had gone over to their opponents, they concluded, only because of appeals to their lower political instincts—prejudice and erratic resentments. The question turning over in Ekern's mind, however, was what he should do now.

IV

Talk soon began that Ekern would not easily accept defeat. This struck close to the truth, for Ekern promptly wrote to LaFollette, pouring out his suspicions that brewers, the Society of Equity, short-sighted anti-fourth-term propaganda, and Governor Davidson had combined to bring him down. Moreover, he asserted, "The Stalwart papers in the county and outside, including the Chicago *Skandinaven*, have been pounding the people here quite strong on my opposition to Davidson and there is no question that this [Norwegian] circular had some influence."[54]

Some of Ekern's allegations, such as Governor Davidson's private opposition, did have a basis in fact. An outside representative of the liquor interests had also done some work in Trempealeau county, and Democrats in the western section had been urged by liquor men to vote as Republicans against Ekern. But notwithstanding his accusations, no evidence appeared that insurance companies had taken a hand in Trempealeau county politics and only slight indications surfaced that the Society of Equity seriously opposed his re-nomination.[55]

Outraged pride and factional spirit brought Ekern, LaFollette, Lenroot, and others together in Madison the following week. Incensed about the defeat of LaFollette's lieutenant and suspicious that Governor Davidson had made a calculated effort to discredit the senator and displace his supporters, they decided Herman Ekern must challenge Twesme as an independent in the general election. To do so, however, presented special problems. Three in particular needed to be met. First, Ekern would have to re-ignite his fading Norwegian support while reducing both Governor Davidson's magnetic appeal among his countrymen and Twesme's pro-Davidson image. Second, he needed to explain why the Trempealeau primary vote should be disregarded, thereby repudiating the intent of the very law that he himself had been so active in framing. Finally, Ekern knew his independent candidacy might cost him votes because it now lacked the official backing of the Republican party.

A two-stage strategy emerged, based on the central argument that the verdict of the primary should be reversed because his defeat had been engineered by scurrilous methods. The first stage called for Ekern to demonstrate that the people – indignant over the wrong perpetrated – desired his candidacy. Ekern's friends would carefully canvass the county to amass signatures imploring him to run as an independent. Simultaneously, to add credence to his accusations, Ekern would launch a "conspiracy" suit against Twesme and stalwart John C. Gaveney for libel. This would effectively diminish Twesme's reputation among Norwegians because suing Gaveney and Twesme jointly would make Twesme appear a stalwart by association; the suit, it was hoped, would convey the impression that Gaveney was the power behind Twesme's candidacy. Once Ekern's popular support reawakened, the second stage of the campaign would summon LaFollette to tour Trempealeau's Norwegian towns on Ekern's behalf.[56]

With no time to lose, Ekern's friends earnestly began their campaign to reverse the primary's outcome. By the last week of September they had harvested over fifteen hundred signatures. Ekern then waited two weeks to announce his independent candidacy in order to help ripen public opinion around his libel suit.

At his day in court, Ekern charged that Twesme and Gaveney had induced the editor of the Arcadia *Leader* to publish a story about Isaac Stephenson having rewarded Ekern with a $1,000 check after the assemblyman cast his vote for Stephenson to be United States senator. This insinuation of payment for his vote, Ekern contended, had damaged his reputation and contributed to his defeat. The money, Ekern insisted, had amounted to nothing more than a campaign contribution in his role as secretary of LaFollette's presidential campaign. Twesme freely admitted to having written the article and contended that the facts were true. He only meant to show that Stephenson owed LaFollette a large debt for delivering legislative votes such as that of Ekern. Moreover, the twenty-nine year old Galesville lawyer offered to make public those who contributed to his campaign fund if Ekern would do the same. The judge ultimately dismissed the case against Gaveney, finding that the former state senator had only paid for the advertisement and been reimbursed by Twesme. The remainder of the legal action was suspended until the following spring.[57]

With his widely heralded lawsuit now postponed amid charges that it had "been a fizzle," Ekern announced his candidacy. He released to newspapers a five-thousand-word statement explaining the action he felt compelled to take and laying down charges of the sort with which Norwegians usually sympathized: "A combination of big Life Insurance Companies, the liquor lobby, and candidates for high office, all from outside the district, with local Stalwart leaders, aided by unprincipled Democratic support, dominated the primaries."[58] As proof of outside interference by the brewing interests, Ekern claimed, for example, that members of the brewers' organization admitted to having put in ten thousand dollars to defeat him. Twesme and the conservative press gleefully ripped into the announcement. "Mr. Ekern must think the people of the county are fools," exclaimed the editor of the Blair *Press*. "He might with equal propriety have said also that he was told that the railroads had put in ten thousand dollars and the insurance companies ten thousand dollars for is not one statement just as well supported by evidence as the other."[59]

While the rattle of Ekern's and Twesme's charges was gaining publicity, Senator LaFollette and Governor Davidson entered the fray and a new and final stage of the battle began. Now the intense county struggle transformed itself into a fierce test of strength between Davidson and LaFollette that drew statewide attention. And supremacy in this section of the state boiled down to who could best command the loyalties of the Norwegian-American voters.[60]

Traveling through the Norwegian townships in northern Trempealeau county a week before the election, Governor Davidson and Twesme appealed to the voters to stand behind the duly elected regular Republican nominee. In his modest, homespun rhetoric, richly infused with west Norwegian accent, Davidson told the standing-room-only meetings at Strum and Blair that he was not there to interfere in local affairs but only to support the Republican ticket and to uphold the integrity of the primary law. The polished Twesme, on the other hand, aimed his shots squarely at Ekern, cautioning the audience "not to trust the embittered attacks of a disappointed candidate." Ekern supporters grew plainly worried. Davidson's presence, a friend confided to Ekern, "may cause us to lose considerable," and he wished that "there was a way to discount the harm he will do." At the same time they hoped that LaFollette, when he arrived the next day, would effectively reclaim the loyalty of Norwegians.[61]

The fatigued but scrappy senator, together with Ekern, met enthusiastic though somewhat smaller crowds than had greeted Davidson on his whirlwind trip through the county. The senator's voice, hoarse from a cold and numerous speaking engagements, nonetheless still carried that magnetic quality that made him a favorite reform spokesman in Norwegian communities. The strenuous schedule involved speeches in Blair and Ettrick and an evening talk in Twesme's hometown, Galesville. Immediately plunging into his subject, LaFollette called his supporters to action. He characterized the primary that nominated Twesme as a fraud controlled by special interests. Undoubtedly with Davidson in mind, he intimated that the fight against the praiseworthy Ekern was actually part of a larger fight aimed at his own undoing. The wily campaigner disdainfully wrote off Twesme as merely "the tool of evil," whose libelous acts should cause voters to "consider the dangerous character of a man who would resort to such means to secure office." The Democrats' political trickery had showed itself, he declared, when usually solid Democratic enclaves such as the predominantly Polish Dodge township suddenly switched to Twesme in the primary. As for the Norwegian circular distributed in Trempealeau county and other Norwegian areas, LaFollette denounced it as "a bigoted and cowardly appeal to national prejudices" put out by the same people who were attacking Ekern. He repeated the same speech at each of the three rallies.[62]

But the end was not yet. Governor Davidson meant to insure that his work would not be nullified and he reentered the county, appearing this time in Galesville, Ettrick, and southern Trempealeau townships. In response, Ekern's faction reportedly tried but failed to get LaFollette also to return. Still, Ekern remained confident. "The appeal made by the Governor on account of nationality goes a very long way," he admitted, but he was sure that bringing the governor back into the county amounted to "a confession of their weakness" and that he would have the necessary votes providing his workers could "overcome the party cross."[63]

Intense public interest had developed and so too had a mood of bitterness. Twesme accused Ekern of hypocrisy in courting the anti-saloon vote at the same time that a brother of the editor of the progressive Whitehall *Times-Banner* "daily made the rounds of the saloons, assuring the keepers and bartenders between drinks that Ekern was against 'County Option.' " The exasperated editor of the Blair *Press* declared Ekern's candidacy "a sham" in which "his greed for office has become chronic and he plays the baby act in his first defeat in a most pitiable way." Conversely, rumors spread in Norwegian communities that Twesme had pulled off a crooked advertising scheme in Northfield, Minnesota, while a student at the University of Wisconsin. Upon being informed about it, Ekern tried to obtain affidavits from the affected parties during the last days of the contest. Bitterness had reached the boiling point, according to the Milwaukee *Sentinel*, "feeling being so strong in some families that brothers do not speak to each other.[64]

By election day much statewide attention focused on Trempealeau county. As with the earlier primary, the outcome was close. Twesme nonetheless again narrowly defeated Ekern—this time by a mere 152 votes out of a total Ekern-Twesme vote of 4,172. Once again the people had spoken and found Ekern wanting.

Critical Norwegian townships and villages had, since the primary, swung back slightly toward Ekern. But the additional 5 points he picked up there failed to offset losses elsewhere. Even in Norwegian areas, this net gain had occurred only with considerable shifting about in sentiment among Norwegian communities. Compared to the earlier primary vote, Ekern's support had advanced nearly 10 percentage points in Preston and Unity while failing to hold onto 13 points of previously won gains in both Hale township and his former stronghold of Pigeon township. As had occurred in the primary, Ekern's poorest showing remained in Twesme's home township, Ettrick, followed by the far northern areas.

V

Examining Herman Ekern's shifting fortunes between 1904 and 1908, one sees three indications of how political events had unsettled traditional Norwegian allegiances. For one thing, Ekern's vote in elections after 1904 dropped remarkably more in Norwegian townships than it did in the county as a whole. Furthermore, the usually like-minded votes cast by predominantly Norwegian precincts diverged more from one another in the 1906 and 1908 elections than they had in 1904. Finally, the average turnout rate of Norwegian townships during the 1906–1908 period exceeded that of the county as a whole, thus demonstrating their intensified interest in the political struggle. LaFollette and his protégé Ekern had, by their efforts to replace Governor Davidson, spawned general Norwegian defections. With ethnic issues brought to the fore, Norwegian solidarity buckled and fell apart. That individual Norwegian townships reacted differently, however, merits attention.

Anti-Ekern feeling seems not to have arisen from any one particular social, cultural, or geographic segment of the county's Norwegian areas. While economic differences among settlements appear to have mattered little, his support slipped to a greater extent in the more recently settled Norwegian townships of northern Trempealeau county than in those to the south. Perhaps here voters placed greater reliance on political advice contained in the Norwegian-language press, especially *Skandinaven*.

Ekern may also have drawn stronger support from the more Americanized Norwegian communities where a mix of people of different Norwegian dialects tended to overcome such barriers to communication by more readily adopting English. Viewed in such terms, the more linguistically mixed townships averaged almost 7 percentage points less favorable to Davidson in the 1906 primary than did the tradition-perpetuating ones where more similar dialects prevailed.[65]

Evidently voters in village and countryside areas also departed from one another in their attraction to LaFollette's socioeconomic rhetoric and Ekern's county-option stance. For while six out of ten voters in rural Norwegian precincts cast their ballots for Ekern in the 1906 primary, fewer than four in ten voted for him in Blair and Eleva villages.

But of likely more importance than social or economic concerns in producing differences was the impact of local political circumstances. Personal rivalries, family connections, newspaper editorial positions, political organization, and the host of other influences that made up a local township's situation—these were what muted or enhanced the force of statewide politics by a few percentage points or more. Ekern's family ties in the central county townships helped make these his principal strongholds. He also counted on his professional and personal association with such men as his law partner in Whitehall, the highly respected H. A. Anderson. And for direct political support he could depend on his connection with J. B. Beach, the longtime county Republican leader and editor of the county-seat newspaper, the Whitehall *Times-Banner*. Likewise, on the other side, Albert Twesme and conservative Judge Cowie maintained similar ties to yet other influential local Norwegians.

Personal political qualities also influenced voters differently from one locality to another. Ekern, though gifted with a knack for political organization and legislative maneuvering, remained hamstrung by his devotion to LaFollette. This made him insensitive to differences among his local critics, all of whom he tended to label "stalwarts." In the northeastern township of Sumner and Osseo village, for instance, people resented Ekern's attacks against local attorney Glenn O. Linderman because, despite the attorney's stalwart affiliations, he was "looked up to as a good Republican and highly respected by all."[66]

If local political circumstances had proved important only in local contests, they might not be worth noting. But in fact the character of grass-roots political organization made a difference as well in statewide political contests. This can be seen in 1906, where Norwegian precinct support for Governor Davidson proved weaker in communities supporting Ekern, for there Ekern's friends had labored on Lenroot's behalf. Otherwise, Davidson would have carried all heavily Norwegian towns by similar majorities.

Norwegian Americans of Trempealeau county had rejected neither LaFollette nor his progressive ideas. But defection did reveal the limits of LaFollette's appeal among them. Although voters appreciated the ardent anti-monopolism of Ekern and his mentor, both learned that neither anti-trust slogans nor blurry political exhortation could shove national pride and prejudice into the background.

The defection punished those who forgot that Norwegians had aligned themselves with LaFollette not simply because they took his reform position seriously and respected his vigorous leadership, but because they valued and expected political recognition for their aspiring Norwegian leaders. Ekern erred politically by being blind to these concerns, instead forthrightly championing Lenroot's candidacy against Davidson. Local conservative leaders such as Judge Cowie ably capitalized on the assemblyman's mistake and, reinforced by unfavorable press reaction, saddled Ekern with an image as one opposed to Davidson. And once Twesme appeared in 1908, the temptation proved irresistible to throw over ideology for retribution by those Norwegians unwilling to believe that the cause of progressivism would suffer under Davidson, as LaFollette and Ekern suggested.

It took the 1906–1908 debacle before progressives learned that the tail went with the hide–that ethnic concerns were inseparable from the success of reform progressivism in Wisconsin. Failure to recognize this had inaugurated a new round of Republican factionalism in the state.

IV

World War I in the Norwegian-American Midwest

CHAPTER 8

Authority Challenged in Minnesota

"Once lead this people into war," President Woodrow Wilson sadly predicted to a newspaper publisher on the eve of his war message to Congress, "and they'll forget there ever was such a thing as tolerance." In the brutality that war brings to a people, he feared, "conformity would be the only virtue."[1] Events would bear out his melancholy prophecy. Perhaps nowhere else did abandonment to wartime hysteria become more pronounced than in the upper midwestern states.

Progressivism had spent most of its force by the 1916 elections in Wisconsin, Iowa, and Minnesota. Economic and political issues that had animated earlier struggles between stalwarts and progressives no longer provoked widespread public interest. Republican factions had burnt themselves out and people seemed to yearn for a breathing spell. But the war in Europe and prospects for American intervention now intruded, injecting into politics national, intensely emotional wartime issues that cut across and shattered divisions engendered by progressive reform. America's entry into the war in 1917 unleashed an intensified patriotism into politics, imposing special strains in Minnesota, Iowa, and Wisconsin. Intent on assuring that their respective states would contribute their full share to the war effort, some state and local leaders stood ready to advocate extreme measures. These they believed were needed to surmount what they saw as lingering neutralist sentiment and the unreliable loyalty of many among their disproportionately large foreign-born populations, the most sizable of which was the German-speaking minority. Consequently, while the declaration of war brought an immediate public response, so too the resulting measures brought a severe tightening of the public mood.

The drive to unify public sentiment increasingly took two pernicious forms. Leaders began to insist repeatedly that what they termed "radicalness" promoted political divisions and therefore must be set aside for the war, and, secondly, that everything smacking of "foreignism" ought to be eliminated. Where authorities let matters drift or yielded to popular prejudices and hysterical public clamor for stern action, their failure to stand against lawlessness allowed local hatreds and passions to get out of hand. Mob spirit gripped many localities — would-be patriots used unofficial witch-hunts and terrorism to ferret out disloyalty. German Americans, of course, faced the worst of this, but Norwegian Americans suffered their share of indignities along with other foreign groups.

In particular, the "anti-radical" campaign in Minnesota to halt organizing efforts of the Nonpartisan League and the anti-foreign-language proclamation of Governor Harding in Iowa imposed severe political choices on Norwegian settlements. These two wartime measures would soon cause them to scatter their votes among Democratic, Republican, and third-party candidates.

I

Neutrality and the drive toward preparedness had already begun to agitate national politics when yet another large-scale agrarian movement took hold of people's interest on the Dakota prairies. Feeling rebuffed by the legislature's failure to act against grain marketing practices, wheat farmers welcomed organization. Under the leadership of Arthur C. Townley, the Nonpartisan League appeared with a socialistic program that called for state ownership and operation of grain elevators, stockyards, packing houses, and mills, state inspection of grain and dockage, and rural credits. In short order, they had ignited a farmers' revolt that in the 1916 elections captured control of North Dakota's government. The movement's stunning success, its radical program, and its vigorous leadership infused with socialists alarmed established interests that League leaders denounced as the same old gang controlling North Dakota as though it were a subsidiary of Minneapolis and St. Paul milling, banking, and railroad interests. But soon Republican party alarm turned to fear as the League's organizers swept on into neighboring states in early 1917, scouting the countryside in Model-T Fords to recruit thousands of new members.

Changing its name to the National Nonpartisan League, in January, 1918, it established new headquarters in St. Paul.[2]

Minnesotans shared the nation's prevailing war hysteria and suspicion of foreign groups, but the onrushing Nonpartisan League movement diverted the administration of Governor Joseph A. A. Burnquist from specific actions to Americanize the foreign-born. Instead, the powerful momentum of the developing movement so frightened Republican leaders that, responding largely through the Minnesota Commission of Public Safety, a temporary board organized to see the state through the war, they wielded arbitrary power, requiring the registration of aliens and their real and personal property and charging the League with disloyalty, in order to quash the movement's force.[3]

"This is no time," declared Governor Burnquist, "to divide our people into factions through the stirring up of untimely issues in contests for public offices."[4] The League soon found itself caught fast—enmeshed in difficulties spawned by the emotions of war.[5] By exaggerating the socialists' ideological coolness to war and by decrying any political dissension that diverted public attention from winning the war, opponents easily attached the stigma of "disloyalty" to the Nonpartisan League. Pressures reached a climax during the weeks preceding the 1918 Republican primary election, when the first major contest occurred between a League-endorsed candidate, Charles Lindbergh, and Governor Burnquist.

Prewar neutrality sentiment, lack of enthusiasm about preparedness, and division of opinion about the European belligerents had convinced many conservative Minnesotans that the air was thick with pacifism, seditious intrigue, and widespread un-Americanism. Two circumstances in the state particularly alarmed conservative Republican leaders. Fully 70 percent of Minnesota's people in 1910 were either of foreign birth or the son or daughter of someone who was.[6] Germans, Swedes, and Norwegians predominated, and superpatriots suspected them all. Minnesotans knew of the traditional Swedish distrust of Russia and of Swedish respect for things German that had evoked a measure of sympathy for Germany's cause. Raised eyebrows about neutralist-minded Norwegians had been partly offset by their tendency to sympathize with the Allies, but when many Norwegian Americans began joining the farmers' Nonpartisan League, suspicions heightened of their pacifistic radicalism.[7] To invigorate the patriotism of his wavering countrymen, an agitated Senator Knute Nelson saw to it that Nicolay A. Grevstad, his loyal friend and the former editor of the Chicago *Skandinaven*, obtained appointment by the Minnesota Commission of Public Safety to monitor non-English newspapers and, in particular, to exercise close surveillance over the Scandinavian-American press.[8]

Rather than form a third party, the Nonpartisan League aimed to dominate the majority party. Demanding that the Republican party adopt the League's economic measures and issues as its own, the League used the party's primary election to select candidates sympathetic to its cause. To do this, League leaders continually stressed tight organization as necessary both to expand their membership and to concentrate their voting strength at election time. Arthur Townley, a master of high-pressure salesmanship who had apparently concluded that reform could not be sold unless it was hustled, steadily recruited and carefully trained a body of organizers. Once instructed and effectively motorized, they began in 1917 to fan out across western Minnesota. The $16 membership fees soon came rolling in.[9]

Making Minnesota the keystone of its efforts, the League proceeded with its organizing activities relatively unopposed through the summer months of 1917. But by the time its leaders began their scheduled series of fall farmer meetings, opposition had hardened. Republicans increasingly saw their dominance to be threatened and, encouraged by the Minnesota Commission of Public Safety, "patriotic" opinion leaders among them effectively turned sentiment against the League. Twin City newspapers kindled the opposition, promoting the argument that politics ought to cease in the interest of wartime unity, especially political activities that might increase class antagonism or in any way dampen public support for the war. Endless repetition of this effective argument in many country weekly newspapers soon condemned nearly every proposed League meeting to accusations of disloyalty. Nineteen Minnesota counties by March, 1918, had adopted measures barring all meetings of the League.[10]

Wartime hysteria reached its peak during the bitterly contested campaign leading to Minnesota's primary election of June 17, 1918—the first major test of League strength. At their state convention in St. Paul on March 17, League delegates endorsed the candidacy of former congressman Charles A. Lindbergh—father of the future famous aviator—against Governor Burnquist. But though the League may have seen in Lindbergh a well-known Republican politician of Swedish extraction, endorsing him during wartime proved a serious mistake.

His anti-war stance before America's entry into the conflict made him especially vulnerable to charges of pro-Germanism and disloyalty. In fact, hardly had Lindbergh received his endorsement before Twin Cities newspapers wrenched passages and phrases from his recently published *Why Is Your Country At War* (1917), printing and reprinting them with devastating effect.[11] Governor Burnquist had been invited to give a welcoming address to the convention, but instead grasped the occasion to send a scathing refusal based on the League's alleged disloyalty. The League, he accused, had closely aligned itself with pro-German, I.W.W., and Red Socialist elements. So from this point on, vowed the Governor, Minnesota would have only two parties, "one composed of the loyalists and the other of the disloyalists."[12]

The loyalty issue dominated the ensuing campaign, pushing debate on the League's agrarian reform program out of sight. When the ballots were counted, it could be seen that Minnesota's Norwegian Americans, as during the earlier Populist era, had contributed much to the dissenting vote. Senator Knute Nelson, despite his immense prestige among his countrymen, nevertheless found much of his partisan "unity" and "loyalty" politics rejected. "The Norwegians put the nonpartisan league into power in North Dakota," he confided two years later to a friend, adding in exasperation, "they are at the bottom of our troubles in Minnesota."[13]

He was right. Norwegian and Swedish farmers–mainly wheat and barley producers–had been the first to join the Nonpartisan League as it expanded into Minnesota in 1916. Into this core body of middle-level farmers who supported the League's economic program streamed large numbers of relatively wealthy German corn and livestock producers in 1917 and thereafter. Charges of disloyalty and anti-German hysteria had driven this second contingent of members to join the Nonpartisan League.[14]

II

This core participation of Norwegian farmers does not mean that most Norwegian Americans sympathized with the League or voted for its candidates. The response of Norwegian settlements in Minnesota, Wisconsin, and Iowa resembled that of Populist times in that the movement made little headway outside the western counties of Minnesota. Hence, the Nonpartisan League movement failed to affect Norwegian settlements in Iowa or Wisconsin.[15] Even within Minnesota, Norwegian farm settlements outside the western grain region avoided the movement. In the southeastern dairy region, for instance, Fillmore county voters cast only 25 percent of their ballots for the League's candidate, and vote tallies in seven of the county's nine predominantly Norwegian precincts failed even to reach that level.

Table 5 Agrarian-Supported Candidates' Share of the Vote for Governor
from Three Regions of Minnesota[a]

Region	1890–1896 Percent	1918–1924 Percent
Southeastern counties	16.9	28.3
West Central counties	45.6	71.0
Northwestern counties	66.9	56.6

[a]Agrarian candidates, 1890–1896, included the nominees of the Farmers' Alliance party, People's party, and Democratic/Populist Fusion party, while all candidates during the period 1918–1924 ran on the Farmer-Labor ticket.

This pattern held throughout diversified crop and dairy sections of the state.

On the surface, therefore, the latest agrarian outburst affected Norwegian settlements much as that of two decades before had. In Minnesota, though, as Table 5 reveals, the locus of Norwegian-American farmer discontent had shifted southward since the 1890s to the west-central region. "This wholly unsound movement," remarked Ole Sageng of Otter Tail county, had carried away "a very large part of our really substantial and ordinarily cautious Scandinavian farmers."[16] But in fact League organizers found even greater success in their membership drives when scouring Norwegian townships in the west-central counties of Kandiyohi and Swift.

A second important change had also taken place: town-country antagonisms among Norwegian settlements showed themselves by the early 1920s to be far deeper than they had been in the 1890s (Table 6). It is no accident that in Rushford City (Fillmore county), where Norwegians comprised nearly two-thirds of the voting age males in 1905, Charles Lindbergh won a lower percentage of the votes cast than in any of the several surrounding Norwegian farm precincts of the county. The same differences marked western counties. In Norwegian precincts of Polk county with small towns, for example, votes for Lindbergh in the primary election sagged 20 percentage points beneath their farm-precinct counterparts. Such antagonisms in Minnesota had invariably accompanied every farmer movement, but this time two circumstances widened the gulf. One was the heightened mood of farmer anger arising from the acts of small town "patriots" during the war. The other drew from efforts of both Nonpartisan League organizers and their detractors to capitalize on urban-rural hostility.

By its very nature, the 1918 "loyalty" campaign against the Nonpartisan League rang with overtones of bitterness between Main Street and the countryside. League opponents who raised the specters

Table 6 Agrarian Candidates' Share of the Vote for Governor from
Norwegian Settlements of Minnesota, Classified by Percentage of People
Living in Incorporated Towns[a]

Region	1890–1896 Percent	1918–1924 Percent
Low Urban (16.7% or less)	47.2	56.1
Moderate Urban (16.8%–34.9%)	45.4	44.6
High Urban (35% or more)	38.1	34.0

[a]Agrarian candidates, 1890–1896, included the nominees of the Farmers' Alliance party, People's party, and Democratic/Populist Fusion party, while all candidates during the period 1918–1924 ran on the Farmer-Labor ticket in general elections. Population percentages for incorporated towns and villages are drawn from the *Thirteenth Census of the United States, 1910; Vol. I: Population.*

of radicalism, class division, socialism, disloyalty, and un-Americanism, all with their implied anti-foreignism, lived chiefly in cities and small towns. Consequently mutual respect broke down; the farmers turned defensive and antagonistic toward townsmen. When prominent citizens from several Swift county towns came together in a mass meeting at Benson to demand the suppression of "seditious and unpatriotic public meetings" by Nonpartisan League speakers, farmers from heavily Norwegian townships reacted. "We claim we are just as loyal and doing as much to win this war as citizens of our cities and villages," declared a caucus of Camp Lake farmers. Similarly, Kerkhoven farmers resented the fact that townsmen would "accuse and convict law-abiding farmers of Swift county of being traitors and harboring sedition without a hearing."[17]

"Look out for Appleton," warned another Swift county farmer whose automobile had sported a banner favoring the League's candidate for governor. "When some of us farmers asked . . . [the town marshal] to protect our property, he offered his star to a bystander and asked to see if he could do it, and boys walked right up in front of the Marshal and tore my Lindbergh banner off." Another prominent "good citizen" "told me I ought to be ashamed to have a sign like Lindbergh's on my car as I have a boy in the army." But "the likes of the 'good citizen' could not make me ashamed, for I saw him wash the yellow paint [the stigma of disloyalty] off of his building a short time ago."[18]

Hoping to turn this to their advantage, League newspapers and their supporters breathed with feeling against the towns, perpetuating Townley's call for farmers to take control away from "the smooth-tongued, bay-windowed fellows that looked well, talked well, lived will, lied well."[19] When a Swift county farmer visited town and found his car covered with yellow paint defaming his patriotism "in plain

Ole O. Sageng, 1913, who represented Otter Tail county as a Republican state senator for several terms beginning in 1906. When the Nonpartisan League approached this popular farmer-politician to be their candidate in 1918, he refused and fought the movement during the ensuing election. Photo courtesy of Minnesota Historical Society.

view of the business men of the village, who offered to give the name of the painter for a reward of $100," an editor sympathetic to the League asked: how can "the sore heads . . . think for a moment that any self-respecting farmer will take the abuse accorded to him, and then come back and kiss the hand that hit him?"[20]

Simultaneously, the League's tactics offered opportunities to opponents trying to mobilize the small-town vote. During Ole Sageng's anti-League bid for reelection to the State Senate from Otter Tail county, he published an open letter to voters of Fergus Falls on the day before the election. The Nonpartisan League's demand to exempt farm improvements from taxation, he said, meant that the city's business and laboring men would have to pay higher taxes. When this had been pointed out to the League organizer who "spent a day of his time" trying to "organize" him, the answer Sageng said he got from the "sleek political profiteer" was " 'Let the other fellow look out for himself.' "[21]

Sageng's opponent—Norwegian-American and League-endorsed Martin W. Odland—later summarized the urban character of opposition to this movement:

"All the big city papers were against them; all the small daily papers in the smaller cities were against them, and at least nine out of every ten of the rural weeklies were fighting them.

Martin W. Odland, editor
of the Fergus Falls *Free
Press*, who was endorsed
by the Nonpartisan
League in 1918 in an un-
successful race for the
state senate against Ole
O. Sageng. Photo courtesy
of Minnesota Historical
Society.

"The cry that this was no time to agitate and discuss problems influenced thousands of voters and the charges of disloyalty, hurled with
such fierceness and persistency, frightened thousands more from the
support of the League candidates."[22]

The events that provoked this melancholy summation continued to
hang over the League and radical farm politics in the twenties—
evoking bitterness that kept the breach wide between Norwegian rural and small-town settlements. It helped guarantee that Norwegian
settlements in the western counties would vote disproportionately in
favor of agrarian candidates for governor through 1924. Their average
1918–1924 agrarian vote exceeded by 9 percentage points that of the
western counties in which they were located.

Nevertheless, votes from Norwegian farm settlements in western
Minnesota also revealed mixed feelings. Some localities supported the
League less strongly than did others in the June primary. Lindbergh
won over three-fourths of the vote cast in Norwegian farm precincts
of Kandiyohi county while getting barely one-half of the vote from
those of Otter Tail county.

III

A few of these differences between Kandiyohi and Otter Tail counties are worth recounting in some detail to show how local leadership and events spun contrary results. Even though the Nonpartisan League forcefully voiced its agricultural grievances through publications and organizers, local success grew undependable where respected opponents to the League stood up and argued effectively.

Among the farmers of Kandiyohi county, Nonpartisan League organizers met an enthusiastic response. Over eleven hundred enrolled members had by late summer of 1917 made Kandiyohi the second strongest League county in the state.[23] Although many opposed the League there, as later incidents demonstrated, no major party politicians felt willing openly to challenge the farmers' organization. In addition, Victor E. Lawson, who edited the county's largest newspaper, the Willmar *Tribune*, threw his support behind the reform program of the Nonpartisan League. This influential editor, whom Senator Knute Nelson described to a friend as "a bad egg because he has a newspaper," helped set a tone of local tolerance toward League opinions.[24] Even the county sheriff raised little complaint. After traveling first to neighboring Meeker county in early October, 1917, to preview a speech by Arthur Townley, the sheriff found nothing objectionable enough to warrant stopping the League's leader from speaking before a similar meeting at Willmar the following week.[25] Townley made his speech at the Willmar Opera House, despite what the Willmar *Tribune's* editor called "repeated efforts . . . especially in the Minneapolis papers, to impugn the patriotism of Mr. Townley."[26]

Holding such a meeting in Otter Tail county, however, was entirely another matter. A few days after the Willmar speech, Townley's schedule called for him to appear before a farmers' meeting at the Lyceum Theater in Fergus Falls. Certain parties there, however, moved to block the event. Most remarkably, Louis Keane, secretary of the Otter Tail County Public Safety Commission, sent a threatening letter to the president of the Nonpartisan League. It read as follows:

"Information has reached this office to the effect that you contemplate speaking here in this county on Octo. 20.

"I am instructed to notify you that this Association will not tolerate any kind of talk here except that which honors our flag and the country for which it stands.

"So you will construe this notice as an invitation *not to come*.

"If after the receipt of this notice you persist in trying to talk here we have made arrangements with our Mayor who has given orders to the police force not to interfere if small boys (and others) use ancient eggs and other missiles wherewith to punctuate your discourse."[27]

Local League defenders immediately protested this threat. Martin Odland, the Norwegian-American editor of the Fergus Falls *Free Press* and a representative in the state legislature, declared that the act called into serious question the city's reputation as a "respectable, law-abiding community."[28] Although Mayor Leonard Eriksson denied that "he would sanction any such disgraceful lawlessness," he nevertheless banned any meeting at which Townley would be the speaker. The people of the city, said the mayor, "do not invite bankrupt and meddlesome agitators of any kind to come into their midst for the purpose of breeding and disseminating without cause, dissension and disloyalty, especially during the stress of war."[29] Consequently, the League arranged to have former congressman Charles Lindbergh and James Manahan appear in his place. At the October 20 meeting, a packed-to-capacity audience overwhelmingly passed a resolution calling upon Governor Burnquist to remove the mayor from office.[30]

Despite large numbers of local Nonpartisan League members and Martin Odland's presence as a vigorous spokesman for their interests in Otter Tail county, foes of the League organized and expressed themselves far more openly than in Kandiyohi county. First of all, Otter Tail's leading newspaper loudly opposed the Nonpartisan League. Owned by Elmer Adams – a man wise in the ways of pressing a political advantage – the Fergus Falls *Journal* remained staunchly Republican and did not shy away from attacking the League. Adams, also the president of Fergus Falls' First National Bank, had served four terms as a state representative and now stood once again as the party's candidate.[31] Even more dire for League prospects among Norwegian-American farmers, prominent local politicians among the ethnic group openly turned against the Nonpartisan League. In particular, the popular state legislator, Senator Ole Sageng, refused pleas by the League to lead their effort there.[32] His credentials could not easily be assailed.

A farmer near Dalton in the Norwegian township of Tumuli, Sageng had back in 1900 won state office first as a Populist and after 1906 as an independent, serving one term in the House and three terms in the Senate.[33] Even when in 1918 Martin Odland became the League's candidate for the State Senate against Sageng, Odland praised his opponent as a "forceful speaker, a skilled parliamentarian, and one of the best-known men in the senate," this before noting the "keen disappointment to his farmer friends that, owing to the course he has recently pursued, his endorsement for reelection by the organized [League] farmers was out of the question."[34] In addition to Ole Sageng, O. P. B. Jacobson of the State Railroad and Warehouse Commission came out for Governor Burnquist's reelection against Lindbergh. He owned, although no longer edited, the local Norwegian-language newspaper, *Ugeblad*.[35] Schooled in the rough and tumble politics of Populist times and unintimidated by the force of agrarian rhetoric, Adams, Sageng, and Jacobson conspired to bring about the League's defeat.

Still, there were limits to the influence that county leadership could exert. All had to cope with the timing of events at state and local levels, which both colored and intensified voter impressions in Norwegian settlements.

Kandiyohi county, for example, had been one of the best organized in the state. For this reason Lindbergh chose to open his campaign there on April 25 for the Republican nomination for governor. The gathering crowd at the courthouse in Willmar became so immense that organizers had to move it to the city fairgrounds so that all could hear.[36] For some weeks thereafter, statewide matters such as Arthur Townley's indictment by Martin county authorities for sedition dominated local discussion. But then, in the closing days of the primary contest, two local events took place that stirred farmer feeling.

The first occurred a few hours after a speech by Governor Burnquist in Willmar. All went well during the afternoon. A large parade preceded the Governor's address, at which the governor insisted that since "this is no time to divide our people into factions" by making political speeches, he would confine his remarks to a stirring plea for 100 percent loyalty.[37] Later that evening, however, things turned sour. Perhaps carried away by the emotional appeal of the governor's speech, certain of the town's citizens smeared yellow floor paint on the front of the Willmar *Tribune*'s printing office and slipped a note under the door accusing editor Lawson of pro-Germanism and of being a disloyal Swede. In his next issue, Victor Lawson highlighted the emotional impact of the event, calling it a "cowardly and contemptible attempt" to besmirch his loyalty, an attack that had been quickly "denounced by the best element of the City of Willmar." But then, tying it to the farmers' movement, he explained: "Instinctively also the country people felt that the editor was being punished for having been fair to their movement and the resentment shown was intense. Intended as a slam that would injure the editor, and destroy the influence of the paper, the outrage proved a blessing in disguise, for it aroused the people and resulted in a spontaneous rally of popular support such as we doubt has ever before been received by a local newspaper in Minnesota.

"As for our stand of fairness towards the farmers and the organization they have made for the avowed purpose of bettering economic conditions in this country, we have no apologies to make. We know that our action is displeasing to politicians who feel that they are losing their grip on the political situation, but we cannot for that reason change our attitude that we believe right, nor can we countenance the wrongful use of patriotic activities for the furtherance of partisan advantages. We have tried our very best to avoid needless friction between town and the country people, and believe that this is a time when public men should remain cool and use tact in dealing with public questions during the heat of political campaigns."[38]

To demonstrate their protest and their commitment to the League, a farmers' parade began two days later, motoring from Svea to Raymond and then continuing on to Willmar and other towns of the county. As ever more cars joined the parade on the way, editor Lawson remarked: "The impression made on the spectators as mile after mile of automobiles passed loaded with quiet but determined country people, and decorated with flags and banners cannot be described. It was soul gripping."[39]

By the time the procession reached Willmar, over three hundred cars were in a line. Owing to reported threats of violence, the parade passed through town without stopping. Even so, Lawson reported that "a number of people disgraced themselves by pulling off banners and hurling jibes at the paraders." Before its end, the procession had grown to nearly seven hundred cars stretching for several miles. The farmers, mindful of what had been done earlier to Lawson's newspaper business, paused on their way home that evening and asked Lawson to come down to his office where he "found a crowd of tired but happy paraders who proceeded to unload lists of subscriptions pledged to the Willmar *Tribune* taken on the trip."[40]

Nothing of this dramatic nature occurred in Otter Tail county during the primary campaign. Except for a well-attended Lindbergh campaign speech at Fergus Falls the first week of May, which drew people from a considerable distance, the League appeared less active in the county.[41] Martin Odland, the League's candidate against Sageng, editorialized for the League in his newspaper. But his commentary waxed defensive—responding to attacks from others.

Here, the League's enemies took the initiative and continued to hold it. Decades of experience as a leader of political opinion in the region helped Elmer Adams of the Fergus Falls *Journal* to probe every weak point that might undermine or discredit the League. Arguing less in the fashion of an angry diehard than of a shrewd demagogue, he subjected the League to attack over the weeks with trip-hammer regularity. The *Journal* pounded on three themes leading up to the primary election. During the initial months of 1918, editorials charged that Townley, not farmers, ran the League and sent outsiders into the county to hoodwink each farmer out of sixteen dollars.[42] After the local League conventions in mid-March, the theme switched for a time to sniping at the League's endorsement of non-farmer candidates such as editor Martin Odland to the state legislature.[43] In the last six weeks before the primary, however, editorial comment increasingly aimed at associating the League with disloyalty and pro-Germanism. How could loyal farmers continue to stay with the League, asked typical editorials, when the League was supported by all the disloyal? Other commentary suggested that votes for Lindbergh came from those who favored a weakened prosecution of the war.[44]

Meanwhile, Senator Ole Sageng began making the rounds of Norwegian settlements speaking for Governor Burnquist. He often traveled with O. P. B. Jacobson. The addresses became especially frequent during the final two weeks of the primary campaign—taking Sageng to nearly every heavily Norwegian township: Leaf Mountain, Folden, Norwegian Grove, Trondhjem, Oscar, and Aastad. A report in the *Journal* expressed confidence that although Leaf Mountain and Folden townships "are probably the strongest of all the townships in Otter Tail for Townleyism, the senator is of the opinion that Townleyism has passed its peak and that many people who favored the League when it was organized are beginning to see it in a different light."[45] Being an ardent prohibitionist himself, as were many Norwegians, Sageng stressed that Governor Burnquist had always backed legislation asked by the county, especially county option and statewide prohibition. Standing before suspicious farmers, the angular, thin-featured Sageng eloquently lauded efforts of the controversial Minnesota Commission of Public Safety to crack down on the liquor traffic. As for the Nonpartisan League, "there are some in every township," he declared, "who have gone so crazy over the proposition that they are disgusting others so that they are quietly quitting, even though forced to wear the buttons 'We'll Stick.' "[46] And then after saying to his audience that "the pro-German element and the I.W.W. element in Minnesota is against Governor Burnquist," Sageng asked if farmers there "intended to line up with those elements against Governor Burnquist."[47]

Although some were convinced, others resented his message. At Leaf Mountain, for example, people came away with a wholly different view of the matter. One farmer wrote that "to say a majority of the audience were disgusted is putting it mildly.

"We thought Ole knew better than to come out among intelligent people and tell them that any vote cast for Lindbergh is a pro-German vote.

"I venture to say that Leaf Mountain will cast a majority vote for all League candidates, and they are not pro-Germans either.

"People have come to the conclusion that they were given a set of brains of their own to use and have decided that they do not need a bell cow in the form of a slick man like Ole to tell them how to vote. This matter of a man wrapping the American flag around him and calling everybody else disloyal is so disgusting that any self-respecting man will pay no attention to such gush of hot air."[48]

The Leaf Mountain farmer proved to be right. When election officials counted the ballots, results showed that nine out of ten voters in the township had supported Lindbergh. In Folden township 80 percent of the voters stood by Lindbergh and 70 percent went for him in two other heavily Norwegian townships. But elsewhere the efforts of Sageng and others had clearly paid off. In Aastad, Oscar, Nidaros, Sverdrup, Dane Prairie, and Sageng's own township of Tumuli, voters cast majorities for Governor Burnquist. Meanwhile, in the townships of Kandiyohi county, Charles Lindbergh drew three-fourths or more of the votes cast in every Norwegian settlement.

Statewide, however, Lindbergh had been defeated by a vote of 199,325 to 150,626. The governor of Minnesota and his war agency, the Minnesota Comission of Public Safety, had dealt the Nonpartisan League a blow. But difficult times soon beset the Republican party as it tried with mixed success to stem the League's postwar successor, the Farmer-Labor party. Without wartime fears to capitalize on, Burnquist and his successors found it more difficult to further their political interests by sowing seeds of distrust, dissension, and hatred.[49] Their wartime measures to maintain power had succeeded, but not without cost: thousands of Norwegian farmers had been alienated from the Republican party—angered more than intimidated by aspersions on their loyalty.

CHAPTER 9

Authority Imposed in Iowa

In Iowa, the Nonpartisan League claimed no more than 15,000 members.[1] Unrelenting antagonism of the Greater Iowa Association and the overwhelming amount of anti-League literature being actively distributed took its toll on the League. Also, the League threw few of its resources into the Iowa fight, concentrating instead on trying to organize Minnesota. The League established no official newspaper in Iowa, and although James Pierce, the publisher of the politically powerful *Iowa Homestead*, took up their cause, organizing efforts never got off the ground.[2] A different issue appeared in Iowa, one spawned by the overheated war atmosphere. It mightily disturbed Norwegian-American voters, among others, and directly threatened Governor Harding's wartime administration.

William Lloyd Harding, a politician of great skill, occupied the center stage of Iowa politics during the second decade of the twentieth century. Guided by the influential George D. Perkins, editor of the Sioux City *Journal*, and equipped with a likable personality and a moderate Republican record, Harding had secured the lieutenant governorship in 1912. Gifted as an off-the-cuff orator, the ambitious Sioux City politician had by 1916 brought the exhausted faction-ridden party under his leadership. And in the general election of that year, he gained an overwhelming victory over his Democratic opponent after a hard-fought campaign.

But then, Harding as governor began to stumble and his administration floundered. George Perkins's death in 1914 had left Harding drifting politically rudderless and, without his strong, steady hand, legislative inaction took its toll and exploitation by friends brought scandal to his administration. His fortunes improved, however, with the coming of war. Iowans immediately and enthusiastically rallied behind their government and Harding quickly capitalized on his oratorical skills to marshal public support for the war effort.[3]

Iowa's prospects looked especially bright in the spring of 1918. Abnormal wartime demand for the state's grain, livestock, and livestock products had brought welcome prosperity to the farms and brisk trade to the main streets of nearby towns and cities. Traveling through the city of Des Moines, the governor could see nearly everywhere signs of commercial expansion: construction of Hotel Fort Des Moines was well underway, the new Court Avenue bridge was about ready for dedication, and a variety of retail and apartment buildings were nearing completion. As for the war effort, public opinion had swung strongly behind the war policies of Governor Harding and his State Council of Defense. The vigor with which he mobilized Iowa's manpower and agricultural and industrial resources and his sometimes overzealous but effective patriotic speeches in support of new policies and fund drives had stilled all but an occasional critic of his administration. Harding's renomination now seemed assured.

Still, a few advisors and Harding himself fretted about public mobilization. Some remained especially perturbed about purported lukewarmness toward the war among foreign elements. In particular, Lafayette Young, editor of the Des Moines *Capital* and chairman of the powerful State Council of Defense, agitated the issue. Becoming nearly obsessed with disloyalty, he urged aggressive policies to eradicate roadblocks to "Americanism" posed by foreign groups. In the first war-loan drive, Iowa had fallen over 28 million dollars short of its assigned quota, and the embarrassed Council blamed the failure partly on foreign groups that did not appreciate the meaning of the campaign. The authorities in subsequent Liberty Loan drives abandoned thrift or investment features of the bonds and traded almost exclusively on patriotism. They also shifted the sales approach, as one contemporary writer put it, away from "requests for purely volunteer subscriptions to what amounted to forced levies for specific amounts."[4]

But beyond concerns about lack of interest in loan drives among the foreign born, leaders saw a broader problem to be the language barrier between foreign-born and English-speaking Iowans. "Americanizers" believed that it accounted for the increasing instances of bitter suspicion and misunderstanding around the state that occasionally flared into violence.

The temper of the times is expressed in this wartime cartoon from the Des Moines *Capital*, May 29, 1918. Foreign-language newspapers fell under a cloak of continual surveillance, suspicion, and distrust during this period of hyper-Americanism and anti-foreignism.

Lafayette Young advocated the necessity for one language in a series of editorials in his Des Moines newspaper, beginning in August, 1917.[5] One month later Governor Harding officially suggested a specific Americanization campaign aimed at awakening by persuasion the "latent" loyalty of foreign elements. But Young, not at all quiet about his views, pressed on—convinced that only a more aggressive approach by the governor would do. Events helped. Increasing instances of mob violence, property damage, and "kangaroo court" convictions had accompanied the recent third Liberty Loan drive. In addition public protests accumulated against the use of the German language on the telephone lines.[6] These cases, interpreted by Young and others as proof that foreign language use had annoyed and angered people, strengthened their arguments.

Their efforts finally brought results. On May 23, 1918, Governor Harding issued a Language Proclamation compelling an almost immediate change to English.[7] This most controversial action of his wartime administration required that English should be the sole medium of instruction in the schools and that citizens should not converse in anything but English in public places, on trains, over the telephone, and in church services for the duration of the war.[8] The balance of Harding's proclamation contained his apologia, in which he pointed out that controversy over the use of foreign languages had made the rules necessary in order to return peace and harmony to the people. Although admittedly "inconvenient to some," he urged that the "rules be adhered to by all," so that "united as one people with one purpose and one language, we fight shoulder to shoulder for the good of mankind."

Four weeks later he pressed the matter further before the State Bar Association's annual meeting. "There were practically three hundred communities," said Harding, "where the public school had been driven out almost, by a foreign language school." But now, he said with pride, "two hundred preachers in Iowa . . . will have to quit business, because they cannot use the language. They ought to quit." Of course, he went on, "Freedom of speech is guaranteed by the Federal and State Constitutions. But this is not a guaranty of the right to use a language other than the language of this Country, the English language." Nor does the Constitution "entitle a person who cannot speak or understand the English language, to employ a foreign language, when to do so tends, in times of national peril, to create discord among neighbors and citizens, or disturb the peace and quiet of the community."[9]

Neither Norwegians nor other Scandinavians were the first to react to the assault. Instead, Bohemian Americans of Cedar Rapids, supported by the editor of the Cedar Rapids *Evening Gazette*, took the lead. Residents sent dozens of telegrams and the newspaper printed several editorials from the group's prominent citizens. But after fuming for a week, the editor of the *Gazette* stopped discussing the issue, apparently satisfied by Harding's clarifying letter to Bohemian-born Iowans to the effect that the edict had been aimed not directly at foreign languages but at German propaganda being spread through them.[10] This shift in interpretation–the first of many to follow– satisfied some. But where the *Evening Gazette* and the Bohemians stimulated discussion of the issue, the editor of the Des Moines *Register* and Iowa's Danish-born population mounted a major campaign against Harding's proclamation.

After hesitating until the first week of June, the editor of the Des Moines *Register*, almost by himself, kept the controversy alive from that time on by relentless public airing of grievances against the language proclamation. He did this partly through the newspaper's own staff editorials, but primarily by opening its columns to all public comment and by reprinting accounts from other newspapers. While righteous indignation may have impelled the *Register* to act, the part played by a long-standing, bitter opposition to Governor Harding and his policies cannot be discounted.[11] Be that as it may, the editorial stance taken by the largest of the state's daily newspapers was a factor to be reckoned with, even though the preponderance of public opinion may well have supported Harding's proclamation.[12]

The *Register* twice gave especially heavy coverage to the language question: the first period followed Harding's proclamation itself, which prompted a good deal of reaction from Danish areas of the state; the second followed Governor Harding's Fourth of July speech at Sac City. There, perhaps carried away by the patriotic zeal of his own extemporaneous remarks, the governor made disparaging remarks about the Danes, about how they "never can repay" what Iowa had done for them after they were "brought from the filth of Denmark."[13] While Norwegian-related comment added up to only 3 percent of the column space devoted by the *Register* to the language issue, Danish views consumed fully 25 percent. The *Register*'s own staff editorials on the controversy absorbed only 17 percent of the total.[14]

It would be a mistake, however, to think that because the Danes protested more visibly Norwegians were any the less hurt and angered by the language order. A review of voting results shows that Governor Harding's vote in 1918 dropped in both Norwegian and Danish settlements by about 39 percentage points from average past levels of support given to Republican candidates.[15] Quite evidently, Danish-born Iowans gave off sparks; less visible fires smoldered elsewhere.

At the first hint of criticism, Governor Harding let all know that to doubt was disloyal: "Those who question my authority to issue the proclamation belong to a class who are always looking for trouble and opportunities to find fault and some are anxious, apparently, to give aid and comfort to the enemy."[16] Meanwhile, support for Harding's arguments continued to flow from the editorial pen of Lafayette Young, who saw all this as a grand opportunity to eradicate foreignism. "The people of Iowa," he vociferated, "have a chance now to clean up the state as far as language is concerned." Politically, he believed, Americanism is thwarted when "men have been elected to congress because they were Germans, or because they were Swedes. And they bragged about it. They bragged because they did not have to ask any American for his vote."[17]

As one perhaps uneasy about such talk, Minnesota's Republican senator, Knute Nelson, busily engaged himself in getting Norwegian Americans behind the war effort, but also acknowledged to a friend that "All sensible men agree that the governor of Iowa is going too far in this matter, both from an ethical and a legal standpoint." Nevertheless, he cautioned obedience: "All our people can do under the circumstances is on all occasions and under all conditions to support the government in word and deed and let the native-born Americans see that our people are worthy of American citizenship."[18]

Most distressing to Norwegian Americans, the language order encroached upon their religion. It stunned them that the governor's edict had forbidden foreign language use in religious gatherings, except among families in their own homes. To this the editor of an Iowa Norwegian-language newspaper, the Story City *Visergutten*, responded: "It practically drives American loyal citizens out of the church buildings they themselves have built, sanctioned under the law, for their religious services." Saddened by the implications, the editor lamented the loss to foreign-born housewives too busy "to take up the study of languages." What also, he asked, of the mothers with sons fighting overseas, for whom devotional services have "been her best consolation?"[19]

Decorah-Posten and *Skandinaven* also voiced constitutional and other criticisms, but editors of non-English-language newspapers had to be especially careful in stating their views, for their attempts at political expression had been effectively muzzled in late 1917 when Congress required such newspapers to submit complete translations of every article concerning government policy or the war, or to be exempted by obtaining a permit. This burden of translation and the intimidation it implied toward voicing any criticism of government policy made the editor of the Story City *Visergutten* consider "not publishing anything about the war."[20]

Editors of most local English language newspapers avoided the issue, partly because they agreed that politics ought to be adjourned for the war and partly because they recognized, as one newspaper put it, that the governor's proclamation "unquestionably conforms to popular prejudices in Iowa against foreignism of all kinds."[21] In counties where many Norwegians lived, editors either pretended that the language edict did not exist, as in the case of the Northwood *Worth County Index* (the county's major newspaper), or they simply fell silent after making a comment or two regretting its issuance. Not more than a half-dozen items relating to the controversy appeared in any newspaper of a heavily Norwegian county from the time the proclamation was issued to the day of the general election in November, 1918. And, of these, hardly an item appeared after August.[22] Still, what did appear often proves revealing. Just after Harding announced his proclamation, the editor of the Forest City *Summit* printed on his front page a letter from Pastor William Jorgenson of the local Norwegian-Danish Methodist church. Harding's was a "harsh" proclamation, wrote Jorgenson, one based on the "absurd" notion that while the United States Constitution guaranteed religious liberty, state governments could proscribe its form and practice. "I, for one," he added, "am unable to express my thoughts in English as freely as I can in my mother tongue. Instead of helping me in assisting our government, this proclamation is hampering me in my work as a Scandinavian pastor among the Scandinavian people, inasmuch as I can much better bring home to my people the necessity of buying Liberty Bonds and War Savings Stamps, giving to the Red Cross, Y.M.C.A., etc., when I use the Scandinavian language instead of the English."

Eight of ten men in the armed forces from his one-hundred-member congregation had been volunteers, he said, and all members had contributed their fair share to war campaign drives. "It is impossible for us to understand why" Harding should have issued a proclamation "against the use of our language in our own church." Ending on what seemed a defiant note, he declared that of the seventy-eight members who attended the previous Sunday's service all but two had "expressed themselves in favor of continuing our church services in the Norwegian-Danish language."[23]

Surprisingly, however, some local newspaper editors not only failed to defend the interests of their many Norwegian constituents but also failed to respect them. In the heavily Norwegian town of Decorah, for example, two out of three newspapers actually supported the governor's proclamation while the third distinguished itself by a single instance of token resistance.

In the columns of the city's largest newspaper, the Decorah *Public Opinion*, several favorable editorials appeared about a month after the governor issued his proclamation. Mincing few words, the Republican editor found the language edict to have "the approval and endorsement of every citizen of the State who has reached the point where he is ready to submerge his own dinky personal views and opinions in the one great and absorbing question that is up to the American people to settle." Likening the governor's situation to that of a battlefield commander who in time of war must be autocratic, the editor held that the good soldier "obeys orders without quibbling or calling a halt to discuss the constitutionality of the order." Inconvenience there will be, he said, but war makes that necessary, and anyone at home who does not expect some inconvenience "is either despicably selfish or lamentably ignorant."[24]

The editor of the second Republican newspaper, the Decorah *Republican*, voiced milder opinions. Only in the June 6 issue did he address the question. It would have been wiser, he suggested, had Governor Harding adopted the approach toward foreigners taken by the federal government, which involved positive educational efforts to enlist their support for the war.[25]

Most interesting and puzzling, however, was the stance taken by the city's third largest newspaper, the Decorah *Journal*. Democratic in its politics and edited by a Norwegian American, Fred Bierman, the newspaper did not respond when Harding first enunciated his policy. Yet no one could doubt the anti-foreign tone of two editorials in September. Both demonstrated that editor Bierman bore little sympathy for his countrymen or others who clung to their foreign heritage. The first, a reprint from the Des Moines newspaper of arch-Americanizer Lafayette Young, accused Norwegians of perpetuating their control over Winneshiek county politics by refusing to Americanize. "What chance," asked Young, "would a boy born in America of American parentage have in Winneshiek county? The Norwegians are good politicians. They know that just so long as they can perpetuate their language and keep up their groups, no other nationality need apply. If Americanization had done its work properly the Norwegians would not be in control of everything in Winneshiek. If the melting pot had melted, Winneshiek county would not be filled with Norwegian newspapers and Norwegian ministers. We say that these foreign groups should not exist. They interfere with the unity of the republic. Ninety percent of the discord in America is caused by these foreign groups in the various cities and states of the union. If the American people will keep their courage and stand together at the present time the foreign settlements can be compelled to blend with the other people."[26]

The second piece, an independent editorial, attacked a recent decision by the Danish Young People's Society to hold its convention at Omaha because of the "undemocratic conditions" existing in Iowa. With this action, editor Biermàn had no patience. "This republic cannot endure in peace and prosperity," he declared, "while it remains a 'polyglot boardinghouse.'" The Danish young people should not scorn the American language, he said. After all, it "was good enough for the Constitution, good enough for Lincoln's Gettysburg speech, why is it not good enough for the Danish Young People's Society of America?"[27]

Quite obviously, Norwegian Americans were not of one mind on Americanization, but the intense wartime situation now forced the issue – leaving them little choice but to accelerate their transition. Editor Fred Bierman's impulses led him to break sharply with his past. "I've been as guilty as anybody," he stated emphatically near the war's end. "I used to say 'I'm a Norwegian.' No more of that for me: 'I'm an American' now: This war will do much for our country, unless we lose our balance after the war. It should Americanize America. That's the big job àt home."[28]

Shades of opinion had long existed within Norwegian-American church congregations as to how quickly to make the transition to English. Norwegians' attachment to their language had steadily loosened as a bilingual second generation filled church membership rolls. Many a congregation accordingly now gave a larger place to the English language in its activities. Although the delicate transition, if mishandled, could split members into two quarrelsome elements, roughly one-fourth of all Norwegian Lutheran congregations in America had made the transition and regularly conducted their services in English by the time America entered the war.[29] But it was one thing to accept inevitable gradual adoption of English from within their national group and quite another to accept compulsion from without.[30]

Editors of the official English organ of the Norwegian Lutheran Church of America expressed only contempt for Harding's proclamation. "With possible patriotic intentions," a spokesman began, "persons entrusted with power and authority have yielded to the public clamor for a display, a vainglorious patriotism, and given out entirely uncalled-for orders and proclamations . . . so drastic and sweeping that they have been an insult and an injury to many law-abiding and patriotic citizens." The church spokesman denounced Iowa's proclamation as "illogical prejudice and an entirely uncalled-for infringement of personal and religious liberty" that would no doubt soon be abandoned. Every citizen had a duty to learn the language of the country, but governmental attempts to "prohibit the preaching of the Gospel in any language which the people may desire" must be considered unconstitutional. "Let us not," he appealed, "stultify ourselves before the world and try to build a Chinese wall around our country and glory in the stupidity of advocating the use of only one language."[31]

The panic brought on by Harding's language order extended beyond Norwegian Lutheran congregations in Iowa to complicate another issue that anti-foreignism pushed to the surface. Many of the fearful began agitating to drop the word "Norwegian" from the name of their national church. When the Norwegian Lutheran Church of America convened its meeting at Fargo, North Dakota–barely two weeks after Governor Harding's proclamation–the matter quickly reached the floor for debate.[32]

On the second day of the meeting, two questions–increased church work in English and changing the organization's name–dominated the morning session. On the English question, President Hans Gerhard Stub lamented that loyalty demanded forbearance and "because we are loyal, we obey such instructions as may seem unreasonable. For instance, that we cannot preach in any language but English. This has worked a hardship in some places, and it might be advisable to seek a modification of such rulings, for instance, in the state of Iowa, where it came so suddenly and unlooked for." As soon as the "name change" matter opened for discussion, Reverend Johan Skagen of Fenton, Iowa, questioned whether they should even refer to the Iowa matter. The state's authorities, he feared, might misconstrue its meaning and "involve the churches [at present] using the Norwegian language in special difficulties." He wanted to take a vote on the name change without discussion, but when another tried to help by moving to table the whole matter, President Stub ruled the motion out of order. Still other Iowans persisted. A Worth county pastor tried to postpone action by deferring the matter to a later meeting; Reverend Nils Brun of Winnebago county regretted that the time seems to have arrived to "give our 'mother' a kick by tearing ourselves away from the church of Norway"; Pastor Daniel Jordahl of a congregation located near Decorah protested that the change in name "would be looked upon with disfavor by the large country charges."[33]

Nevertheless, President Stub and other leaders who felt Americanization pressures most keenly favored the change. Retaining the current name, they argued, would stigmatize them as a "foreign" church and hamper their work. Times had indeed changed. In 1916, President C. L. Preus of Luther College had stood up for his "hyphenated" brethren, saying "it is not well that the immigrants Americanize too rapidly, for they thereby tear away the roots binding them to the traditions and culture of their home people and they drift about aimlessly."[34] Now wartime hysteria had reduced him to arguing before the convention: our members' faith "is the same regardless of language or nationality." And, as for the name, he thought, "American Lutheran" would be more fitting than "Norwegian Lutheran." "The best news which we can send Governor Harding of Iowa," said another, "is to tell him that the Norwegian Lutheran Church of America has struck the word 'Norwegian' from its name."[35]

Discussion finally ended and one question lay before the delegates: should a committee prepare a resolution to change the name to one that the next convention in 1920 could adopt by constitutional amendment? Whether because of wartime patriotism or a fateful sense of urgency demanded by the political situation, delegates overwhelmingly approved the motion in a standing vote of 533 to 61.[36]

Before adjourning, the convention delegates designated a committee of three emissaries to meet with Governor Harding in hopes of adjusting the language question. When they were finally able to meet with the governor on June 25, he informed them that where necessity demanded use of the Norwegian language, a satisfactory arrangement was possible. A pastor, for instance, might repeat a sermon first in Norwegian and then in English or give a morning sermon in English followed by a sermon in Norwegian in the evening. But this should not be done, Harding warned, until the pastor first wrote to the governor and explained the conditions that warranted departing from the provisions of his proclamation. If satisfied that real difficulties rather than any antagonism to English impelled the pastor to make his request, the governor would issue his consent. With permission thus in hand, the pastor stood protected from accusations of disloyalty for disregarding the proclamation.[37]

By August, 1918, however, the arrangement had clearly broken down at the governor's end. Pastors who wrote one or more times requesting permission to use the Norwegian language on certain occasions had never received answers. Evidently the governor's silence "gives consent to the arrangements suggested," inferred a Winnebago county editor, adding that "the majority of the ministers will conclude that he takes this method of granting his permission to disregard the drastic conditions of his language proclamation."[38]

In light of the governor's inaction on the church matter as well as his numerous explanations and clarifications of the edict, rumors naturally circulated before the election that Harding had "backed down"on his proclamation. Actually he rather seemed to vacillate than retreat, depending on the circumstances of the moment.

When he stood before the overflow crowd at the Decorah Opera House on September 26, the moment seemed to call for firmness. Although confining his speech mainly to general patriotic subjects, he offered a few forthright remarks on the language question. He thought he had been right in issuing the proclamation, and now, Harding said, he knew it. After loud applause by the friendly audience, he continued. Never could an immigrant grow an American soul so long as he was "thinking of his mother country, speaking her language, and living her life," he said. Although Harding recognized that "the variety of opinion on the language question was bound to hurt his popularity," he indicated that the question of the popular vote bothered him very little.[39]

The actual campaign between Governor Harding and Claude R. Porter, the Democratic candidate, opened only two weeks before the election. Spirited charges flew back and forth as to who should be considered the more patriotic candidate. Porter made little mention of the language controversy and he did not have to. The Democratic candidate contented himself with oblique remarks about how Iowa needed a governor "who can Unify, Not Divide; Who Will Classify Citizens Not By Race Or Creed, But By The Sole Test of Patriotic Service."[40]

Perhaps sensing that nativist votes might offset losses elsewhere, Governor Harding seemed far more willing to discuss the language question. "Why don't you come out in the open for or against one language in this country?" challenged the governor. He further accused Porter of having been afraid, as United States District Attorney, to act against German propaganda being spread through the use of foreign languages.[41] Throughout this brief political battle, however, public apathy reigned—numerous newspapers commented about the lower than usual level of voter interest in this off-year election.[42]

Predictions proved correct; Iowa voters cast one of the lightest votes in years. In disaffected Norwegian settlements, however, greater numbers of people showed up to vote, holding declines in their turnout to less than one-half that of the state generally.[43]

The vote against Harding visibly demonstrated the trend of Norwegian feeling. Contrary to years past when Norwegian precincts cast Republican majorities of 20 to 30 percentage points over that of the state at large, this time the vote plummeted to 13 percentage points beneath the victorious incumbent's statewide average.[44] This plunge

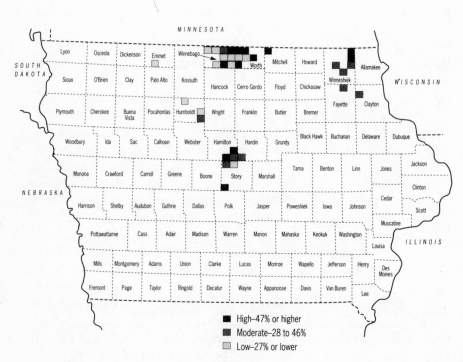

Figure 16. Norwegian Support for Governor Harding, 1918 Election.

of 43 percentage points from the average Republican vote cast since 1900 leaves no doubt about Norwegian dissatisfaction. Claude Porter piled up a large majority of votes in Norwegian-dominated Winnebago county to make him the first Democrat since the Civil War ever to receive a majority there for state office. Norwegians clearly had joined with foreign language-speaking residents elsewhere to repudiate the governor.[45]

Dwelling on the overall magnitude of Norwegian defection can leave a false impression, however. Despite general disappointment, uniform Norwegian sentiment simply cannot be asserted in the face of precinct returns that ranged all the way from 10 to 69 percent for Governor Harding.[46] Obviously individual settlements had drawn different conclusions about the extent to which Governor Harding should be punished at the polls. What prompted the difference?[47]

In this particular election year, the usual opinion leaders – county newspapers – avoided both the language issue and politics in general. Moreover, the ordinary impact of county political parties had lessened as a result of suspending partisan politics for the war's duration. Winneshiek county Democrats, for instance, put forth no candidates for county offices while the remaining county candidates – Republican and otherwise – made no effort to solicit votes or to get out the vote.[48] In such a political vacuum, otherwise minor voices might work their influence.

Although admittedly difficult to demonstrate, it may well be that Norwegian ministers in this instance were largely responsible for local voting differences. Here, in the language question, appeared an issue that threatened the very heart of immigrant church practices. Its religious prohibitions had particularly galled Norwegian Americans and their anger had focused on that aspect of the edict. When issues of this kind appeared that threatened religious values and cultural institutions, pastors – the local symbols of tradition, language, and learning – typically assumed center stage in shaping community opinion. The language edict probably goaded to action many Norwegian pastors who ordinarily eschewed politics. The likely result: despite giving way to outward conformity demanded by the proclamation, most worked quietly to feed disenchantment with Governor Harding.

Of course, pastors did not uniformly influence their congregations. Some felt more strongly about the issue than others; some felt more intimidated by the loyalty issue than others; some commanded more influence and respect or had lived among their charges for longer periods than others. These and other factors may account for differences in the efforts of voters to punish Harding's action.[49] While it is difficult to prove individual ministerial influence, an occasional clue has survived.[50]

Two examples illustrate the connection between local ministers and the varied vote for Harding. Two heavily Norwegian townships of Winneshiek county, Pleasant and Highland, lay in the northeastern part of the county. Neither settlement had rebuffed Harding as had others and the apparent source of their behavior becomes clear when we see that the two townships formed a single church community where Pastor Thore Olson Tolo served an estimated three-fourths of the total parishioners. The same effect is noticed in Hamilton county, where Harding's vote in Scott township fell to one-half that given by Lincoln and Ellsworth townships. Although two or three pastors served each of the three townships, in Scott township Norwegian language services predominated before Harding's proclamation, while the congregations of Lincoln and Ellsworth attended proportionately more English language services. Furthermore, Pastor Martin Norstad may have felt more called upon than others to defend Harding's wartime measures, for besides ministering to many Lincoln and Ellsworth parishioners, he also became local camp pastor during the war for the United States Army.[51]

In Iowa, a cultural issue had cut to the heart of church tradition and had evoked a strong but varied Norwegian-American response, one that likely reflected the personal views of local ministers. The differing votes among settlements did not stem from disagreement between pietist and ritualist religious elements, for the issue this time had nothing to do with the state enforcing standards of public or private morality; nor was this the brand of "activist" government for which Norwegian-American pietists yearned. Instead, the language question had arrayed foreign-born against native-born citizens after Governor Harding promulgated his "Babel" edict. The question of how much cultural diversity the government should tolerate had twisted itself into a different form, and individual ministers faced this direct assault upon traditional Norwegian church practices in light of their local circumstances and personal convictions. This close involvement of Norwegian-American pastors in gubernatorial elections did not repeat itself in Minnesota, where different conditions produced different sources of Norwegian-American leadership.

Once again in this and other situations variety characterized Norwegian settlements. In different ways, a mix of issues and national, state, or local circumstances had combined with varying Norwegian-American leadership to shape election outcomes.

Norwegian Americans: the Political Experience

"The truth is, there is no use disguising it," wrote Senator Knute Nelson in 1920, "the Norwegians are at the bottom of our political troubles in the N[orth] W[est]." Disheartened by the great influx of Norwegians into the radical Nonpartisan League—hardly his notion of a loyal and public-spirited organization—Nelson saw his countrymen's association with it as unworthy and an embarrassment. To this admired Norwegian-American Republican, not only did it seem that "the bitterness & malignity of the Norwegian nonpartisan farmers exceeds that of any other class of Nonpartisans," but that while "the older class of Norwegian Immigrants & their descendants . . . stand fast in the Republican faith—the rest seem to be in a state of flux & chaos."[1]

His underscoring of fragmented and shifting alignments in Norwegian-American politics touched a central truth. But as for this being something new, Senator Nelson had evidently forgotten his own political past when Minnesota's Republican leaders made him their gubernatorial nominee in 1892 to stem the rush of recent Norwegian immigrants into Populist ranks.

Selective political memory, of course, is not confined to participants in the events. Former congressman Haldor Boen, for example, lashed out at a writer who misrepresented the past roles played by him and others in Minnesota Populism, saying: "All history not narrated by those who were the chief actors is of very little value."[2] As a consequence of the caprice of memory in history's participants and the particular vantage points of historians, written records have yielded varying, even contradictory, portraits of Norwegian Americans in politics.

Since the 1960s the color and texture of such portraits have been most influenced by historians identified with the ethnocultural interpretation of politics. Their studies have proved a healthy antidote to earlier mechanistic and oversimplified socioeconomic versions of American political history. Under their influence the focus has shifted from broad national issues, class ideologies, and prominent leaders down to the states, counties, and towns. Here is where political parties immediately felt at first hand the force of clashing attitudes produced by European immigration and cultural heterogeneity. These historians found that cultural conflict was rife – that political behavior in large measure stemmed from ethnic hatreds, religious chauvinism, assailed traditions, xenophobia, bigotry, and resistance to conformist pressures.

Its persuasive focus, its insights, and the needed balance it brought to the historical record has given popularity to the ethnocultural interpretation. Some have wondered, however, if the result might not be to replace "a monocausal and simplistic economic interpretation with an equally simplistic and monocausal cultural interpretation."[3] Fortunately, ongoing work has continued to refine and to address certain perceived shortcomings; for example, Paul Kleppner's *Third Electoral System, 1853–1892* (1979), compared to his earlier *Cross of Culture* (1970), gives more attention to ways in which particular conditions – varying settlement patterns and historical experiences – affected differently the relation of social attributes to partisan behavior. Also Samuel P. Hays finds an "underemphasized" type of analysis to be that dealing with "subcultural variation within each identifiable ethnocultural group, for each group was far from homogeneous," while Kleppner has noted the need for studies that deal with political behavior of a single group "across a variety of different states."[4] As the thrust of this present study is in that very direction, an appropriate question to ask is, what do the findings about Norwegian Americans suggest?

I

Most striking is perhaps this: complexity and contradiction are central to any story of Norwegian-American politics. The temptation to make complicated stories manageable by ignoring troublesome inconsistencies and characterizing Norwegian-American voters as having acted predictably out of class or nationality or religious impulses or its leaders as being unyielding advocates of reform or defenders of individual liberty is a mistake.[5] In particular, three circumstances – the political peculiarities of each state, the date of each settlement, and the urban or rural location of each settlement – are seen to have acted as separating or dividing influences on Norwegian communities.

Patterns of Norwegian-American party alignment reveal that no particular ethnocultural or economic effect operated independently of the intervening influence of a state's political culture. State boundaries made for real differences, for each state is unique. Its political culture – arising as it does from historical experiences relating to party arrangements, social structure, regional economic differences, ethnic divisions, and so on – controlled ways in which issues were raised and resolved. And, as a breakdown of votes in Chapter Two indicates, Norwegian-American voters responded accordingly. In Iowa their Republicanism remained steadfast but unenergetic, their internal divisions rooted in ethnoreligious conflicts, while economic forces and movements that shaped people's lives in Minnesota produced strikingly different effects. Political alternatives in Wisconsin encouraged voters in heavily Norwegian settlements to exhibit stronger than average turnout rates and tend toward left-of-center Republicanism.

The great questions animating politics between 1880 and 1924 – prohibition, Populism, progressivism, and the internal security issues during World War I – all played themselves out differently in each state and the votes of Norwegian-American settlements showed these differences. Prohibition so marked Iowa politics during the 1880s that Norwegian settlements divided on the question here, but not elsewhere. Populism strongly moved voters in the group's wheat-growing settlements of northwestern Minnesota, but not elsewhere. Candidates of the progressive wing of the Republican party drew great support from Wisconsin's Norwegian settlements, but not elsewhere. And, for vastly different reasons, the political acrimony of World War I sowed defection among Norwegian settlements in Iowa and polarized sentiment among their counterparts in Minnesota, but not in Wisconsin.[6]

Just as a state's political culture opened up or choked off chances that particular economic or cultural questions would find political life, a second factor – period of settlement – worked its influence within this framework. For as each set of new immigrants established their communities and involved themselves in political activity, they absorbed a partisan perspective unlike that of Norwegians settling at other times and places. This sensitized the immigrants to some issues and not others, depending in part on how closely the issue touched upon and activated old-country attitude. Meanwhile, other attitudes and feelings from Norway, without an American outlet for their political expression, receded into the background and so failed to pass themselves on to the next generation of Norwegian-American voters.

Because massive swings of public opinion and impetus for reform separated political eras and effectively stamped certain emerging electorates with a shared set of experiences and attitudes, Samuel P. Huntington singles out "differing experiences and priorities of successive generations" as one of the two most significant forms of past conflict in America.[7] This "generational rhythm of American politics," as Daniel J. Elazar terms it, has in fact been noted since the time of Thomas Jefferson.[8] Its subdividing influence on arriving immigrant groups, however, has been largely ignored.

Each wave of Norwegian immigrants saw American political life a bit differently because its time of arrival coincided with different moments in the evolution of national and state politics. The initial period of a community's settlement proved especially important. Unencumbered by the inertia of past party loyalties handed down from native-born fathers, the first immigrant generation proved exceptionally sensitive to immediate political issues, and their own resulting partisanship then set the allegiances that their children in the settlement generally followed.

The more turbulent the politics of the period, the more distinct generational impression they apparently left on the newest Norwegian-American settlements. America's great electoral realignments of the 1860s and the 1890s coincided with the emergence of conspicuous political generations of Norwegian Americans—the first clinging to Republicanism and the second engulfed by agrarian third-party radicalism. A third, less cohesive, group of settlements, established during the more uncertain decade following the Civil War, embraced Republicanism, but less enthusiastically than earlier arrivals, as shown by their more ambivalent vote during times when economic questions assumed center stage.

The Norwegian-American experience of generational realignment in their party loyalties suggests that parties won their new adherents from among heretofore inactive voters with weak party attachments, not by converting loyal party followers to another party.[9] Thus, when a large contingent of immigrant Norwegians went Populist and then returned without enthusiasm to Republicanism until an agrarian party alternative reappeared, Norwegian-American voters in recently established settlements had no tradition of Republican voting.

To understand a man, goes the saying, you must know his memories. What made political generations of immigrants differ from those of the native-born was that their party affiliations stemmed from values and recollected experience drawn partly from the politics and regional economies of their new home and partly from their country of origin. With both sources of political attitudes and loyalties in a state of flux, the dynamics of old-country life meshed with the pace of events in America to help divide Norwegian Americans among themselves. New political currents in America heightened differences between earlier and later arrivals, as did strife within the immigrant group over such issues as predestination and public versus religious schools. Earlier leaders consequently failed to maintain their authority as social arbiters or mediators while others moved forward to speak for the more secular, class-oriented, politicized newcomers as religious controversies burned themselves out and yielded preeminence to political ones. Senator Knute Nelson's disparaging view of recent Norwegian Americans who joined the Nonpartisan League, noted at the beginning of the chapter, reflects this unsettled state of affairs.

As Norwegian immigrants' time of settlement shaped their political inclinations, so too did it matter whether they chose to live in the countryside or in town. For if they chose farming during times of agricultural discontent, chances increased that it would nurture their abiding Norwegian agrarianism.

The disproportionate involvement of Norwegian Americans in Farmers' Alliance, Populist, and Nonpartisan League politics as well as their visible association with Robert LaFollette's cause in Wisconsin underscores the strength of their agrarian heritage. This, once unleashed, resonated with recalled old-world feelings of dislike of officials and distrust of towns and cities.

Prudence dictated, so many Norwegian farmers thought, that a suspicious eye be kept on townsmen lest they use the advantage of their monopolistic position to gouge the unwary smallholder. The thrust of their grievances was directed against urban interests, especially those that threatened efforts by farmers to sustain market prices for their goods, relieve the burden of expensive credit on which smallholders relied, or restrain and regulate those who controlled their livelihood—middlemen, retailers, bankers, and financiers.

Aggravating these suspicions were the hidden injuries of class inferiority felt by Norwegian-American farmers who remembered the tension of past town-countryside relations. Norway's rural-urban antagonisms had been visible and ran deep. The "bitter feeling" wrote one visitor to Norway in the 1890s, left many a freeholding farmer believing himself to be "despised"; he learned from a farmer elected to the Norwegian parliament that "many people in the cities believe that we are no better than cattle." Further confirmation came to the traveler when he reserved rooms at an inn for himself and several farmers from Upper Telemark. There he found them rebuffed. The owner of the inn "said he thought the room had been secured for gentlemen and their wives. I answered, 'Never mind; they are honorable, straightforward bønder, well-known in your district.' I ordered dinner for twelve. He said he could not accommodate me, that he had no food, no bread, etc.

"At last I became annoyed, and told him that it was all nonsense; that a good honest farmer, even if he wore a peasant costume, was as good as anybody. Finally, I said that, if he refused, I would expose him in the public print. He then relented, but with bad grace; he never gave us enough to eat, and his charges were exorbitant."[10]

The immigrants' sensitivity to such class differences neither faded away nor went unnoticed. Kristofer Janson wrote of his immigrant countrymen that when a few gave in to their longing for the mountains and fjords of home and returned, he heard time and time again of their having come back to America within a few months because "they cannot stand the class distinctions at home."[11]

To Norwegian immigrants building their midwestern prairie farms in 1885, there seemed little reason to abandon their fear and animus toward townsmen. Main Street's business and professional men may have lacked the aristocratic haughtiness shown back home, but they held, so it seemed to many, just as sure a grip on the small farmers' livelihood and political prospects. These country towns of middlemen—grain buyers, bankers, dealers in groceries, hardware, and farm implements, and other buyers and sellers of goods—and everyone else who, so it seemed, lived indirectly off the farmers, were the centers of economic and political power. Many Norwegian immigrant farmers would find plenty to agree with in the critical characterization of Main Street given by the midwestern son of Norwegian immigrants, Thorstein Veblen: "Anyone who knows anything about the country towns of the prairie states, knows that the established retailers of the place habitually act in collusion in all matters which seriously interest them, such as prices and competition. The usual organ of this collusion, or of the conspiracy to restrain competition is the local Commercial Club; and back of the Commercial Club, and serving its purposes is the town government, which is much the same thing under another name."[12]

What Robert R. Dykstra found for Kansas and Stanley B. Parsons for Nebraska's rural political life in the late nineteenth century proved no less true in nearby states – the key leadership of both parties rested in the hands of village newspaper editors, town fathers, and local entrepreneurs.[13] It was a hierarchy of county and state party leadership that admitted few farmers to its ranks. This group of bustling village promoters, although interested in farm prosperity, supported farm programs for relieving burdensome freight rates or curing grain market abuses only so long as these programs did not interfere with the status quo or jeopardize their local promotion schemes or disrupt community amicability. With this social and political distance persisting between town and country in an era of agricultural discontent, lingering old-country suspicion of official and business classes lived on among immigrant Norwegians, ready to express itself when American political issues turned in that direction.

The rural class-conscious aspects of Norwegian agrarianism began to find political outlets as Civil War issues lost their ability to mobilize partisanship and agricultural discontent loomed larger in political discussions. While generally the major party organizations and political leaders strove mightily to keep economic grievances and class conflict out of campaigns, regional situations often made major party leaders cut and trim their rhetoric to fit the demands of their constituents. Accordingly, during the years when numerous Norwegian-American settlements were developing in an atmosphere of flourishing agricultural discontent, the immigrants felt the tug of "anti-monopolist" rhetoric from Democrats who were seeking inroads into Republican constituencies, while Republicans countered with "low tariff" promises. Left unsatisfied, the recent settlements of Norwegian Americans disproportionately joined agrarian third-party movements once they appeared.[14]

The political loyalties of Norwegian Americans thus depended greatly on where they lived, when they came, and what livelihood they chose. That being said, it needs also to be recognized that Norwegian immigrants did share one attitude that cut across all of these as a constant partisan influence – anti-Catholicism. It assumed such strength that it defied state Republican politics, state boundaries, generations, and rural-urban divisions in predictably prompting Norwegian-American settlements to reject Democratic party candidates. The consistently solid majorities they cast against Democratic candidates reflected their animus toward what they considered the political home of Catholic nationalities, the party of Popery. The pattern dissolved only on rare occasions when a Scandinavian Democrat reached for high office, or in places like Otter Tail county where flourishing agrarian discontent kept Norwegian settlements voting the Populist ticket even after several positions of leadership on it had been captured, as one Norwegian American put it, by a "handful of oily-tongued Irish Democrats."[15] True, Norwegian anti-Catholicism found its limits in the failure of the American Protective Association to expand into these areas of economic discontent. But the record of anti-Democratic voting continued to be a far more uniform and predictable feature of Norwegian-American settlements than did their support for Republican candidates.

II

To a view recognizing political complexities within the immigrants' world must be added a second finding: in Norwegian-American politics, religion and class were inevitably intertwined. In Norway pietism had found life among those with an agrarian antagonism to central authority. In America this persisted in instances of heated rebellion against Norwegian ministerial authority and the class distinctions it implied, all of which figured in the origins of numerous pietist congregations under the Eielsen and Haugean synods. When Norwegian Lutheranism in America broke apart into synods, the divisions "represented only a new form for the substance of older conflicts and differences which had their origins in Norway," differences "not only religious in nature but social, political, and cultural as well."[16]

The ethnocultural interpretation of politics has focused not on this agrarian class heritage of Norwegian-American pietism, but instead on the differing doctrinal orientations of pietist and liturgical elements as the key shaping force behind voter attachments. Norwegian-American Lutherans after 1890 were divided mainly among churches of the liturgical Norwegian Synod, the moderately pietist United Norwegian Lutheran Church, and the highly pietist Hauge's Synod. Voters, according to ethnocultural scholars, cast their ballots in support of the political party that appealed to their pietist or liturgical beliefs. "Liturgicals" opposed Republicans' espousing moral reform on the grounds that such matters should be left to the individual and his church, while pietists supported Republicanism because of its willingness to see state authority regulate and control public morality, the pietists' thrust of which, in Paul Kleppner's words, was to "reach out and purge the world of sin."[17]

This concept, though it plausibly may explain variability between ethnic groups, lacks persuasiveness within Norwegian-American settlements.[18] Here party votes differed greatly among those belonging to the very same pietist or liturgical synod and, conversely, differed little between pietist and liturgical settlements in either Wisconsin or Minnesota throughout the period under study. Instances when pietist settlements departed politically from liturgical settlements occurred only in Iowa, where prohibition specifically had been made a dominant issue – perhaps *the* dominant issue – in politics since before the Civil War. Norwegian-American settlements divided sharply on prohibition, in other words, only where encouraged – indeed, perhaps, required – to do so by the state's own deep and energized divisions on this issue within its political culture.

Pietist-liturgical conflict among Norwegian-American settlements thus proved an inconstant and minor political force. Class feeling limited the minister's influence in politics and religions indifference among large numbers of only nominal Lutherans exacerbated it. Together they muted, eroded, or reduced the political perceptibility and impact of pietist-liturgical controversy.

III

Just as the class dimension of immigrant Lutheranism demands recognition in an ethnocultural interpretation, so too does agrarian class feeling among Norwegian Americans need to be recognized in an expanded meaning of ethnocultural.

Remembered Norwegian class animosities were embedded within and expressed as part of such census attributes as "nationality" and "religion" that ethnocultural researchers have found to be strongly correlated with votes. When so recognized, the extent to which class sentiment underlay statistical correlations of party votes with religion or nationality – serving to buoy or depress the relationship – will receive greater notice. Lamentably, Alan Dawley reminds us, "class and ethnic identity are often seen as antithetical: the more ethnic identity, the less class consciousness. On the crudest level 'ethnicity' and class are reduced to variables, to be toted up in the fancy gridwork of a pseudo-social science alongside religion, party affiliation, years of schooling, distance from work, etc."[19]

Nationality is in fact a broad "global" attribute of several component values and attitudes – class feeling interweaving with such factors as region of origin, kinship, and language – that rural Norwegian immigrants carried within themselves, each aspect of which lived on or gradually perished according to what was activating American politics at the time of settlement. Too often what is "inseparable" is assumed to be separate as political historians strive to treat "each genre of attributes independently in order to determine whether, when, and how they overlapped and interacted with each other."[20] The risk of misinterpreting results thus grows when studying complex variables with numerous component aspects and other associated characteristics.[21] One simply cannot easily distinguish whether members of an ethnic group voted solidly because of their clannish regard for the candidate, their shared Protestantism, their remembered agrarian class animosities, or for all of these and other reasons. Thus to see significant correlations of nationality with votes as denying the influence of economic class is to risk misjudging a phenomenon that may be richly infused with class content.

This cultural expression of inherited or shared class experiences found its formulation by E. P. Thompson in *The Making of the English Working Class*. To him, as people construed the events of social conflict through which they lived, their inheritance "of remembered village rights, of notions of equality before the law, of craft traditions," and of the recollected past helped those disposed to behave as a class to define themselves in relation to other groups in class ways.[22] Class, thus being a dynamic and evolving "historical relationships not exclusively defined by one's economic relations to the means of production," fit the situation of Norwegian immigrants who found old-world points of reference useful to locating themselves and encountering New World situations.[23]

Such aspects of nationality have not gone entirely unrecognized. Michael Paul Rogin, for example, scrutinized Populist voting patterns in North Dakota and asked what led a group such as the Scandinavians to support Populism while another such as the Russian Germans resisted the movement. He concluded that "an ethnic tradition" seems to have "predisposed Scandinavians to support agrarian radical movements" and fostered their "concern with economic demands." Russian-German communities, on the other hand, being tightly knit, "fearful of alien influence, rigid and tradition-bound," manifested a "refusal to support economic change" and proved "resistant to class appeals."[24]

Given the past class experience and other cultural aspects of nationality groups, the focus of historical explanation ought to be on the particular blend of their influence jointly operating at different political levels. For while ethnicity and class might be analytically distinct principles of social organization, they nevertheless "interpenetrate in complex and varying ways."[25] The Norwegian-American experience suggests that party differences resulted from situations faced when their legacy of class and other social aspects of their cultural identities converged with national, state, and local political cultures. Expanding settlement and evolving economic networks, maladjustments in transportation, an era of single party dominance, restive farmers, good harvests, an influential editor, a dynamic leader – these and a multitude of other long-term, intermediate, and short-term influences combined at each level to shape distinctive combinations of party allegiance.

IV

The Norwegian-American experience shows also that local situations and leadership made predictions risky about the impact of larger long-term forces at work such as the influence of a community's ethnic or religious makeup or economic profile.

This study found that the sum total influence of social and economic indicators examined never accounted statistically for more than half the observed voting differences. This held true among Norwegian settlements in each state as well as for the region as a whole. Although the linear relationship of these characteristics to votes often accounted for from 20 to 40 percent of variations – thus making such research surely worth one's time – analyses that look mainly to the singular force of these factors evidently miss a good deal of what was going on.

The quantitative analysis undertaken here – although involving mainly frequencies and percentages – uncovered great variety. This is consistent with the view that differences between settlements often seemed due to the uneven qualitites of political leaders working in a township, county, or state – juggling issues and events to capitalize on immediate voter aspirations and discontents.

Qualities of political figures and the issues they espoused – the short-term influences – must not be treated as uninfluential in their own right, important only as they ignited the underlying ethnic or religious predispositions assumed to have "really" divided voters. Stories of political struggle in Otter Tail and Trempealeau counties and elsewhere underscore the intrinsic importance of short-term localized influences in directing election outcomes.

In Otter Tail county from 1891 to 1894, for example, agrarian politics breathed with factionalism involving Haldor Boen, John Hompe, Charles Brandborg, and others. Factionalism prompted Boen's ouster from Alliance circles, it underlay the disruptive events surrounding the killing of the young Swede, it brought about Boen's sudden return to leadership over the new Populist party, and it exacerbated his bitter 1894 reelection defeat by allowing enemies to transform his fading prospects into a permanent political exile. Boen's admirers praised his courage and indomitable leadership, while his enemies castigated him for his all-consuming ambition for office and his reckless dictatorial manner. Boen still felt the bitterness a decade later: "I was so shamefully abused, vilified and slandered, that I determined to withdraw from political life. I longed for some one to raise his voice in my defense; but nothing but abuse did meet me."[26] Norwegian-American Populists naturally took sides. Boen succeeded in some Norwegian townships far more than in others, depending on the political influence of his local friends and the strength of his Norwegian-American opponents. In Boen's home township of Aurdal, for instance, the weaker than expected support that he received was evidently due in large measure to the intense personal antagonism of a staunch Republican, the Reverend Ole N. Fosmark. Whatever the reasons—Boen's divorce, his secularism, or their clashing personalities—relations between the two so deteriorated that Fosmark ultimately forced Boen's dismissal from the congregation.[27]

Election campaigns proved to be acrimonious, personally bitter, and divisive, aimed as much at undermining the personal popularity of candidates as with cultivating ethnic and religious animosities. Voter reactions to a politician's winning personality and to immediate political issues reached to every level of politics. Who would deny the effect, for example, of the powerful Chicago *Skandinaven*'s repeated allegations that Minnesota's Ignatius Donnelly was an "industrious liar" and "unscrupulous demagogue," fastening himself on the farmers' movement only for the sake of his own "personal benefit and ambition"?[28] And who could ignore the polarized personal reactions of Wisconsin's press to Robert M. LaFollette and Herman L. Ekern through their years of political struggle in that faction-ridden state, years when politicians dated their own careers "W. B." and "A. B."—"With Bob" and "Against Bob"?[29]

Leaders and political issues were not merely incidental aspects of stubborn cultural determinants. Issues and events and party organizations decided which Norwegian-American politicians rose to power. And the effect of these, when combined with a politician's own personal qualities, aided or curbed what he might do, and often decided how the Norwegian-American electorate might vote. The bland politics of Wisconsin's Republican congressman Nils Haugen would have stood little chance among western Minnesota farmers. Conversely Minnesota's radical Populist congressman, Haldor Boen, undoubtedly would have got nowhere in Congressman Gilbert Haugen's orthodox Republican district in northern Iowa.

V

A comprehensive picture of electoral change and its determinants will remain unfinished until the values and attitudes distinctive to a group are treated not as being held by all its members but as shared with varying intensity by elements of it with different livelihoods, living in different regions and types of localities, and hailing from different parts of the old country. The question always to be asked, Samuel P. Hays reminds us, is "what particular people, at what particular time, in what particular place thought and acted in what particular way?"[30] And, we must recognize the significant impact of the local situation on how elements of a group voted, where politicians witnessed at first-hand the election effect of bad choices, wrong turnings, lost opportunities, factional spirit, and the entanglement of unstable loyalties, issues, mutual obligations, compromises, and indifference.

Yes, differences of religious, ethnic, and economic status set boundaries for political action, but they were of a kind within which a remarkable amount of variation occurred. American electoral politics had truly been caught in endless cultural conflict, but so too had one or another group predisposition surfaced at times, only to be later neutralized by the crosscurrents of other issues, their immediate political cultures, and the qualities of men that events lifted to leadership.

Notes

Notes

INTRODUCTION

1. Statement of Charles Francis Adams in the first annual address delivered before the State Historical Society of Wisconsin, as reported in R. B. Anderson, *Life Story of Rasmus B. Anderson* (2nd revised ed., Madison, Wisconsin, 1917), 68.

2. Three important recent studies of midwestern politics are Richard Jensen, *The Winning of the Midwest: Social and Political Conflict, 1888-1896* (Chicago, 1971); and Paul Kleppner's two works, *The Cross of Culture: A Social Analysis of Midwestern Politics, 1850-1900* (New York, 1970), and *The Third Electoral System, 1853-1892: Parties, Voters and Political Cultures* (Chapel Hill, North Carolina, 1979). For discussion of these and other major voting analyses and the thrust of their interpretations see: Allan G. Bogue, Jerome W. Clubb, and William H. Flanigan, "The New Political History," in *American Behavioral Scientist*, 21 (1977), 201-220; Richard L. McCormick, "Ethno-Cultural Interpretations of Nineteenth-Century American Voting Behavior," in *Political Science Quarterly*, 89 (1974), 351-377; James E. Wright, "The Ethnocultural Model of Voting," in *American Behavioral Scientist*, 16 (1973), 14-33; Robert P. Swierenga, "Ethnocultural Political Analysis: A New Approach to American Ethnic Studies," in *Journal of American Studies*, 5 (1971), 59-79; Walter Dean Burnham, "Quantitative History: Beyond the Correlation Coefficient, A Review Essay," in *Historical Methods Newsletter*, 6 (1972), 17-26; Bogue, "United States: The 'New' Political History," in *Journal of Contemporary History*, 3 (1968), 5-27; James R. Green, "Behavioralism and Class Analysis: A Review Essay on Methodology and Ideology," in *Labor History*, 13 (1972), 89-106.

3. See Lee Benson, *Turner and Beard: American Historical Writing Reconsidered* (Glencoe, Illinois, 1960), chapters I-II.

4. Benson, *The Concept of Jacksonian Democracy: New York as a Test Case* (New York, 1966), 165.

5. They have also searched in new places for information. Where historians had conventionally dug among the shards of surviving manuscript collections,

books, and newspapers to piece together the stories of great national struggles and the influential figures who shaped them, several in the 1950s began to probe deeper, trying to recover the political experience of ordinary Americans from election and census records and from mounds of information collected by institutions and official agencies. And, aided by the computer and quantitative techniques of varied complexity, historians were soon exploring the social bases of community and state history and relating them to sociological and anthropological concepts. Gradually, as they imaginatively pursued these new leads, the patterns they saw in past elections and popular voting alignments changed their perceptions as to what had historically mattered in politics and in other of life's aspects.

6. Benson, *Concept of Jacksonian Democracy*, 165.

7. The statistical problems of multi-collinearity existing in tests of linear relationship among variables give ample evidence of what social scientists describe as the "block-booked" nature of social characteristics.

8. The cultural dimension of class, though hardly new, has yet received little application in popular voting studies. Green, in his "Behavioralism and Class Analysis," 97-98, notes the need to deal with the persistence of European class differences after immigration, but as of 1972 he found examples of such writings only among general histories of Jewish immigration.

9. Letter to the author from Peter A. Munch, February 24, 1972.

10. See Frank Thistlethwaite, "Migration from Europe Overseas in the Nineteenth and Twentieth Centuries," in *Xle Congres International des Sciences Historiques, Stockholm 1960, Rapports, V: Histoire Contemporaine* (Gothenburg, 1960), 32-60; Oscar Handlin, *The Uprooted: The Epic Story of the Great Migrations that Made the American People* (New York, 1951); Marcus Lee Hansen, *The Immigrant in American History* (Cambridge, 1941).

11. See Rudolph Vecoli, "Contadini in Chicago: A Critique of *The Uprooted*," in *Journal of American History*, 51 (1964), 404-417; Frederick C. Luebke, *Immigrants and Politics: The Germans of Nebraska, 1880-1900* (Lincoln, 1969); Jon Gjerde, *From Peasants to Farmers: The Migration from Norway to the Upper Middle West* (New York, 1985); Robert C. Ostergren, *A Community Transplanted: The Trans-Atlantic Experience of Swedish Immigrant Settlement in the Upper Middle West, 1835-1915* (Madison, Wisconsin, 1988); Walter D. Kamphoefner, *The Westfalians: From Germany to Missouri* (Princeton, 1987). For an excellent summary of scholarship on the complexity and variability of emigrant homeland and migration experiences, see John Bodnar, *The Transplanted: A History of Immigrants in Urban America* (Bloomington, Indiana, 1986), chapter 1.

12. Al Gedicks, "The Social Origins of Radicalism Among Finnish Immigrants in Midwest Mining Communities," in *The Review of Radical Political Economics*, 8 (1976), 1-31; Walter Galenson, "Scandinavia," in Galenson, ed., *Comparative Labor Movements* (New York, 1952), 109-111.

13. See, for example, Herbert Gutman, "Work, Culture, and Society in Industrializing America," in Milton Cantor, ed., *American Workingclass Culture: Explorations in American Labor and Social History* (Westport, Connecticut, 1979).

14. Edward P. Thompson, *Making of the English Working Class* (New York, 1963), 9-10. For analyses of Thompson's place in attempts to incorporate a sociocultural dimension into what had come to be a static mechanical Marxism, see Richard R. Weiner, *Cultural Marxism and Political Sociology* (Beverly Hills, California, 1981), chapter 1; and Alan Dawley, "E. P. Thompson and the Peculiarities of the Americans," in *Radical History Review*, 19 (1978-1979), 33-59.

15. The vigorous debates within "cultural Marxism" are eloquently stated in writings by two of its leading protagonists: Perry Anderson, *Arguments Within*

English Marxism (London, 1980), chapters 2 and 3; and Thompson, *The Poverty of Theory and Other Essays* (London, 1978).

16. Pierre L. van den Berghe, in *The Ethnic Phenomenon* (New York, 1981), 241–247, holds that class attachments, being segmental and based on shared economic interests, are more tenuous and fleeting, hence less permanent, than ethnic affinities, viewed as kinship ties. This "primordialist" position, grounded in "kinship" sociobiology, which emphasizes cultural over situational factors in ethnic identities, can be easily exaggerated. If shared economic interests persist after migration, class attachments would find mutual reinforcement and endure. This happened with aspects of Norwegian class heritage which found new life in America's small farmer class relations and drew sustenance from agrarian political issues. Abner Cohen—examining the "situational" nature of ethnicity—points out, in linking ethnic distinctions to the pursuit of interests, that "the members of interest groups who cannot organize themselves formally will . . . tend to make use, though largely unconsciously, of whatever cultural mechanisms are available in order to articulate the organization of their grouping. And it is here, in such situations, that political ethnicity comes into being." Abner Cohen, "Introduction: The Lesson of Ethnicity," in Cohen, ed., *Urban Ethnicity* (London, 1974), xvi–xviii. Kleppner, in *The Third Electoral System*, 368–369, argues a related point: that American ethnoreligious-based identifications with the major political parties found reinforcement in "a host of ethnoreligiously exclusive secondary institutions" such as churches and parochial schools. Emergent farmer-labor parties, on the other hand, were "not accompanied by the development of a parallel class-oriented infrastructure of secondary institutions." Given these observations about what worked against class identity, it is noteworthy indeed that agrarian politics took semi-permanent hold upon a sizeable segment—the post-1875 generation—of rural Norwegian-American settlements, more so than other nationality groups living in the same area. Perhaps, as John S. Saul writes, ethnicity may best reveal its secrets "when the *simultaneity* of class and centre-periphery contradictions is placed front and centre as a key factor within our analytic framework." See his "The Dialectic of Class and Tribe," in *Race & Class*, 20 (Spring, 1979), 371.

CHAPTER 1

1. From a Norwegian-language political circular translated and reprinted in the Arcadia (Wisconsin) *Leader*, October 23, 1908.

2. H. H. Boyeson, "The Scandinavians in the United States," in *North American Review*, 155 (1892), 530. A variety of such attempts are discussed in Kendric C. Babcock, *The Scandinavian Element in the United States* (Urbana, Illinois, 1914), 172–177.

3. Arthur C. Paulson, "The Norwegian-American Reaction to Ibsen and Bjørnson 1850–1900" (Ph.D. dissertation, State University of Iowa, 1933), 3.

4. Babcock, *Scandinavian Element*, 181.

5. Munch, *A Study of Cultural Change: Rural-Urban Conflicts in Norway* (Oslo, 1956), 32–33; Ronald G. Popperwell, *Norway* (New York, 1972), 24, 36–37; Odd Sverre Lovoll, *A Folk Epic: The* Bygdelag *in America* (Boston, 1975), 2–5.

6. Kristopher Janson, "Norsemen in the United States," in *Cosmopolitan*, 9 (1890), 681.

7. Babcock, *Scandinavian Element*, 181. See also Munch's essay, "Social Class and Acculturation," in *The Strange American Way: Letters of Caja Munch from Wiota, Wisconsin, 1855–1859, with An American Adventure (exerpts from "Vita Mea," an autobiography written in 1903)*, trans. by H. Munch and P. A. Munch (Carbondale, Illinois, 1970), 224.

8. G. Amneus, "Population," in *Norway: Official Publication for the Paris Exhibition, 1900* (Kristiania, 1900), 88; Popperwell, *Norway*, 19-20, 299-300; O. T. Bjanes, *Norwegian Agriculture* (Oslo, 1926), 18-19.

9. See Axel Steen, "Climate," in *Norway: Official Publication for the Paris Exhibition*, 45-57; Popperwell, *Norway*, 19; Bjanes, *Norwegian Agriculture*, 21, 23.

10. Amneus, "Population," 90, 99-100; Michael Drake, *Population and Society in Norway 1735-1865* (Cambridge, 1969), 81-82, 95-99, 101, 106; Bjanes, *Norwegian Agriculture*, 24.

11. The capsule summary of political developments is drawn from several sources, including B. J. Hovde, *The Scandinavian Countries, 1720-1865: The Rise of the Middle Classes*, 2 vols. (Boston, 1943), 1:177-228, 2:510-572; Karen Larsen, *A History of Norway* (New York, 1948); Thomas K. Derry, *A History of Modern Norway 1814-1972* (Oxford, 1973), 1-96; Popperwell, *Norway*, 65-142; Per Bang, *Norway La Norvege* (New York, 1971), 23-24.

12. The tone of Norwegian sensitivities toward their Swedish "big brother" in the 1830s is related in Samuel Laing, *Journal of a Residence in Norway during the Years 1834, 1835, 1836* (2nd ed., London, 1837), 196-199.

13. Laing, *Residence in Norway*, 321.

14. Moneyed people sometimes entered this class—persons who had succeeded in sawmilling, small industry, shipping and wholesaling businesses, or who owned sizable agricultural holdings.

15. Munch, "Social Class and Acculturation," 198-200, and his "Authority and Freedom: Controversy in Norwegian-American Congregations," in *Norwegian-American Studies*, 28 (1979), 4-8; Stein Rokkan, "Geography, Religion and Social Class: Cross Cutting Cleavages in Norwegian Politics," in S. M. Lipset and S. Rokkan, eds., *Party Systems and Voter Alignments* (New York, 1967), 368-369; Derry, *History of Modern Norway*, 27-31.

16. Dorothy Burton Skårdal, *The Divided Heart: Scandinavian Immigrant Experience through Literary Sources* (Lincoln, Nebraska, 1974), 56.

17. Johan Bojer, *The Emigrants*, trans. by A. G. Jayne (New York, 1925), 23-24.

18. Larsen, *A History of Norway*, 334.

19. A. Crichton and H. Wheaton, *Scandinavia*, 2 (New York, 1841), 291-292.

20. Theodore C. Blegen, *Land of Their Choice: The Immigrants Write Home* (Minneapolis, 1955), 197.

21. *The Life of Reginald Heber, D.D., Lord Bishop of Calcutta, By His Widow, With Selections From His Correspondence, Unpublished Poems, and Private Papers; Together with a Journal of His Tour in Norway, Sweden, Russia, Hungary, and Germany, and A History of the Cossaks*, 1 (London, 1830), 56.

22. Bayard Taylor, *Northern Travel* (New York, 1881), 271-272.

23. Anticlericalism and religious indifference among Norwegians are treated in three articles by Frederick Hale, "Anticlericalism and Norwegian Society Before the Breakthrough of Modernity," in *Scandinavian Studies*, 52 (1980), 245-263; "An Embattled Church," in *Scandinavian Review*, 69 (1982), 52-60; and "Transatlantic Norwegian Religion and Ethnicity," in *Fides Et Historia*, 17 (1984), 6-24.

24. Arne Garborg, *Peace*, trans. by Phillips Dean Carleton (New York, 1929), 58.

25. Garborg, *Peace*, 140-141.

26. The background and ramifications of this issue are ably summarized in Rokkan, "Geography, Religion and Social Class," 372-374. See also Derry, *History of Modern Norway*, 76-77; Oscar J. Falnes, *National Romanticism in Norway*

(New York, 1933); Hovde, *Scandinavian Countries*, 2:467–469; Harry Eckstein, *Division and Cohesion in Democracy: A Study of Norway* (Princeton, 1966), 43–47; Popperwell, *Norway*, 192–194, 198, 210.

27. This runs contrary to the idea that attachment to democracy strongly marked the Norwegian character. Historians of Norwegian immigration, perhaps anxious to show Norwegian-American respectability in the face of anti-foreignism, have been quick to assert that Norway's immigrants closely resembled Americans in that they, too, had acquired the political knowledge and experience of living in a democratic country. "They hail from one of the two most democratic countries of Europe," claimed a typical enthusiast, "and have come, as they are coming, to the United States thoroughly schooled in popular government." N. A. Grevstad, "Participation in American Politics," in Harry Sundby-Hansen, ed., *Norwegian Immigrant Contributions to America's Making* (New York, 1921), 107. See also Sigvart Luther Rugland, "The Norwegian Press of the Northwest, 1885–1900" (M.A. thesis, State University of Iowa, 1929), 55–56; Babcock, "The Scandinavian Contingent," in *Atlantic Monthly*, 77 (1896), 663; Babcock, *The Scandinavian Element*, 140; Boyesen, "Scandinavians in the United States," 527. As evidence of strong democratic impulses, they fondly point out that the people had never known bondage and that, after Norway established her constitutional government in 1814, the people lived under an extremely democratic form of government by the standards of the time. Because Norway had always been too poor and thinly populated to support a nobility with extensive political or economic privileges, a feudal system had never evolved. Instead, from earliest times, peasants had without royal charter held the right, under ancient *udal* laws, to own and inherit land. Danish and Swedish rulers alike chose not to interfere with Norway's landholding system. As for Norway's liberal constitution of 1814, with over one in ten of its people enfranchised, Norway led other countries of western Europe in its level of early democratization. See Leola Nelson Bergmann, *Americans From Norway* (Philadelphia, 1950), 33–35; Laing, *Journal*, 115, 203–207; Rokkan, "Geography, Religion and Social Class," 379.

28. Rokkan, "Geography, Religion, and Social Class," 371; Ingrid Semmingsen, "The Dissolution of Estate Society in Norway," in *Scandinavian Economic History Review*, 2 (1954), 187.

29. Rasmus Sunde, "Emigration from the District of Sogn, 1839–1915," in *Norwegian-American Studies*, 29 (1983), 120–121.

30. Derry, *History of Modern Norway*, 27, suggests that "by the 1870s Norway, with an enfranchised population of only 7 or 8 percent, restricted the right to vote to a very much smaller section of the community than did Disraelian Britain or many nations of the Continent."

31. Rokkan, "Geography, Religion and Social Class," 379–385; Derry, *History of Modern Norway*, 25–27; Oyvind Osterud, "The Transformation of Scandinavian Agrarianism," in *Scandinavian Journal of History*, 1 (1976), 207; Merle Curti, *et al.*, *Making of an American Community* (Stanford, 1959), 296.

32. This is a leading theme in Gjerde, *From Peasants to Farmers*. See also Andres A. Svalestuen, "Emigration from the Community of Tinn," in *Norwegian-American Studies*, 29 (1983), 82–83.

33. Nico and Beatrix Jungman, *Norway* (London, 1905), 137.

34. Several classes of *husmenn* (cotters) are concisely identified in Svalestuen, "Emigration from the Community of Tinn," 86. The classes, in his words, included: " 'husmenn med jord,' cotters with a piece of land to till; 'husmenn uten jord,' cotters without land; and 'innerster' (lodgers) who did not even have a hut to live in but lodged with and worked for others. In 1855, when the cotter system was about

at its height, there were in Norway 65,060 cotters with land, 21,982 cotters without land, and 13,350 'innerster'. Besides these cotters, properly speaking, there were day laborers and servants, who usually were sons and daughters of cotters. In 1855 there were 28,984 day laborers and 54,631 servants in Norway. 'All these together composed the cotter class. When we combine them they were absolutely the most numerous social class in Norway'." Svalestuen quotes the last sentence from Einar Hovdhaugen, *Husmannstida* (Oslo, 1976), 91–92.

35. Gjerde, *From Peasants To Farmers*, 8, 96, 104, 123.

36. Drake, *Population and Society in Norway*, 120, 148, 159; Derry, *History of Modern Norway*, 29–31.

37. Semmingsen, "Dissolution of Estate Society in Norway," 187.

38. In treating the Thrane movement, this study relies on the analysis of modern research relating to the movement's appeal, purposes, and varied sources and distribution of membership contained in Kåre Tønnesson, "Popular Protest and Organization: The Thrane Movement in Pre-industrial Norway, 1849-55," in *Scandinavian Journal of History*, 13 (1989), 121–129. See also Terje I. Leiren, *Marcus Thrane: A Norwegian Radical in America* (Northfield, Minnesota, 1987), chapter 1.

39. Garborg, *Peace*, 85–86.

40. The latter expressed conflict between urban power and rural culture and aspirations while the former embraced a regional struggle reflecting age-old differences between East and West Norway. See Rokkan, "Geography, Religion and Social Class."

41. Hale, "Anticlericalism and Norwegian Society," 256.

42. Rokkan, "Geography, Religion, and Social Class," 368–277. See also Munch, *Study of Cultural Change*, 30–63; Popperwell, *Norway*, 32–33.

43. Paulson, "Norwegian-American Reaction to Ibsen and Bjørnson," 5.

44. Semmingsen, "Norwegian Emigration in the Nineteenth Century," in *Scandinavian Economic History Review*, 8 (1960), 156.

45. Laurence M. Larson, *Log Book of a Young Immigrant* (Northfield, Minnesota, 1939), 68.

46. Semmingsen, "Norwegian Emigration in the Nineteenth Century," 150–160; Einar Haugen, *The Norwegian Language in America: A Study in Bilingual Behavior*, 2 vols. (2nd ed., Bloomington, Indiana, 1969), 1:23–29; Carlton C. Qualey, *Norwegian Settlement in the United States* (Northfield, Minnesota, 1938), 4–9. Recent studies which question the relative importance to emigration from Norway of economic hardship wrought by excessive population growth include: Aage Engesæter, "Poverty, Overpopulation, and the Early Emigration from Sogn," in *Norwegian-American Studies*, 32 (1989), 31–51; B. Lindsay Lowell, "Sociological Theories and the Great Emigration," in *Norwegian-American Studies*, 32 (1989), 53–69; and Gjerde, *From Peasants to Farmers*.

47. Blegen, *Norwegian Migration to America: The American Transition* (Northfield, Minnesota, 1940), 310.

48. Arlow W. Andersen, *The Norwegian-Americans* (Boston, 1975), 41, quoting Knud Langeland, *Nordmændene i Amerika* (Chicago, 1888), 97.

49. *The North* (Minneapolis), August 23, 1893.

50. Babcock, *Scandinavian Element*, 142–144. Local examples are detailed in Curti, *Making of an American Community*, 103–104, 302–303, 315–319, 339–341, and Larson, *Log Book*, 75–78.

51. Burnham, "The Changing Shape of the American Political Universe," in *American Political Science Review*, 59 (1965), 7–11.

52. The only exception to the average spread in turnout rates occurred in the

election of 1916 when 8.3 percentage points divided Norwegian farm from small town/village precincts.

53. Fergus Falls (Minnesota) *Weekly Journal*, June 23, 1892, February 15, 1894; John W. Mason, ed., *History of Otter Tail County Minnesota*, 2 vols. (Indianapolis, 1916), 2:34–35.

54. Babcock, *Scandinavian Element*, 147. See also Larson, *Log Book*, 77–78; Janson, "Norsemen in the United States," 686; Andersen, "Senator Knute Nelson: Minnesota's Grand Old Man and the Norwegian Immigrant Press," in Lovoll, ed., *Makers of an American Immigrant Legacy: Essays in Honor of Kenneth O. Bjork* (Northfield, Minnesota, 1980), 31.

55. Olaf M. Norlie, *History of the Norwegian People in America* (Minneapolis, 1925), 483. See also Babcock, "The Scandinavian Contingent," 667. A contrary view concluding that "Norwegians have had about their 'share' of public offices," is Grevstad, "Participation in American Politics," 117.

56. Norlie, *History of the Norwegian People in America*, 489–491.

CHAPTER 2

1. The shaping influence of the Civil War on one such state is discussed in Leon D. Epstein, *Politics in Wisconsin* (Madison, 1959), 35–36. The relative importance of translocal politics to local ethnocultural conflict is emphasized in Burnham's review essay, "Quantitative History," 63–64.

2. Blegen, *Norwegian Migration To America: The American Transition*, 297–298.

3. The term Slave Power was first popularized by Senator Thomas Morris of Ohio and later embraced by Salmon P. Chase and other anti-slavery advocates. This was their name for the conspiracy, as they saw it, by southern slaveholders to dominate the national government. The type of partisan atmosphere created by the Republican critique of the South and the aristocratic Slave Power is described in William E. Gienapp, *The Origins of the Republican Party, 1852–1856* (New York, 1987), 358–364, and in his "The Republican Party and the Slave Power," in Robert H. Abzug and Stephen E. Maizlish, eds., *New Perspectives on Race and Slavery in America* (Lexington, Kentucky, 1986), 51–78. See also Eric Foner, *Free Soil, Free Labor, Free Men* (New York, 1970), chapter 2, especially 64–65.

4. "The Letters of Mons H. Grinager: Pioneer and Soldier," trans. by C. A. Clausen, collected by Per Hvamstad, in *Norwegian-American Studies*, 24 (1970), 66–67.

5. A. C. Preus, "De norske præsters politiceren," in *Emigranten*, December 5, 1856, quoted in Munch, "Authority and Freedom," 31.

6. H. Fred Swansen, *The Founder of St. Ansgar: The Life Story of Claus Laurits Clausen* (Blair, Nebraska, 1949), 124.

7. Blegen, *Norwegian Migration to America: The American Transition*, 435. See also Todd W. Nichol, ed. and trans., *Vivacious Daughter: Seven Lectures on the Religious Situation Among Norwegians in America* (Northfield, Minnesota, 1990), 162–166, 172–173.

8. Banned from Norway since Reformation times, not until 1845 were Catholics allowed to establish a congregation in Christiania. Popperwell, *Norway*, 250, note. The political force of one's party preferences oriented in opposition to other ethnic or religious groups is discussed in several studies. See Samuel P. Hays, "Political Parties and the Community-Society Continuum," in William Nisbet Chambers and Burnham, eds., *The American Party Systems* (New York, 1967), 158–159; Benson, *The Concept of Jacksonian Democracy*, 184, 278–281, 301, 303; Michael F. Holt, *Forging a Majority: The Formation of the Republican Party*

in Pittsburgh, 1848–1860 (New Haven, 1969), 218; McCormick, "Ethno-Cultural Interpretations of Nineteenth-Century American Voting Behavior," 359–361.

9. To help identify sources of these differences, six quantitative indicators were compiled of circumstances that might have influenced divisions among Norwegian-American precincts. They were: a precinct's predominant Lutheran affiliation, estimated time of principal settlement, geographic location, ethnic predominance, region of origin in Norway, and proportion of Norwegian Americans in small towns. To the extent that these indicators corresponded or failed to correspond to differences in voting, their importance has been stressed or called into question in this study. This interpretation does not rest simply on quantifiable relationships, however, as the final three chapters show. But where possible an attempt has been made to capitalize on clues that they may offer.

10. To make comparable the standard deviation of one election to that of another because each measures dispersion of votes around an entirely different mean, the standard deviation of each has been divided by the mean of the distribution of Republican votes. The resulting "coefficients of variability" yield what amounts to the percentage of scatter in votes from the mean and thereby permits one year's percentage figure to be compared to others.

11. Kleppner, *The Cross of Culture*, 71. Another leading interpreter of midwestern politics from a "pietist versus liturgical" group perspective is Jensen, *The Winning of the Midwest*.

12. Although this story of ecclesiastical turmoil is lengthy and complex, the broad theological outlines of the conflict are clear. Disagreements between "high-church" and "low-church" elements expressed themselves in three graduated theological orientations: orthodox, Grundtvigian, and Haugean. Orthodoxy, representing high-church ideals, stressed orderly institutional church life: church authority, conservative doctrine, and a relatively elaborate ritual conducted by properly trained ministers. In contrast, the low-church impulses reflected the pietistic Haugean movement of early nineteenth-century Norway, which stressed lay preaching, personal religious experience (awakening), repentance (public confession), and conversion. Although they had deep respect for the Bible and doctrine, low-church adherents attached particular importance to practicing a "true Christian life" by abstaining from such worldly pleasures as card playing, tobacco smoking, alcohol, and social dancing. Between these two polar church positions stood a third tendency of moderation—one that reflected in large measure the influence of N. F. S. Grundtvig (1783–1872), a Danish theologian. This approach underscored the churchly function to provide the sacraments, but attacked the "high-church" tendency toward religious indifference that theological rationalism had allegedly brought, and minimized the "low-church" demands for awakening, conversion, and ascetic living. Attacks by both high- and low-church groups against this more optimistic, yet restrained, approach condemned it to an irregular and flickering life. But the blend of views comprising this orientation helped pave the way by 1890 for the new United Norwegian Lutheran Church in America. The above relies on discussion of the matter in Clifford Nelson and Eugene Fevold, *The Lutheran Church Among Norwegian-Americans*, 1 (Minneapolis, 1960), 13–23, 123–270; Haugen, *The Norwegians in America* (New York, 1967), 20–22; Bergmann, *Americans From Norway*, 145–162; Blegen, *Norwegian Migration: The American Transition*, 100–103, 131–174; J. T. Flint, "State, Church and Laity in Norwegian Society" (Ph. D. dissertation, University of Wisconsin, 1957); Norlie, *Norwegian People in America*, 189–190.

13. Bergmann, *Americans From Norway*, 147–148.

14. Munch, "Social Class and Acculturation," 196–197. See also Blegen, *Norwegian Migration: The American Transition*, 172–173.

15. Some possibility for error exists here because few of the townships examined were entirely of a "single church" character. Classifications are based on an estimated fifty percent or more of a locality's communicants belonging to a single synod as of 1915, and statistical correlations are based on the estimated percentage of each synod's members in a township.

16. Most of the predominantly Haugean precincts identified turned out to be in Wisconsin, where Robert LaFollette, feeling that Theodore Roosevelt had stolen the presidential nomination from him, evidently succeeded in turning the votes of Norwegian settlements to Taft.

17. Munch, "Authority and Freedom," 4. Part of the reason may be that the liturgical Norwegian Synod was high church only in a relative sense; some low-church ideals had crept into the state church of Norway. But the idea that a basic pietism characterized all Norwegian churches probably overstates the case, for it seems odd indeed that Lutherans in Norwegian settlements, unlike Swedish and Danish churches, fragmented as much as they did. Pietist influences within the state church are noted in Blegen, *Norwegian Migration: The American Transition*, 170–171; Fevold, "The Norwegian Immigrant and His Church," in *Norwegian-American Studies*, 23 (1967), 10; Kleppner, *Cross of Culture*, 85–86. Lower correlations between Republican votes and Lutheran synod affiliations may also be partly due to the invariable margin of error involved in deriving estimates of each synod in the settlements and also to the numerous immigrants who did not join any church.

18. Nina Draxten, *Kristofer Janson in America* (Boston, 1976), 18.

19. Eva Lund Haugen and Einar Haugen, eds. and trans., *Land of the Free: Bjørnstjerne Bjørnson's America Letters, 1880–1881* (Northfield, Minnesota, 1978), 220. The intertwined nature of religious and class feeling made for a volatile situation in America where, in its freer religious atmosphere without state restraints, the pot all too quickly boiled over. The turmoil that rolled across St. Luke's congregation in Ole E. Rølvaag's novel *Peder Victorious* illustrates the difficulties of keeping a lid on percolating tensions. Here in the Spring Creek settlement, what began as a series of Sunday meetings by the more "quickened ones" soon grew to a desire among them for a new congregation "consisting exclusively of confessing Christians." When the remaining members of St. Luke's tried to hold back the dissenters on grounds that the church constitution gave them no right to resign, "anti-official" antagonism erupted. "Oh, ho – so that was the idea," argued the dissenters. "St. Luke's intended to set up a state church and coerce people by force? What about Hans Nielsen Hauge? Did he ask the State Church of Norway for permission to go the way the Lord pointed out to him?" Ole E. Rølvaag, *Peder Victorious*, trans. by Nora O. Solum and Rølvaag (New York, 1929), 65.

20. Blegen, *Land of Their Choice*, 197–198.

21. Draxten, *Kristofer Janson*, 18.

22. Munch, *The Strange American Way*, 29–30. That the immigrant readily abandoned such peasant customs of linguistic deference toward Old Country betters in favor of the informality of their new country is well treated in Skårdal, *The Divided Heart*, 124–125.

23. Munch, "Authority and Freedom," 21.

24. Gerhard Lee Belgum, "The Old Norwegian Synod in America, 1853–1890" (Ph. D. Dissertation, Yale University, 1957), 137.

25. Belgum, "The Old Norwegian Synod," 137.

26. Letter to *Skandinaven*, October 29, 1869, quoted in H. Fred Swansen, "The Norse in Iowa to 1870" (M.A. thesis, State University of Iowa, 1936), 164.

27. Letter to *Skandinaven*, December 1, 1869, quoted in Swansen, "Norse in Iowa to 1870," 165.

28. Munch, *Strange American Way*, 231.

29. Note, for example, the reminiscences of Johan Storm Munch, "An American Adventure: Excerpts from 'Vita Mea,'" in Munch, *Strange American Way*, 170, 182.

30. Gjerde, "Conflict and Community: A Case Study of the Immigrant Church in the United States," in *Journal of Social History*, 19 (1986), 689–693. A similar instance involved the split-off of Hadlanders from the Valdres-dominated Old York Church congregation in Green county, Wisconsin, as noted in Munch and Robert B. Campbell, "Interaction and Collective Identification in a Rural Locality," in *Rural Sociology*, 28 (1963), 27–28. See also Ann M. Legreid and David Ward, "Religious Schism and the Development of Rural Immigrant Communities: Norwegian Lutherans in Western Wisconsin, 1880–1905," in *Upper Midwest History*, 2 (1982), 18.

31. Paulson, "The Norwegian-American Reaction to Ibsen and Bjørnson," 26–27.

32. Paulson, "The Norwegian-American Reaction to Ibsen and Bjørnson," 25.

33. Paulson, "The Norwegian-American Reaction to Ibsen and Bjørnson," 23.

34. Haugen, *Land of the Free*, 151.

35. Haugen, *Land of the Free*, 195.

36. *Beretning om sjette ordentlige Synodemøde for den norsk-evangeliske-lutherske Kirke i Amerika, afholdt i Rock River Kirke fra 10de til 17de Juni 1863*, 8–10, quoted in Hale, "Transatlantic Norwegian Religion," 16. See also Nichol, *Vivacious Daughter*, 38.

37. Haugen, *Land of the Free*, 220.

38. Belgum, "Old Norwegian Synod in America," 132.

39. The same pattern of religious indifference is found for 1900 by Hale, "Transatlantic Norwegian Religion," 19–20.

40. Observation is based on percentages calculated by dividing the number of Norwegian Lutheran church members in 1906 by the number of first, second, and estimated third generation Norwegian Americans in 1910. The number of Norwegian born and their children was derived from the U.S. Bureau of the Census, *Thirteenth Census of the United States Taken in the Year 1910, Vol. II– Population 1910*, (Washington D. C., 1913), 996–1010. For computing the estimated third generation as of 1906, a factor of 25.79 percent was added based on the calculation established by Norlie, *History of the Norwegian People in America*, 312–313. Norwegian Lutheran church membership data came from the U. S. Bureau of the Census, *Special Reports, Religious Bodies: 1906, Part I– Summary and General Tables* (Washington, D. C., 1910), 327–329.

41. According to statistics contained in *Beretning . . . Den Norsk Lutherske Kirke i Amerika . . . 1923* (Minneapolis, 1923), 626–627, the following percentages of confirmed members communed within the year in the Upper Midwest districts: Iowa District, 53.8%; Southern Minnesota District, 53.7%; Northern Minnesota District, 30.2%; South Dakota District, 44.2%; North Dakota District, 29.6%.

42. Reminiscences of Johan Storm Munch quoted in Munch, *Strange American Way*, 111.

43. Munch, *Strange American Way*, 76.

44. Before the 1860s, narrow provincialism as well as regional and local

cleavages continued to cover up feelings of resentment by the Norwegian peasantry against the alien official classes. The religious revival of Hans Nielsen Hauge had first whetted agrarian aspirations during the years surrounding the turn of the nineteenth century. The latent class antagonism and religious pietism of the country people gave enthusiastic support to Hauge when he sharply attacked the professional competence and exclusive authority of the official pastorate. This gradually broadened into what Blegen has called a "struggle of the common people against the aristocracy," in which "the laity tended to be on one side, the state-church on the other." Blegen, *Norwegian Migration: The American Transition*, 101; see also Larsen, *History of Norway*, 358. Whether driven by the Haugean agrarianism of western Norway, the social strains of a pronounced class hierarchy in eastern Norway, or the resentments of fishermen dependent on those who controlled port facilities in the North, commoners understood the party struggles between the Left and the Right. The Left wanted reforms and the Right opposed them. The social roots of ecclesiastical division are well brought out in Munch, "Social Class and Acculturation," 196–211. See also Nelson and Fevold, *The Lutheran Church*, 6–23; Munch, *A Study of Cultural Change* 41–43; Hovde, *The Scandinavian Countries*, 2: 556–557; Halvdan Koht, "Free Men Build Their Society," in *The Voice of Norway* (New York, 1944), 58–60; Blegen, *Norwegian Migration to America, 1825–1860* (Northfield, Minnesota 1931), 163, 167.

45. A political generation is defined as an assemblage of persons whose exposure to the same prevailing events at a formative time in their development leads them to share a political outlook significantly different from earlier and later groups who shared different experiences. Of the many studies of generations that are available, the following proved particularly useful: Norman B. Ryder, "The Cohort as a Concept in the Study of Social Change," in *American Sociological Review*, 30 (1965), 843–861; Alan B. Spitzer, "The Historical Problem of Generations," in *American Historical Review*, 78 (1973), 1353–1385; Seymour M. Lipset, Paul F. Lazarsfeld, Allen H. Barton, and Juan Linz, "The Psychology of Voting: An Analysis of Political Behavior," in Gardner Lindzey, ed., *Handbook of Social Psychology* (Cambridge, 1954), 1147–1148; Maurice Zeitlin, "Political Generations in the Cuban Working Class," in *American Journal of Sociology*, 71 (1966), 493–508; Philip E. Converse, "Of Time and Partisan Stability," in *Comparative Political Studies*, 2 (1969), 139–144; Daniel J Elazar, *The Generational Rhythm of American Politics* (Philadelphia, 1976).

46. Babcock, *The Scandinavian Element*, 157.

47. Distinct political generations formed when large events such as war, depression, or prosperity converged with tensions of an immigrant society, the prevailing political climate, and the immigrants' transplanted attitudes.

48. On Norwegian party alignments of the 1840s and 1850s, see Andersen, *The Immigrant Takes His Stand: The Norwegian-American Press and Public Affairs, 1847–1872* (Northfield, Minnesota, 1953), chapters 2 and 4. On the rise of the Republican party, see Gienapp, *Origins of the Republican Party*, and Foner, *Free Soil, Free Labor, Free Men*, chapters 2 and 4.

49. Andersen, *The Immigrant Takes His Stand*, 54, 118, 140, 147.

50. Andersen, *The Immigrant Takes His Stand*, 121, 122, 135, 155.

51. *Normanna* (Minneapolis), quoted in *The North* (Minneapolis), December 3, 1890.

52. Pearson Product Moment correlations were +.80 for Minnesota and +.68 for Wisconsin. Comparable precinct level data were unavailable for Iowa's average land values.

53. "The Scandinavians and the Presidential Nominations," in *Scandinavia* 1 (August, 1884), 278.

54. Using the computer program, the Statistical Package for the Social Sciences (SPSS), I examined by regression analysis the extent (R^2) to which four social indicators accounted for variance in Republican votes of upper midwestern Norwegian settlements. Of them, the estimated percentage of Lutheran membership in pietist churches (Hauge's Synod, United Lutheran Church, Lutheran Free Church) explained never more than four percent of the variation in votes, while percentage of small town population remained a negligible influence until 1924 when it accounted for eight percent of differences in the vote. Percentage of eligible Norwegian voters accounted for fourteen percent of the variation in the 1880 vote, but then dropped to almost nothing as an explanatory influence. Only the time when Norwegian settlements became established (expressed as the estimated average years of residence in a settlement as of 1895) consistently accounted for from eleven to forty-five percent of the variation in votes.

55. Norwegian communities with very high Norwegian concentrations (81.7 percent or greater) generally voted little differently than did those containing lesser concentrations (50.0 to 68.5 percent). Only during the 1880s, when post-Civil War Republicanism still unified Norwegians, did 10 percentage points separate the moderately concentrated Norwegian settlements from those with very high proportions of Norwegian voters. Thereafter, other issues intruded to make the Norwegian vote less predictable. It took a direct outside threat to get them to vote on strictly ethnic lines.

56. With the exception of 1924, never more than five percentage points separated the average Republican votes of farm precincts (16.7 percent or less nonfarm population) from non-farm precincts (35.0 percent or more non-farm population).

57. An effort was made to learn whether old country sociocultural divisions between western Norway and eastern Norway might have carried over to influence Norwegian-American political behavior. Geographic isolation over the centuries had brought about differences in dialect, religious inclination, and social class structure. Yet no carryover effect on Norwegian-American voting could be found. Although at first it seemed that settlements peopled mainly by western Norwegians occasionally voted more strongly Republican, this simply reflected the fact that most of these settlements were located in the stronger Republican states of Iowa and Wisconsin. Because only 108 settlements could be identified according to their predominant region of origin in Norway, the voting tendencies noted are based on less complete voting returns than are those presented in other figures and tables of this study. On the contrasts between eastern and western Norwegians, see Arvid Sandaker, "Emigration from Land Parish to America, 1866–1875," trans. and ed. by C. A. Clausen, in *Norwegian-American Studies*, 26 (1974), 51; Blegen, *Norwegian Migration: 1825–1860*, 10, 74–76; Haugen, *The Norwegian Language in America*, 2: 338–349; Rokkan and Henry Valen, "Regional Contrasts in Norwegian Politics: A Review of Data from Official Statistics and from Sample Surveys," in Erik Allardt and Rokkan, eds., *Mass Politics: Studies in Political Sociology* (New York, 1970), 199–202.

58. The literature concerning state political culture is sparse. The preeminent work is Daniel J. Elazar's *American Federalism: A View from the States* (New York, 1966), along with his later elaboration, *Cities of the Prairie: The Metropolitan Frontier and American Politics* (New York, 1970). See also Raymond D. Gastil, *Cultural Regions of the United States* (Seattle, 1975), 54–70, and John H. Fenton, *Midwest Politics* (New York, 1966).

59. *Thirteenth Census of the United States, 1910,* 1:30, 929.

60. The same characteristics of Norwegian settlements contributed differently to election outcomes from one state to the next. Only Minnesota's Norwegian townships seemed to follow the regional pattern whereby the dates of settlement assumed importance. In Iowa varying Republican votes corresponded more closely to the percentage of Norwegian voters within townships and to their Lutheran synod affiliations. Votes from Wisconsin's Norwegian townships, on the other hand, bore no consistent relationship to any characteristics examined. Norwegian voting differences, it thus seems clear, grew substantially out of conditions specific to the states in which they were located.

61. Of the ninety combined elections for governor in the three states from 1865 to 1924, Democrats achieved election only ten times. These Democratic victories distributed themselves unevenly, however. Iowa Democrats won but two contests (1889, 1891); Wisconsin Democrats won three elections (1873, 1890, 1892) and Minnesota Democrats captured the governor's chair five times (1898, 1904, 1906, 1908, 1916).

62. During this period, majorities of more than 53 percent went to Republican candidates in eight elections in Iowa, four in Wisconsin, and three in Minnesota.

63. If the relatively higher value of the franchise did not actually diminish an immigrant's interest in politics, Iowa's rules of the game certainly increased chances that election day might catch him ineligible to vote. This reasoning can be easily exaggerated, however. It is instructive to keep in mind that Minnesota's franchise requirements became as restrictive as Iowa's in 1898, although Norwegian turnout in Minnesota did *not* abruptly decline in reponse.

64. This occurred in 1883, 1896–1898, and 1904–1906.

CHAPTER 3

1. Babcock, "The Scandinavians in the Northwest," in *Forum* 14 (1892), 108.

2. Babcock, *Scandinavian Element,* 114. See also Paul Knaplund, *Moorings Old and New: Entries in an Immigrant's Log* (Madison, Wisconsin, 1963), 61, 159, 221; Blegen, *Minnesota: A History of the State* (Minneapolis, 1963), 217; Fenton, *Midwest Politics,* 76–77; Roger Wyman, "Voting Behavior in the Progressive Era: Wisconsin as a Case Study" (Ph. D. dissertation, University of Wisconsin, 1970), 595, 611–612; George H. Mayer, *The Political Career of Floyd B. Olson* (Minneapolis, 1951), 13; Arthur Naftalin, "A History of the Farmer-Labor Party of Minnesota" (Ph. D. dissertation, University of Minnesota, 1948), 73.

3. Babcock, "Scandinavian Contingent," 663.

4. Taylor, *Northern Travel,* 295–296. A similar instance of popular prejudice toward Catholics, noted at Tromsø, is reported by another traveler, John Dean Caton, in his *A Summer in Norway* (Chicago, 1880), 129–131.

5. Taylor, *Northern Travel,* 295–296.

6. Babcock, "Scandinavian Contingent," 663, makes the point that "The distrust of the Irish, which sometimes takes active form, is at bottom religious, and not racial." This view he later repeats in his *Scandinavian Element,* 114.

7. Boyesen, "Scandinavians in the United States," 528.

8. Review comments on Boyesen's article by editor of *The North* (Minneapolis), December 7, 1892.

9. "The Scandinavians and the Presidential Nominations," 25.

10. Rølvaag, *Peder Victorious,* 113–114.

11. Rølvaag, *Their Fathers' God,* trans. by Trygve M. Ager (New York, 1931), 20.

12. Rølvaag, *Their Fathers' God*, 325, 329.

13. *Skandinaven*, April 22, 1914, quoted in Herbert F. Margulies, "Anti-Catholicism in Wisconsin Politics, 1914–1920," in *Mid-America*, 44 (1962), 52.

14. Bureau of the Census, *Special Reports, Religious Bodies: 1906*, part 1: 62. It must be remembered, however, that the Scandinavian constituency for anti-Catholicism also spread itself unevenly across the upper midwestern states. In this respect Minnesota stood foremost, with 28 percent of its residents being of Norwegian, Swedish, and Danish background, while the three combined Scandinavian groups in Wisconsin and Iowa constituted only 11 and 8 percent respectively according to the *Thirteenth Census of the United States, 1910*, 1:30, 929.

15. For discussion of general A.P.A. developments, see Donald L. Kinzer, *An Episode in Anti-Catholicism: The American Protective Association* (Seattle, 1964); Allen W. Burns, "The A.P.A. and the Anti-Catholic Crusade: 1885–1898" (M.A. thesis, Columbia University, 1947); John Higham, *Strangers in the Land: Patterns of American Nativism 1860–1925* (New York, 1963), 62–63, 79–87; Humphrey J. Desmond, *The A.P.A. Movement: A Sketch* (Washington, D.C., 1912); Howard Carl Lundvall , "The American Protective Association: A Study of an Anti-Catholic Organization" (M.A. thesis, State University of Iowa, 1950); Alvin Packer Stauffer, Jr., "Anti-Catholicism in American Politics, 1865–1900" (Ph. D. dissertation, Harvard University, 1933).

16. Mary Callista Hynes, "The History of the American Protective Association in Minnesota" (M.A. thesis, Catholic University of America, ca. 1939), 3; Higham, *Strangers in the Land*, 81.

17. *Loyal American and the North* (Minneapolis), February 17, 1894.

18. *Loyal American and the North*, February 17, 1894, and "Medole" in *Loyal American and the North*, May 12, 1894.

19. See John P. Bocock, "The Irish Conquest of our Cities," in *Forum*, 17 (1894), 186–195; Boyesen, "Scandinavians in the United States," 528; *The North*, September 17, 1890.

20. Quoted in a supplement to *Scandia* (Duluth), May 27, 1893. For expressions of Swedish-American newspaper reaction, see Fritiof Ander, "The Swedish-American Press and the American Protective Association," in *Church History*, 6 (1937), 165–179.

21. *Folkebladet* (Minneapolis), quoted in *The North*, August 16, 1893.

22. *Christian Youth* (Decorah, Iowa), reprinted in *Loyal American*, July 29, 1893.

23. "Medole," in *Loyal American and the North*, May 12, 1894.

24. Bocock, "The Irish Conquest," 186–195; Andersen, *The Immigrant Takes His Stand*, 147.

25. *Skandinaven*, April 12, 1893, as quoted in Jon Wefald, *A Voice of Protest: Norwegians in American Politics, 1890–1917* (Northfield, Minnesota, 1971), 19.

26. Knaplund, *Moorings Old and New*, 159.

27. *Loyal American and the North*, August 11, 1894.

28. Quoted in *Irish Standard* (Minneapolis), March 25, 1893.

29. *Loyal American*, December 2, 1893.

30. According to Grace McDonald, *History of the Irish in Wisconsin in the Nineteenth Century* (New York, 1976), 184–185, the association in Wisconsin "never flourished as well as in some of the neighboring states" although it offered Democrats an opportunity to solidify the Catholic vote. As for Norwegian participation, Desmond, in his *A.P.A. Movement*, 45, writes that "in Milwaukee, the Germans and the Norwegians, in 1894, undoubtedly made up a clear majority in the councils."

31. *Loyal American*, December 30, 1893.

32. *Loyal American*, July 29, 1893, January 27, 1894.

33. *Irish Standard*, as quoted in Hynes, "A.P.A. in Minnesota," 43.

34. Hynes, "A.P.A. in Minnesota," 43.

35. *Irish Standard*, May 6, 1893.

36. Minneapolis *Journal*, reprinted in *Loyal American and the North*, April 28, 1894.

37. *Daily Globe* (St. Paul), *Irish Standard*, and *Guardian* (Adrian, Minnesota), as quoted in Hynes, "A.P.A. in Minnesota," 44, 52.

38. *Loyal American and the North*, July 7, 1894.

39. *Loyal American and the North*, November 10, 1894; Hynes, "A.P.A, in Minnesota," 91.

40. Kinzer, *Episode in Anti-Catholicism*, 171.

41. *Sentinel* (Iowa Falls, Iowa), October 23, 1867.

42. Babcock, *Scandinavian Element*, 171.

43. Norlie, *History of the Norwegian People in America*, 435, 517–518.

44. Kenneth Smemo, "The Immigrant as Reformer: The Case of the Norwegian American," paper delivered at the Sixty-Sixth Annual Meeting of the Organization of American Historians, Chicago, April 13, 1973, 14. Evidently Nelson's leadership of dry forces amounted to a later political conversion, however; according to Millard L. Gieske, "as the prohibition drive became a kind of crusade, he joined up." See Gieske, "The Politics of Knute Nelson, 1912–1920" (Ph.D. dissertation, University of Minnesota, 1965), 2: 400–401.

45. Norlie, *History of the Norwegian People*, 518.

46. Andersen, *Immigrant Takes His Stand*, 122.

47. As quoted in Jean Skogerboe Hansen, "*Skandinaven* and the John Anderson Publishing Company," in *Norwegian-American Studies*, 28 (1979), 48.

48. *The North*, June 29, 1892.

49. Semmingsen, "Dissolution of Estate Society in Norway," 174.

50. The relationship of the temperance crusade to pietist movements in Norway is noted in Blegen, *Norwegian Migration: The American Transition*, 223; Rokkan and Valen, "Regional Contrasts in Norwegian Politics," 209; Smemo, "Immigrant as Reformer," 5–6.

51. Derry, *History of Modern Norway*, 37; *The Cyclopaedia of Temperance and Prohibition* (New York, 1891), 454.

52. Blegen, *Norwegian Migration: The American Transition*, 204.

53. *Cyclopaedia of Temperance and Prohibition*, 455.

54. *The North*, September 28, 1892.

55. From an article by Edith Sellers describing her observations of the practical operation of the Gothenburg system in the Scandinavian countries, as excerpted in the United States Brewers' Association, *The Year Book with Proceedings of the Fifty-Third Annual Convention Held in Atlantic City, N.J., October 3-4, 1913* (New York, 1914), 80–81.

56. Rokkan and Valen, "Regional Contrasts," 193, 209, 216.

57. John Martin Vincent and Milton Offutt, "Norway's Decisive Vote to Repeal Prohibition," in *Current History*, 25 (1926), 422–423; Popperwell, *Norway*, 278–279; Larson, *History of Norway*, 521; Derry, *History of Modern Norway*, 155–156, 176–177, 291, 300–304.

58. Blegen, *Norwegian Migration: The American Transition*, 205. In St. Paul and Minneapolis, liquor-related charges comprised about one-half of the total arrests during the 1880s. Taking 1882 as a guide, arrest records suggest that, in proportion to their population, policemen arrested Norwegians for drunkenness or

for drunk and disorderly behavior more often than they did native-born persons but less often than either the Swedes or the Irish. See James T. Hathaway, "The Evolution of Drinking Places in the Twin Cities: From the Advent of White Settlement to the Present" (Ph.D. dissertation, University of Minnesota, 1982), 53–56.

59. Paul Reigstad, *Rølvaag: His Life and Art* (Lincoln, Nebraska, 1972), 88; C. Somner Sorenson, "A Comparison of the Views of Hamsun, Rølvaag, and Feikema on Rural Society" (M.A. thesis, State University of Iowa, 1955), 52.

60. Rølvaag, *Giants in the Earth*, trans. by Lincoln Colcord and Rølvaag (New York, 1929), 178, 281–283; Rølvaag, *Peder Victorious*, 230, 245.

61. For a breakdown of voting percentages from farming and small town areas on anti-liquor referenda in the three states, see Table 1 in Soike, "Norwegian-Americans and the Politics of Dissent" (Ph.D. dissertation, University of Iowa, 1979), 102.

62. Blegen, *Norwegian Migration: The American Transition*, 205; Rokkan, "Geography, Religion and Social Class," 372, 415–419.   63. Catholics were most numerous in Wisconsin, followed by Minnesota and Iowa. And, if membership in the Synodical Conference (led by the Missouri Synod) is taken as an index of liturgical German Lutheran strength, over two-and-one-half times as many German Lutherans lived in Wisconsin in 1906 as in Minnesota and over twice as many lived in Minnesota as in Iowa. Expressed as a percentage of the total estimated state population in 1906, members of the Lutheran Synodical Conference constituted 7 percent in Wisconsin, 3 percent in Minnesota, and 1 percent in Iowa. Bureau of the Census, *Special Reports, Religious Bodies: 1906*, part 1:311, 327, 371.

64. Similar pietist-liturgical differences evidently existed in North Dakota where, upon statehood in 1889, voters had adopted prohibition as an article of its state constitution and a decided majority continued to sustain its life until it was finally repealed at the national level. The diminished liturgical support for prohibition is seen in the weaker support given by the Norwegian Synod to abstinence societies. Duane R. Lindberg explains: "Though the 'Synod' represented 28% of the clergy, it accounted for 9% of the pastors who actively promoted the total abstinence movement. Whereas the Hauge's and Free Church synods, representing 15% and 14% respectively of the Norwegian Lutheran clergy in North Dakota, accounted for 58% of the pastoral leadership in terms of this social-political issue. The United Church, which was the largest synod, accounted for 43% of the clergy and provided 33% of the leadership." See his "Pastors, Prohibition and Politics: The Role of Norwegian Clergy in the North Dakota Abstinence Movement, 1880–1920," in *North Dakota Quarterly*, 49 (Autumn, 1981), 31.

Correlations between Republican gubernatorial votes and five variables that consistently produced individual correlations greater than +-.30 collectively evinced only limited ability to account for more than one-third of the total variations, thus indicating that other important factors were at work. The variables of national background and percentage of liturgical Lutheran church affiliation, however, clearly expressed a linear relationship to the vote in Iowa.

65. According to this view, "pietist-evangelical" groups sought through the Republican party to superimpose their moral values on society in such forms as Sunday blue laws, prohibition, and parochial school restrictions. Conversely, the Democratic party attracted those groups of liturgical orientation that opposed a morally activist government intervening to prescribe codes of personal behavior. Such activities liturgicals believed fell most properly within the sphere of the church. The influence of this religious dimension on midwestern politics in described in Kleppner, *The Cross of Culture*, 71, 316–368; Jensen, *Winning of the Midwest*, xiii, 58–88, 269–308.

66. Jensen, *Winning of the Midwest*, 89-121; Dan E. Clark, "Recent Liquor Legislation in Iowa," in *Iowa Journal of History and Politics*, 15 (1917), 44-46; Ballard C. Campbell, "Did Democracy Work? Prohibition in Late Nineteenth-Century Iowa: A Test Case," in *Journal of Interdisciplinary History*, 8 (1977), 87-116.

67. See Jensen, *Winning of the Midwest*, 81.

68. Throughout the 1880s Highland township did not further weaken in its Republicanism as did the other three Norwegian Synod townships, but instead continued to vote over 87 percent Republican for governor.

69. Larson, *Log Book of a Young Immigrant*, 57.

70. A post-election report pointed out the Scandinavians' disenchantment with the prohibition amendment: "The Scandinavians are . . . divided on the liquor question. They don't always agree with the Germans in their antipathy to prohibitory laws, and sometimes are even inclined to take just the opposite side to that supported by the German element. The Iowa Democrats reduced, however, in a remarkable degree, the immense Republican majority of the last elections, the gains being especially noticeable in some of the northern Scandinavian counties." "The Scandinavians in the Late American Elections," in *Scandinavia*, 2 (1883), 26.

CHAPTER 4

1. Comment by Haldor Boen in the Fergus Falls (Minnesota) *Globe*, April 25, 1896. Similar reasoning is expressed in *Normanna* (Minneapolis), quoted in *The North*, December 3, 1890.

2. For discussions of regional agricultural patterns see: Oliver E. Baker, "Agricultural Regions of North America," in *Economic Geography*, 3 (1927), 447-465; 4 (1928), 44-73, 399-433; John Fraser Hart, *The Look of the Land* (Englewood Cliffs, New Jersey, 1975), chapter 9; Edward Van Dyke Robinson, *Early Economic Conditions and the Development of Agriculture in Minnesota* (Minneapolis, 1915); John C. Weaver, "Changing Patterns of Cropland Use in the Middle West," in *Economic Geography*, 30 (1954), 1-18; Ladd Haystead and Gilbert C. Fite, *The Agricultural Regions of the United States* (Norman, Oklahoma, 1955).

3. Baker, "Agricultural Regions," 4:426.

4. Theodore Saloutos, "The Agricultural Problem and Nineteenth-Century Industrialism," in *Agricultural History*, 23 (1948), 156, 160-165. Useful on problems of agricultural expansion during this era are: W. A. Coutts, "Agricultural Depression in the United States," in *Publications of the Michigan Political Science Association*, 2 (1896-1897), 1-65; C. F. Emerick, "An Analysis of Agricultural Discontent in the United States," in *Political Science Quarterly*, 11 (1896), 439; Fred A. Shannon, *The Farmer's Last Frontier: Agriculture, 1860-1879* (New York, 1945), chapters 8, 13.

5. Herman C. Nixon, "The Populist Movement in Iowa," in *Iowa Journal of History and Politics*, 24 (1926), 3; Leland L. Sage, *A History of Iowa* (Ames, 1974), 188-192.

6. Sage, *History of Iowa*, 204-209, 211-213; Nixon, "Economic Basis of the Populist Movement in Iowa," in *Iowa Journal of History and Politics*, 21 (1923), 391.

7. From 1891 through 1895, Logan township gave nearly one-half of its vote to third parties and Eden followed with from 28 to 42 percent of its votes. Mount Valley and Linden townships provided lesser but significant portions.

8. An examination of the 1891 Union labor vote and the People's party vote of 1893 and 1895 showed that they correlated most strongly with percentage of crop acreage planted in wheat (1891 = .43; 1893 = .38; 1895 = .53) and also with estimated time of principal settlement (1891 = -.47; 1893 = .44; 1895 = .46). The

Pearson Product Moment Correlation between the two independent variables was .43.

9. The 1892 townships included Jefferson + Springville village (Vernon county), 22.3%; Navarino (Shawano county), 37.8%; Sand Creek (Dunn county), 48.5%; Grant (Dunn county), 62.0%; Colfax township and village (Dunn county), 27.8%. The Populist-leaning settlements in 1894 were reduced to Navarino, 24.4%; Sand Creek, 25.0%; and Grant, 34.4%.

10. Estimated time of major settlement correlated strongly with percentage of vote for Populist gubernatorial candidates, the Pearson Product Moment Correlation being .52 in 1892 and .50 in 1894. An excellent summary of the electoral sources of Wisconsin Populism is Wyman, "Agrarian Working Class Radicalism? The Electoral Basis of Populism in Wisconsin," in *Political Science Quarterly*, 89 (1975), 825–847.

11. Greater average values per acre were negatively related to the vote for Populist gubernatorial candidates, Pearson Product Moment Correlations being -.22 in 1892 and -.23 in 1894. Of the 48 Norwegian townships examined, four of the five Populist-inclined settlements numbered among the ten settlements with the lowest average value per acre and the greatest degree of potato cash-crop farming—this according to the 1905 Wisconsin State Census.

12. This finding differs from Kleppner's analysis in his *Cross of Culture*, 140. The Populist Party in Wisconsin, he suggests, comprised "essentially a coalition of Swedish, Norwegian, and native pietists." This clearly does not apply to Norwegian areas, where the liturgical or less evangelical-oriented Norwegian Synod congregations made up a large portion of the townships that leaned toward Populism. Three of the five most Populist of the Norwegian settlements in 1892 lay in Dunn county. Grant township, the most Populist of the three, was a Norwegian Synod community and in the other two townships an estimated one-half or more of the Norwegians who belonged to Lutheran churches held membership in Norwegian Synod congregations. Estimates based on Norlie, *Norsk Lutherske Menigheter i Amerika, 1843–1916*, 2 vols. (Minneapolis, 1918), 1:123–275; 2:496–520.

13. Jensen, *The Winning of the Midwest*, 135–137; Wyman, "Wisconsin Ethnic Groups and the Election of 1890," in *Wisconsin Magazine of History*, 51 (1968) 269–293.

14. Compared to the vote for the Republican candidate in 1888, the 1890 vote for the Republican incumbent fell in Norwegian settlements by percentages that corresponded to their predominant Lutheran church orientation as follows: Hauge's Synod (pietist) = 6.5%; United Church and Lutheran Free Church (moderately pietist) = 8.6%; mixed pietist and Norwegian Synod congregations = 8.3%; Norwegian Synod (liturgical) = 13.9%.

15. This reasoning about the relation of agrarian radicalism to different farming systems conforms to that first enunciated by Benton H. Wilcox, "An Historical Definition of Northwestern Radicalism," in *Mississippi Valley Historical Review*, 26 (1929), 382–394. Other studies have reached similar conclusions. See, for example, Theodore Saloutos and John D. Hicks, *Agricultural Discontent in the Middle West, 1900–1939* (Madison, 1951), chapters 1, 2, 7.

16. Henrietta M. Larson, *The Wheat Market and the Farmer in Minnesota, 1858–1900* (New York, 1926), 118–119, 126, 142, 149, 255. The east-west railroad lines not touching Minneapolis included the Southern Minnesota, the Winona and St. Peter, and the Northern Pacific.

17. Hays, "Political Parties and the Community-Society Continuum," 158.

18. For analysis of conditions in the northwestern part of the state, see Larson, *Wheat Market in Minnesota*, chapters 5–7.

19. Ada (Minnesota) *Puhler's Red River Valley Journal*, October 2, 1885.

20. *Puhler's Red River Valley Journal*, October 9, 1885.

21. *Puhler's Red River Valley Journal*, October 9, 1885, reprint of story from Minneapolis *Tribune*.

22. Ada (Minnesota) *Norman County Herald*, May 5, 1888; *Puhler's Red River Valley Journal*, October 9, 1885.

23. The impact of the McKinley Tariff is discussed in *Folkebladet* (Minneapolis), quoted in *The North*, November 12, 1890; *Normanna* (Minneapolis), quoted in *The North*, November 19, 1890; *Red River Dalen* (Crookston, Minnesota), quoted in *The North*, December 10, 1890; *Norman County Herald*, October 31, 1890; Battle Lake (Minnesota) *Review*, November 20, 1890; *Inter-Ocean* (Chicago), quoted in Rushford (Minnesota) *Star*, November 20, 1890; *Norman County Index*, quoted in *Norman County Herald*, November 21, 1890.

24. Localities with lower average land values yielded lower Republican percentages and, unlike corn-raising areas, those where wheat assumed importance demonstrated weaker Republican allegiance. Lower Republican votes also came from two other sectors: recently established Norwegian settlements and rural townships situated farther from the county seat. Collectively these indicators accounted for one-half or more of the total voting differences shown by Minnesota's Norwegian settlements during the 1890s, although the individual contributions of each varied somewhat during particular years.

25. This absence of association held regardless of whether the votes for governor from predominantly pietist (Haugean, United Lutheran, Lutheran Free Church) or liturgical (Norwegian Synod plus townships where neither liturgical or pietist congregations predominated) settlements were aggregated by Minnesota as a whole or by region within the state. Furthermore, individual Pearson Product Moment Correlations of the agrarian candidate vote (1890–1896) with estimated church affiliation failed to produce a linear relationship stronger than -.07. This also held for presidential elections.

26. The importance of an index of regional peripherality as it applies to Norway is described by Rokkan and Valen, "The Mobilization of the Periphery: Data on Turnout, Party Membership and Candidate Recruitment in Norway," in *Acta Sociologica*, 6 (1962), 111–158. In the present study, Norwegian-American settlement classifications were assigned according to their central or peripheral location in Minnesota. Centrally situated rural settlements possessed greater advantages of communication, wealth, and services (nearness to the county seat, higher land values, and an incorporated town or village) while peripheral townships lacked these attributes. Classified as "extremely peripheral" were settlements where the center of the township is located 12.9 miles or more from the county seat and which contained 10.5 percent or less of small town/village population (1910) and where the land values were two dollars per acre or more below the mean of such values in the state (1905). Settlements with two of the three attributes became "moderately peripheral" while those with "low peripherality" met only one of the criteria.

27. When Norwegian precincts in the northwestern counties were classified according to whether they contained incorporated small town/village populations in low (0–16%), moderate (16.8%–34.9%), or high (35% or more) proportions, the votes for agrarian gubernatorial candidates between 1890 and 1896 averaged as follows: Low = 70.1%; moderate = 65.2%; high = 57.8%. Conversely, precincts with larger small town/village populations voted more strongly Republican: low = 24.5%; moderate = 24.3%; high = 34.4%.

28. Before 1890 Norwegian settlements voted more as a bloc for the Republican party candidates even though the linear correlation remained low between percent of voting-age Norwegian males and Republican votes for governor. But whatever the reasons behind Norwegian bloc voting for Republicans, the Democratic party was unable to use "nationality" to breach this attachment. Back in 1883 the Democrats sought to overcome their crippled minority status by placing Norwegian-born Adolph Bierman at the head of their state ticket—the first Norwegian to run for governor. Frantically, the Republican press struggled to hold the Norwegian vote in line and met with general success. Only seventeen out of seventy-five Norwegian settlements examined cast majorities for Bierman, and the geographical distribution of Bierman's pluralities was scattered. For press opinion, see Minneapolis *Tribune*, quoted in Rushford *Star*, September 27, October 11, 25, November 1, 1883.

29. He voted for the Morrison Bill in 1884 and for the Mill Bill in 1888. According to the Benson (Minnesota) *Swift County Monitor*, August 24, 1888, after he voted for the Mills Bill, the Republican newspapers "changed their opinion of Knute Nelson," saying that "he is over rated in ability, dishonest to his party, and has held office long enough under false pretenses."

30. *Swift County Monitor*, November 28, 1890; *The North*, November 12, 1890; *Skandinaven*, quoted in *The North*, November 19, 1890; *Amerika* (Chicago), quoted in *The North*, November 19, 1890.

31. From excerpts of a letter dated January 1, 1915, sent to an old family friend in Norway and reprinted as "The Unelected President," in *The Norseman* (1971), 15. On Knute Nelson's overall political career, see Andersen, "Senator Knute Nelson: Minnesota's Grand Old Man and the Norwegian Immigrant Press," in Lovoll, ed., *Makers of An American Immigrant Legacy*, 29–49.

32. Many denounced the move as a blatant appeal to national prejudice. Resolutions "refusing the bait" were passed by two Farmers' Alliances composed solely of Scandinavians (Bear Park in Norman county and Scandia in Polk county) and then published in *Great West* (St. Paul), May 6, 27, 1892. For press opinion, see St. Peter *Herald*, quoted in *Swift County Monitor*, November 4, 1892, and Wabash *Democrat*, quoted in *Swift County Monitor*, August 26, 1892; Also see Carl H. Chrislock, "The Politics of Protest in Minnesota, 1890–1901" (Ph. D. dissertation, University of Minnesota, 1954), 184–186.

33. St. Paul *Globe*, quoted in the *Swift County Monitor*, August 5, 1892.

34. Janson, "Norsemen in the United States," 686.

35. The Swedish language *Svenska Amerikanaren* (Chicago), quoted in *The North*, August 31, 1892.

36. *Svenska Amerikanska Posten* (Minneapolis), quoted in *The North*, September 14, 1892.

37. *Daglig Tidende* (Minneapolis), quoted in *The North*, September 24, 1890. The circular, dated September 10, 1892, is reprinted with comment in *The North*, October 12, 1892.

38. *The North* October 12, 1892.

39. *The North*, October 12, 1892. See also Luth. Jaeger's post-election review in the November 16, 1892, issue.

40. *The North*, October 26, 1892.

41. The four townships included Norwegian Grove, Sverdrup, Tordenskjold, and Folden.

42. Nicolay Grevstad to Knute Nelson, July 18, 1892, Knute Nelson Papers, Minnesota Historical Society, St. Paul.

43. *Irish Standard* (Minneapolis), December 3, 1892. See also its issues of November 26 and December 10, 1892.

44. "The Unelected President," 16. Concerning his larger plurality of 60,000 votes in the next campaign of 1894, Nelson said "I lost a great many Norwegian votes, but the Swedes stood firm, the Americans were more enthusiastic for me than they had been before."

CHAPTER 5

1. Fergus Falls (Minnesota) *Globe*, September 19, 1896.

2. Fergus Falls *Weekly Journal*, November 6, 1884. On small town versus countryside conflicts as a widespread phenomenon during this era, see Robert R. Dykstra, "Town-Country Conflict: A Hidden Dimension in American Social History," in *Agricultural History*, 38 (1964), 195–204; Luebke, "Main Street and the Countryside: Patterns of Voting in Nebraska During the Populist Era," in *Nebraska History*, 50 (1969), 257–275.

3. William Watts Folwell, *A History of Minnesota*, 3 (St. Paul, 1926), 168–169; John D. Hicks, "The Origin and Early History of the Farmers Alliance in Minnesota," in *Mississippi Valley Historical Review*, 9 (1922), 204–205.

4. Fergus Falls *Weekly Journal*, December 3, 1892. See also its issues of November 26 and December 10, 1892.

5. The published summary of the 1905 Minnesota census identified where fathers of persons enumerated were born. Data for Otter Tail county revealed the most frequently noted birthplaces to be as follows: Norway, 29%; United States, 26%; Germany, 18%; Sweden, 13%; Finland, 6%; Denmark, 2%, with the remaining 6% divided among twelve countries. See *Fifth Decennial Census of the State of Minnesota* (St. Paul, 1905), 197.

6. The thirteen Norwegian townships included Oscar, Trondhjem, Norwegian Grove, Aastad, Aurdal, Dane Prairie, Tumuli, Sverdrup, Tordenskjold, St. Olaf, Everts, Nidaros, and Folden.

7. Mixed German Catholic and Lutheran populations lived in Effington and Elizabeth townships.

8. John W. Mason, ed., *History of Otter Tail County*, 2 vols. (Indianapolis, 1916), 1:297–298. Finns were most numerous in the townships of Newton, Otto, Blowers, Paddock, and Deer Creek.

9. Mason, *History of Otter Tail County*, 1:297; Fergus Falls *Weekly Journal*, November 21, 1895; Robinson, *Early Economic Conditions and Agriculture in Minnesota*, 57–119.

10. Fergus Falls *Weekly Journal*, April 10, May 15, 22, June 5, 1884. For biographical information on Hompe, see Fergus Falls *Weekly Journal*, October 30, 1890; Mason, *History of Otter Tail County*, 2:646–647.

11. Fergus Falls *Weekly Journal*, June 23, 1892; Mason, *History of Otter Tail County*, 2:34–35.

12. Fergus Falls *Weekly Journal*, September 18, 1884, October 30, 1890.

13. Fergus Falls *Weekly Journal*, September 8, 1884. Republican townsmen were none too happy about the Alliance demands and heightened antagonism between Main Street and countryside distinguished the ensuing campaign. See an open letter by John Hompe to the Fergus Falls *Weekly Journal*, October 30, 1884, and editorial in Battle Lake *Review* reprinted in the Fergus Falls *Weekly Journal*, November 6, 1884.

14. Boen's decision not to run was despite indications that he might poll more votes than Bjorge in Norwegian areas. Underwood's postmaster informed the Fergus Falls *Weekly Journal*, October 30, 1884, that "if the election district was

limited to the three [largely Norwegian] towns, Aurdal , Sverdrup, and Tordenskjold, where they are both equally known, it is safe to say that Mr. Bjorge would
be badly beaten; and why? Because Boen has a far better education, much more
grit, and a much larger store of experience."

15. Fergus Falls *Weekly Journal*, June 10, 1886.

16. Fergus Falls *Weekly Journal*, June 10, 1886. Anfin Solem edited the
Fergus Falls *Ugeblad*. Born of farm parents near Trondheim, Norway, in 1850, he
graduated from a normal school near his home town and taught school. Coming to
Otter Tail county in 1879, he worked at several odd jobs until 1884, when he purchased a poorly performing Norwegian-language newspaper and became its editor. By 1890 the circulation had grown to 1,500 weekly. See *Album of Biography:
of the Famous Valley of the Red River of the North and the Park Regions* (Chicago,
1889), 429–430.

17. Fergus Falls *Weekly Journal*, June 10, 24, July 1, October 7, 1886. Editor
Elmer E. Adams emerged as one of the most powerful Republican leaders during
the period under study. Born in 1861 of native Vermont parents, he moved to Min-
neapolis with his family in 1879 and finished his education at the Minnesota State
University in 1884. That same year he became editor of the Fergus Falls *Daily
Telegram* and, within a year, had consolidated it with the Fergus Falls *Weekly
Journal* under his editorship. Republican in politics, the *Journal* boasted a weekly
circulation of 2,300 in 1889. Added biographical information is found in *Album of
Biography*, 440–441, and the Fergus Falls *Weekly Journal*, November 21, 1895.

18. Many Alliancemen remained angry after the convention. The Fergus Falls
Ugeblad continued listing the Alliance-endorsed ticket instead of changing to the
new Republican lineup. Republicans expressed concern that the Alliance might
field its own endorsements, but nothing came of it. Fergus Falls *Weekly Journal*,
July 1, 1886.

19. Fergus Falls *Weekly Journal*, October 7, 1884. Voting results for this and
other local elections in the county were secured from the newspaper's post-election
issues.

20. Other reasons for the decline within the state at large are cited in Donald
F. Warner, "Prelude to Populism," in *Minnesota History*, 32 (1951), 131–133.

21. Fergus Falls *Weekly Journal*, April 5, 19, 1888.

22. Fergus Falls *Weekly Journal*, April 19, June 7, 1888. Boen claimed the
fight was a personal attack on him.

23. Fergus Falls *Weekly Journal*, June 23, 1892. The description of Haldor
Boen's personal qualities is based on several sources, the most important of which
include: biographical sketch (author unknown) contained in the township history
files prepared by the W.P.A. Historical Project for the Otter Tail County Historical Society, Fergus Falls; Harald E. Boen, "Side Lights on the Life of Haldor E.
Boen," in Fergus Falls *Journal*, January 5, 1940; Fergus Falls *Weekly Journal*,
June 23, 1892, February 15, 1894.

24. Fergus Falls *Weekly Journal*, June 7, 1888.

25. Fergus Falls *Weekly Journal*, June 14, 1888.

26. Warner, "Prelude to Populism," 136–137; Hicks, "The People's Party in
Minnesota," in *Minnesota History Bulletin*, 5 (1924), 536–538.

27. See Battle Lake *Review*, June 19, 1890, and its editorial reprinted in
Fergus Falls *Weekly Journal*, May 29, 1890, as well as all May and June issues of
the Fergus Falls *Weekly Journal*.

28. Fergus Falls *Weekly Journal*, May 8, 1890.

29. The *Journal*'s account of the *Ugeblad*'s views and reaction to them are contained in the Fergus Falls *Weekly Journal*, May 29, June 5, 1890.

30. Fergus Falls *Weekly Journal*, May 29, June 5, 1890.

31. Fergus Falls *Weekly Journal*, June 5, 1890.

32. *Rodhuggeren*, February 12, 1895.

33. Charles W. Brandborg was a prominent Allianceman who worked closely with John Hompe. Born in 1847 in Halland, Sweden, he learned the stonemason's trade as a youth before immigrating to Wisconsin in 1873. About 1881 he homesteaded near Henning in Otter Tail county. He joined the Farmers' Alliance in 1884 and became affiliated with the Knights of Labor three years later. A man of strong Alliance views and deep Prohibition convictions, Brandborg presided as chairman of the Republican county executive committee in 1888 and, as of 1890, he was both president of the County Alliance and a member of the Alliance campaign committee. Brandborg was offered but declined the nomination for Congress in 1890. For added biographical information, see Charles W. Brandborg and Family Papers, Minnesota Historical Society, St. Paul; and Fergus Falls *Weekly Journal*, July 9, 1891.

34. Fergus Falls *Weekly Journal*, June 19, 1890. Internal friction briefly threatened when someone proposed to empower the executive committee to remove from the ticket any nominee who accepted nomination or endorsement from another political party. A bitter flareup ensued between Boen and Plowman over the 1886 election, when the Republicans nominated Plowman and other Alliance-endorsed candidates but left Boen and Hompe out in the cold. Boen alleged that when he and Hompe mounted independent candidacies the Republican nominees had "knifed them at every opportunity," which prompted Plowman to shake his fist toward Boen, denying Boen's allegations and the "malicious . . . dirty spirit" in which they had been made.

35. Fergus Falls *Weekly Journal*, June 19, 1890. There is some confusion about this. In its issue of May 26, 1892, the *Journal's* editor said that "it was Mr. Boen who smoked out the Republican nominees in 1890 and forced them to declare either for or against the Alliance."

36. Fergus Falls *Weekly Journal*, June 26, 1890. The *Journal* recommended that the four men be guaranteed a Republican nomination, while the *Ugeblad* saw the refusal of nominations as a snub to the working man.

37. Fergus Falls *Daily Journal*, July 2, 1890; A. C. Richardson to Charles Brandborg, August 11, 1890, Brandborg Papers.

38. Fergus Falls *Globe*, June 13, 1896, March 5, November 26, 1898.

39. Fergus Falls *Weekly Journal*, August 21, 1890.

40. Fergus Falls *Weekly Journal*, August 21, October 9, 20, 1890; Hans Nelson to Charles Brandborg, August 22, 1890, Brandborg Papers.

41. Battle Lake *Review*, November 20, 1890.

42. Fergus Falls *Weekly Journal*, October 30, 1890.

43. A. O. Richardson to C. W. Brandborg, October 30, 1890, Brandborg Papers.

44. Fergus Falls *Weekly Journal*, November 6, 1890.

45. Ethnic concentrations are derived from the 1895 Minnesota state census schedules at the Minnesota Historical Society, St. Paul. The *Legislative Manual of the State of Minnesota* provided necessary election data.

46. For the entire city, the Alliance/Populist vote for governor averaged 36.7 percent from 1890 through 1896. The average share from each ward was as follows: First ward, 44.9%; Second ward, 29.8%; Third ward, 33.9%; Fourth ward, 42.5%.

47. Chrislock, "Politics of Protest in Minnesota," 142–143; Hicks, *The Populist Revolt* (Lincoln, Nebraska, 1961), 96–127, 205–237; Hicks, "People's Party in Minnesota," 541–542; Warner, "Prelude to Populism," 138–145.

48. Chrislock, "Politics of Protest in Minnesota," 145.

49. Warner, "Prelude to Populism," 145.

50. Fergus Falls *Weekly Journal*, June 18, 1891.

51. Fergus Falls *Weekly Journal*, July 9, 1891.

52. Fergus Falls *Weekly Journal*, July 9, 16, 1891.

53. Fergus Falls *Weekly Journal*, July 16, 1891.

54. Fergus Falls *Weekly Journal*, July 9, 16, 1891.

55. Fergus Falls *Weekly Journal*, August 13, 1891.

56. Fergus Falls *Weekly Journal*, July 30, August 13, 1891; Battle Lake *Review*, July 30, 1891.

57. Fergus Falls *Weekly Journal*, December 17, 1891, May 26, 1892.

58. See the February and March issues of the Fergus Falls *Weekly Journal*, 1892.

59. Actions of the Otter Tail Alliance at the annual state meeting of the Alliance provide an example of the local attempt to stir up such a revolt. Fergus Falls *Weekly Journal*, December 24, 1891, and January 14, 1892.

60. Fergus Falls *Weekly Journal*, March 10, 1892. See also the issue of March 3.

61. Fergus Falls *Weekly Journal*, March 3, 1892. Evidently, some Donnelly men who distrusted Boen saw Boen's attempt to placate rather than eradicate as an act of betrayal. H. L. Burgess to Dr. E. W. Fish, April 8, 1892, Ignatius Donnelly Papers, Minnesota Historical Society, St. Paul.

62. Fergus Falls *Weekly Journal*, March 17, 1892. The *Journal* reported that editor Solem of the *Ugeblad* concluded that the People's party had no right to enter the county and interfere, for it would only injure the farmers' movement here. Most attending the County Alliance executive committee meeting still held that the Alliance party ought to exist separate from the People's party, but, instead of making a final decision, they called a convention of the entire County Alliance on May 19 to decide the matter. Perhaps this was because four of its members had been named by Boen to be on the People's party central committee.

63. Fergus Falls *Weekly Journal*, March 24, 1892.

64. Fergus Falls *Weekly Journal*, May 26, 1892.

65. Fergus Falls *Weekly Journal*, June 23, 1892. As in past Alliance conventions, twenty-five of the sixty-six townships did not send representatives and the Fergus Falls city wards sent a total of eight delegates. None came from Hompe's home township of Deer Creek or from Brandborg's town of Henning. An attempt to bring the *Ugeblad*'s editor into the People's party by sending him as a delegate to the state convention met with failure. He coldly declined, declaring that he was out of politics.

66. Further Alliance resistance in the state nearly collapsed after the Otter Tail and Seventh District party organizations merged into the People's party. Losing this stronghold of farmer discontent so undermined the bargaining power of the state Farmers' Alliance party that only one-fourth of the eligible delegates attended the state convention in July. Warner, "Prelude to Populism," 144–145.

67. Fergus Falls *Weekly Journal*, June 30, 1892.

68. Battle Lake *Review*, July 17, 1890; Fergus Falls *Globe*, July 17, 1890; Fergus Falls *Journal*, January 5, 1940.

69. Fergus Falls *Globe*, March 21, 1896.

70. Fergus Falls *Weekly Journal*, February 15, 1894, quoting comments by Congressman A. J. Cummings in the New York *Sun*.

71. Fergus Falls *Weekly Journal*, October 30, 1890.

72. Reprinted in the Fergus Falls *Weekly Journal*, July 7, 1892. Boen's ene-

mies had long tagged him as "a political trader" interested more in office than in principles. See, for example, Battle Lake *Review*, October 6, 13, 1892.

73. Fergus Falls *Weekly Journal*, October 20, 1892. Also see its issue of October 30, 1890, and the Fergus Falls *Globe*, October 31, 1896.

74. Examples of *Ugeblad* editorial opinion are described in the following issues of the Fergus Falls *Weekly Journal*, May 12, 19, 26, June 2, August 18, 1892.

75. That the *Ugeblad*'s resistance to the new People's party did prove costly to the newspaper is apparent in a letter from a Scandinavian farmer to Donnelly. "Last Saturday I attended a People's party caucus of what I call 'my own alliance – 336 Leaf Lake,' entitled to four delegates to the county convention, and I tell you, the wind that was blowing then out there boded no good for . . . [the Hompe, Brandborg forces]–even 'Ugebladet' . . . had lost its influence. I attended the county convention at Fergus Falls last Thursday: the same wind was blowing there." A. P. Onsdorff to Ignatius Donnelly, June 18, 1892, Donnelly Papers.

76. Haldor E. Boen to Ignatius Donnelly, July 26, 1892, Donnelly Papers.

77. Fergus Falls *Globe*, August 6, 1892. People's party men lamely countered that the *Ugeblad*'s editor must be in the pay of the Republicans, since he had failed to support candidates of the People's party whose principles he espoused. But later in the campaign the argument gained a little credence when one of Solem's anti-Boen editorials appeared as a Republican circular printed on *Ugeblad* type. Fergus Falls *Globe*, October 15, 23, 1892; Fergus Falls *Weekly Journal*, October 20, 1892.

78. Fergus Falls *Weekly Journal*, October 6, 1892. At this time the Populists' only support came from the Fergus Falls *Globe*, an English-language newspaper of small circulation whose editor strongly espoused prohibitionism and devoted only intermittent attention to People's party politics.

79. Fergus Falls *Weekly Journal*, September 29, 1892; Fergus Falls *Globe*, October 1, 1892.

80. Fergus Falls *Weekly Journal*, October 20, 1892.

81. Fergus Falls *Weekly Journal*, November 24, 1892.

82. Haldor Boen to Ignatius Donnelly, November 22, 1892, Donnelly Papers. In the legislative and county races, voters elected the entire People's party ticket, although with slimmer majorities than in 1890. Fergus Falls *Weekly Journal*, November 17, 1892.

83. Mason, *History of Otter Tail County*, 1:664–666; and all December issues of the Fergus Falls *Weekly Journal*, 1893.

84. Fergus Falls *Globe*, March 31, April 14, 1894.

85. Fergus Falls *Weekly Journal*, April 19, 1894; *Rodhuggeren*, February 27, 1894. References to *Rodhuggeren* articles in this chapter are all based on items translated by Donald Berg.

86. Founded in 1893, *Rodhuggeren* in Fergus Falls quickly acquired the largest circulation in the county, with 4,500 issues weekly compared to the *Ugeblad*'s 1,500. It became the most powerful newspaper politically among Norwegians. Fergus Falls *Weekly Journal*, June 12, 1890; Fergus Falls *Globe*, March 7, 1896, November 27, 1897.

87. English translation printed in Fergus Falls *Weekly Journal*, April 19, 1894.

88. On the Great Northern Railroad strike, see Fergus Falls *Weekly Journal*, April 26, 1894. On the impact of radical rhetoric and events of 1894, see Chrislock, "Politics of Protest in Minnesota," 229–240.

89. Fergus Falls *Weekly Journal*, April 19, August 2, October 4, 25, 1894.

90. Unidentified news clipping titled "Boen Discontinues His Globe," 1912,

contained in miscellaneous township information files of Otter Tail County Historical Society, Fergus Falls.

91. Boen later claimed the Republicans spent $60,000 to defeat him. Undated news clipping titled "Boen Abandons Paper," Minneapolis *Journal*, 1912, in miscellaneous township information files of the Otter Tail County Historical Society, Fergus Falls.

92. Fergus Falls *Weekly Journal*, June 7, July 12, 1894.

93. Fergus Falls *Globe*, July 28, 1894.

94. Fergus Falls *Weekly Journal*, October 11, 1894.

95. *Rodhuggeren*, September 11, November 2, 1894, January 29, 1895; staff editorial in *Rodhuggeren*, February 19, 1895.

96. *Rodhuggeren*, August 14, 21, 28, September 11, 1894; comments by Walter Friberg on Boen and Foss reprinted in *Rodhuggeren*, October 16, 1894; letter from J. B. on Hans A. Foss in *Rodhuggeren*, August 14, 1894; Lars R. Holen letter on Foss in *Rodhuggeren*, November 27, 1894.

97. *Rodhuggeren*, December 9, 1893, April 17, November 13, 1894, January 29, 1895.

98. Fergus Falls *Weekly Journal*, October 11, 1894. See also *Rodhuggeren*, August 14, October 7, 1894.

99. Fergus Falls *Globe*, October 20, 1894.

100. As pointed out by Syver Vinje, "Some Corrections," in *Rodhuggeren*, November 13, 1894.

101. Fergus Falls *Weekly Journal*, October 25, 1894.

102. Fergus Falls *Weekly Journal*, October 25, 1894. Also see issues of October 4, 11, 1894.

103. "The Order Has Gone Forth," printed in English in *Rodhuggeren*, October 23, 1894.

104. Vinje, "Some Corrections."

105. "The Order Has Gone Forth!!: Boen Must Be Defeated," in *Rodhuggeren*, October 13, 1894.

106. *Rodhuggeren*, November 2, 1894.

107. Fergus Falls *Weekly Journal*, November 22, 1894.

108. English translation in Fergus Falls *Weekly Journal*, November 29, 1894.

109. Fergus Falls *Weekly Journal*, November 29, 1894.

110. Interview with Harald Boen, Haldor's son, at his home in Wadena, Minnesota, September 4, 1970. Congressman Haldor Boen, in 1892, had wanted to take his family to Washington, but his wife, an unassuming, quiet woman who desired a simple home life with her family, would not go. In a move he later regretted, Haldor instituted divorce proceedings and the court granted the decree shortly thereafter.

111. It is surprising that Boen could afford the price for the newspaper; in April, 1894, he confided to Ignatius Donnelly that he was over $6,000 in debt, with his creditors demanding payment. Haldor Boen to Ignatius Donnelly, April 5, 1894, Donnelly Papers.

112. Fergus Falls *Weekly Journal*, November 21, 1895.

113. Fergus Falls *Weekly Journal*, February 13, 1896; Fergus Falls *Globe*, February 15, 1896.

114. Fergus Falls *Weekly Journal*, March 26, 1896.

115. *Wheelock's Weekly* (Fergus Falls), October 15, 1895, October 25, 1900; Fergus Falls *Weekly Journal*, April 11, 1907.

116. Fergus Falls *Weekly Journal*, May 21, 1896.

117. Fergus Falls *Globe*, May 9, 28, 1896; Fergus Falls *Weekly Journal*, May

14, June 6, 1896. Two excellent accounts of the political situation are in the Fergus Falls *Weekly Journal*, May 14, June 4, 1896.

118. Fergus Falls *Globe*, May 30, 1896.

119. Fergus Falls *Weekly Journal*, June 4, 1896. The effect of the new revised apportionment is seen by considering the proportions of delegates from two towns. Boen's home town of Aurdal cast 111 Populist votes and got seven delegates, which is only one delegate to sixteen voters whereas Star Lake cast only eleven Populist votes and received two delegates which was one delegate to five voters.

120. Fergus Falls *Globe*, June 6, 1896.

121. Fergus Falls *Weekly Journal*, June 25, 1896.

122. Fergus Falls *Weekly Journal*, June 25, 1896; Fergus Falls *Globe*, June 27, 1896.

123. Fergus Falls *Globe*, July 18, 1896. See also Fergus Falls *Weekly Journal*, June 25, July 23, 1896.

124. St. Paul *Dispatch*, quoted in Fergus Falls *Weekly Journal*, September 24, 1896.

125. Fergus Falls *Globe*, July 18, 1896.

126. Fergus Falls *Globe*, October 10, 1896.

127. See, for example, incidents noted in the Fergus Falls *Weekly Journal*, September 3, 10, 17, 1896; Fergus Falls *Globe*, September 5, 12, 1896.

128. Fergus Falls *Weekly Journal*, September 24, October 1, 22, 1896.

129. The German precincts included Effington, Edna, Corliss, Gorman, Dora, Pine Lake, Perham, and Elizabeth.

130. Fergus Falls *Weekly Journal*, November 12, 1896.

131. Fergus Falls *Weekly Journal*, November 12, 1896. A similar comment about Populist success in Norwegian areas appeared in the next week's issue of November 19.

132. Fergus Falls *Globe*, November 14, 1896. See also Fergus Falls *Weekly Journal*, October 22, 1896.

133. Fergus Falls *Globe*, November 12, 1898. Some surmised that the falling off in the Populist vote was due to a change in the Minnesota constitution which disfranchised many immigrant voters. The Minnesota legislature of 1895 proposed to amend the elective franchise by disqualifying aliens from exercising the suffrage and voters approved it on November 3, 1896. Voters disfranchised by the amendment were people of foreign birth who had declared their intention to become citizens but had not carried through to become full citizens.

134. Fergus Falls *Globe*, November 10, 1900.

CHAPTER 6

1. For general information on the period of progressive movements in each state, I have relied on the following: Margulies, *The Decline of the Progressive Movement in Wisconsin, 1890–1920* (Madison, 1968); Wyman, "Voting Behavior in the Progressive Era"; Robert C. Nesbit, *Wisconsin: A History* (Madison, 1973), 399–456; John E. Visser, "William Lloyd Harding and the Republican Party in Iowa, 1906–1920" (Ph. D. dissertation, University of Iowa, 1957); Sage, *History of Iowa*; Chrislock, *The Progressive Era in Minnesota, 1899–1918* (St. Paul, 1971); Folwell, *History of Minnesota*, vol. 3.

2. Chrislock, *Progressive Era in Minnesota*, 18–19; Charles B. Cheney, *The Story of Minnesota Politics* (Minneapolis, 1947), 27.

3. See Knaplund, *Moorings Old and New*, 195; Val Bjornson, *The History of Minnesota*, 1 (West Palm Beach, Florida, 1969), 435–436; Cheney, *Minnesota Poli-*

tics, 17–18, 35–36, 43; Theodore Christianson, *Minnesota: A History of the State and Its People*, 2 (New York, 1935), chapter 16.

4. Nesbit, *Wisconsin*, 405.

5. Robert S. Maxwell, *LaFollette and the Rise of the Progressives in Wisconsin* (Madison, 1956), 60. See also David L. Brye, "Wisconsin Scandinavians and Progressivism, 1900–1950," in *Norwegian-American Studies*, 27 (1977), 172.

6. Anderson, *Life Story*, 617. As one dismayed conservative Republican politician in Trempealeau county lamented, "The *Skandinaven* is taken by about every one, and it is their political bible." John C. Gaveney to Elisha Keyes, June 20, 1901, Elisha Keyes Letterbooks, State Historical Society of Wisconsin, Madison. See also A. N. Freng to Herman Ekern, August 27, 1906, Ekern Papers, State Historical Society of Wisconsin; Margulies, *Decline of the Progressive Movement*, 27.

7. Anderson, *Life Story*, 617, 626. Owing to the deeply strained relations between Rasmus Anderson and John Anderson, publisher of *Skandinaven*, Rasmus Anderson firmly believed that John Anderson had been led to espouse LaFollette's cause in order to avoid, as he put it, embracing "any candidate for office who recognized me as his friend," as had party regular Senator John C. Spooner.

8. Robert M. LaFollette, *LaFollette's Autobiography: A Personal Narrative of Political Experiences* (Madison, 1913), 7; Norlie, *History of the Norwegian People in America*, 502; Maxwell, *LaFollette*, 60; Margulies, *Decline of the Progressive Movement*, 26.

9. The mean Republican vote of the entire state was as follows: 1881–1898 = 51.4%; 1900–1912 = 51.7%; and 1914–1924 = 54.7%.

10. The varied Scandinavian response to LaFollette has not gone completely unnoticed. See, for example, Dykstra and David R. Reynolds, "In Search of Wisconsin Progressivism, 1904–1952: A Test of the Rogin Scenario," in J. H. Silbey, A. G. Bogue and W. H. Flanigan, eds., *The History of American Electoral Behavior* (Princeton, 1978), 321–322.

11. Substantial differences showed in the extent to which the Republican share of votes for governor increased in Norwegian settlements from the period 1892–1898 to that of 1900–1910. They ranged as follows: 8 settlements increased 4%, or less; 11 increased 5–9%; 12 increased 10–14%; 8 increased 15–19%; 6 increased 20–24%; and 2 increased by 25% or more.

12. In an effort to identify variables that asserted considerable long-term influence in the settlements, I initially examined a variety of cultural and socioeconomic characteristics of Norwegian precincts to see which ones correlated most strongly with Republican votes for governor. This involved computing Pearson Product Moment correlations between votes cast in general elections and twenty-two independent variables on which data could be found for nearly all selected Norwegian precincts. These tabulations showed that only socioeconomic characteristics displayed linear relationships to the election results of +-.30 or greater. Then, probing further, I tried by partial and multiple correlation to determine: (a) the relative impact of five of the most prominent variables when the influence of each on the other is removed, and (b) the extent of the total variation that they collectively explain.

13. The five independent variables that demonstrated consistent recurring correlations included, in order of their frequent impact: (1) percentage of farms being rented by foreign born plus native born of foreign parents; (2) percentage of value that potatoes comprised of the total harvested crop; (3) average value per acre; (4) average value per farm; and (5) value of total harvested crops per farm.

14. Dykstra and Reynolds, "In Search of Wisconsin Progressivism," 322;

Michael Paul Rogin, *The Intellectuals and McCarthy: The Radical Specter* (Cambridge, Massachusetts, 1967), 69.

15. W. A. Hartman and J. D. Black, "Economic Aspects of Land Settlement in the Cut-Over Region of the Great Lakes States," *United States Department of Agriculture Circular No. 160* (1931), 2–3, 27–36.

16. This included Norwegian settlements in the cutover counties of Waupaca, Portage, Shawano, Adams, Jackson, and Dunn.

17. Unlike Iowa or Minnesota, research revealed no single characteristic of settlement or combination of characteristics to have exerted more than minimal impact on the Norwegian-American vote in Wisconsin.

18. See Wyman, "Voting Behavior in the Progressive Era."

19. Examples of anti-Catholicism affecting Norwegian reactions are the 1914 Republican primary race, when progressive forces put up a Catholic for senator, and in 1918 when Roy P. Wilcox, a Catholic state senator, ran for governor in the Republican primary. See Margulies, "Anti-Catholicism in Wisconsin Politics," 51–56.

CHAPTER 7

1. For pre-1880 development of the county, see Curti, *Making of an American Community*; also Franklyn Curtiss-Wedge, *History of Trempealeau County, Wisconsin* (Chicago, 1917).

2. Curti, *Making of an American Community*, 328, 331, 344, 378, 436. It has been suggested that Curti and others have given insufficient attention to the influence of these small controlling cliques of leaders in frontier communities. See Dykstra, "Stratification and Community Political Systems: Historians' Models," in Allan G. Bogue, ed., *Emerging Theoretical Models in Social and Political History* (Beverly Hills, California, 1973), 86–87.

3. Curti, *Making of an American Community*, 104, 321.

4. Curti, *Making of an American Community*, 341.

5. Biographical data in Curtiss-Wedge, *History of Trempealeau County*, 673–676.

6. Curtiss-Wedge, *History of Trempealeau County*, 386–387.

7. Biographical data from introduction to and campaign sketches from Herman L. Ekern Papers, State Historical Society of Wisconsin, Madison; Albert Erlebacher, "Herman L. Ekern: The Quiet Progressive" (Ph. D. dissertation, University of Wisconsin, 1965).

8. Erlebacher, "Herman L. Ekern," 18.

9. After Ekern had served two terms as county attorney, Cowie's influential Norwegian friends among his wife's relatives, remembering that rotation was the general rule, may have helped press for Cowie to have his turn at the position.

10. On 1898 county politics, see Arcadia (Wisconsin) *Leader*, August 11, October 6, 1898; Galesville (Wisconsin) *Republican*, October 6, 20, November 10, 1898; Trempealeau (Wisconsin) *Herald*, November 4, 1898.

11. The largest-circulating newspaper, the Whitehall *Times-Banner*, was located in the county seat and became the major pro-LaFollette organ. Although its clever and cautious editor often straddled divisive issues, he nonetheless remained editorially responsive to the progressive sentiments of the central and northern towns. Leading the conservative press assault was Bert Gipple's boldly written Galesville *Republican*. From the time it began in 1897, Gipple needled LaFollette, castigating him as one who had an unhealthy desire for power and who magnified the errors of others while setting himself up as the only honest man in politics. His

newspapers's position found periodic support from the brash Trempealeau *Herald*, and the Arcadia *Arcadian* and, in the 1906 campaigns, from the Blair *Press*.

12. On the 1900 situation in county politics, see Trempealeau *Herald*, August 10, September 7, September 28, October 5, 1900; Galesville *Republican*, July 26, August 23, 1900; Arcadia *Leader*, September 21, November 9, 1900; O. J. Hawkenson to H. L. Ekern, August 22, 1908, Ekern Papers.

13. On Ekern's approach to political organization, see Erlebacher, "Herman L. Ekern," 46–50.

14. Galesville *Republican*, October 2, 1902.

15. Whitehall *Times-Banner*, quoted in Galesville *Republican*, September 18, 1902. Gale township and Galesville conservatives later claimed that Arnold's defeat was due to treacherous trading of votes by which he had been sacrificed by his friends in the southern part of the county. See Galesville *Republican*, October 2, 1902, for a review of the convention.

16. Trempealeau *Herald*, May 13, 1904.

17. Galesville *Republican*, July 21, 1904.

18. Letter to editor from F. A. George, Hale township, in Galesville *Republican*, September 1, 1904.

19. LaFollette went into the county to work personally against his legislative opponent, State Senator Gaveney, while Gaveney followed on his heels trying to counteract his being branded a political hireling and corporate tool. See Galesville *Republican*, November 3, 1904.

20. Galesville *Republican*, October 20, 1904.

21. Senators were not elected directly by the people until passage of the Seventeenth Amendment to the United States Constitution in 1913.

22. Born in the western Norway district of Sogn in 1854, Davidson arrived in Wisconsin at age eighteen. From 1877 he had resided at Soldiers Grove, a small hamlet in the Mississippi River county of Crawford, where he eventually established a prosperous general merchandise store. After he had served in a variety of local public positions, the district's voters elected the likable Norwegian to the State Assembly in 1892, where he served until 1898. Davidson's friendship with, or at least connections to, the new reform element within the party secured for him the nomination for state treasurer, a position that he held until 1904 when he was elected lieutenant governor. See James O. Davidson, Scrapbooks of Newspaper Clippings Relating to Wisconsin Politics and Government, 1897–1910, and to Davidson's Governorship, Number 8, State Historical Society of Wisconsin, Madison; Galesville *Republican*, February 22, 1906; Arcadia *Leader*, August 25, 1898. That Davidson's relationship to LaFollette's new reform coalition was uneasy—mixing friendship with mistrust—is indicated in Kenneth Acrea, "The Wisconsin Reform Coalition, 1892 to 1900: LaFollette's Rise to Power," in *Wisconsin Magazine of History*, 52 (Winter 1968–1969), 152, 157.

23. Nils P. Haugen to Robert M. LaFollette, April 2, 1906, Robert M. LaFollette Papers, State Historical Society of Wisconsin, Madison. See also Haugen, *Pioneer and Political Reminiscences* (Evansville, Wisconsin, 1930), 275–278.

24. Haugen, *Pioneer and Political Reminiscences*, 277–278.

25. A. T. Rogers to LaFollette, January 11, 1906, LaFollette Papers, as quoted in Margulies, *Decline of the Progressive Movement in Wisconsin*, 90.

26. Galesville *Republican*, June 15, 1905; Margulies, *Decline of the Progressive Movement*, 87.

27. Galesville *Republican*, February 1, 1906.

28. Galesville *Republican*, May 10, 1906.

29. Sigvart Luther Rugland, "The Norwegian Press of the Northwest" (M.A. thesis, State University of Iowa, 1929), 9, 40–41.

30. Haugen to LaFollette, April 2, 1906; Ekern to LaFollette, February 17, 1906, in LaFollette Papers, Correspondence; Anderson, *Life Story*, 623–624. *Skandinaven*'s agent, Gryttenholm, also became a leading figure in writing and circulating among Norwegian communities pro-Davidson and anti-Lenroot-LaFollette circulars in both the 1906 primary and the 1908 effort to unseat Herman Ekern in Trempealeau county.

31. Ekern to LaFollette, February 17, 1906, LaFollette Papers, Correspondence.

32. Haugen to LaFollette, April 2, 1906, LaFollette Papers, Correspondence.

33. A. N. Freng to Ekern, August 27, 1906, Ekern Papers. The political importance of *Skandinaven* is noted in Margulies, *Decline of the Progressive Movement*, 27; Maxwell, *LaFollette*, 60; Anderson, *Life Story*, 617.

34. Ekern to Freng, August 28, 1906. For another instance, see Erlebacher, "Herman L. Ekern," 67.

35. Something had to be done, concluded Ekern at LaFollette's urging in late May, when a *Skandinaven* reader wrote a letter saying that all of Senator LaFollette's supporters backed Davidson. Together Ekern and LaFollette's law partner drafted a reply that they mailed to *Skandinaven* in early June, but which the newspaper did not publish until mid-July. See Erlebacher, "Herman L. Ekern," 67.

36. *Skandinaven*, August 1, 1906, contained – all printed in English – the item from the *Blair Press*, Ekern's article on "LaFollette and the Governorship," which he had written for the *Milwaukee Free Press*, and *Skandinaven*'s editorial reaction to Ekern's arguments.

37. Ekern to J. E. Holden, August 22, 1906, Ekern Papers.

38. A. T. Rogers to Ekern, August 16, 1906, Ekern Papers.

39. LaFollette had traveled to Blair village on August 21 to offset strong Davidson sentiment there. Perhaps a greater proportion of recent Norwegian arrivals lived here, for Ekern commented before the election that he had the support of "the businessmen and about every farmer," while complaining that the younger element was being worked very hard by the opposition. See Ekern to Thomas Herried, August 22, 1906, Ekern Papers. That he may have garnered greater support from those who had made a better go of life in America is also suggested by the somewhat stronger support Ekern received from places with higher average personal property values. Average assessed values for rural townships giving strong support to Ekern were: Pigeon, $248; Unity, $249; Hale, $225. Less support came from: Ettrick, $213; and Chimney Rock, $144. Of course, it was to be expected that his uncle's family played an influential role in this respect. Personal property values for the year 1905 in Trempealeau county are derived from Tax Roll records located at the LaCrosse Area Research Center, State Historical Society of Wisconsin.

40. The following figures reveal the extra margin that Davidson attracted over Ekern's vote in predominantly Norwegian precincts: Albion township plus Eleva village, 67 percent; Preston township plus Blair village, 35 percent; Ettrick township and village, 28 percent; Chimney Rock township, 25 percent; Unity township, 17 percent; Hale township, 4 percent; Pigeon township, 2 percent.

41. Galesville *Republican*, April 30, 1908. See also Erlebacher, "Herman L. Ekern," 142.

42. See, for example, Galesville *Republican*, August 20, 1908.

43. Erlebacher, "Herman L. Ekern," 142.

44. Ekern's opponents recognized Twesme's potential at least as far back as May 17, 1906, when he spoke at a Norwegian independence day celebration in Galesville. Galesville *Republican*, May 17, 1906. For biographical information see Buffalo county (Wisconsin) *News*, quoted in Galesville *Republican*, July 23, 1908, and Curtiss-Wedge, *History of Trempealeau County*, 457–458.

45. Quoted in Galesville *Republican*, May 21, 1908.

46. Galesville *Republican*, June 25, August 13, 1908; O. J. Hawkenson to Ekern, August 20, 1908, Ekern Papers.

47. Galesville *Republican*, August 13, 1908; Hawkenson to Ekern, August 15, 22, 1908, Ekern Papers.

48. Ekern to several friends and party workers, August 26, 1908; Ekern to 0. H. Moe, August 31, 1908, Ekern Papers.

49. Trempealeau *Herald*, August 21, 1908; Ekern to Henry Schafer, August 31, 1908, Ekern Papers.

50. Robert Cowie to James O. Davidson, August 21, 1908, James O. Davidson Papers, State Historical Society of Wisconsin, Madison. An earlier invitation by an influential Twesme supporter, Alex A. Arnold, had been turned down. See A. A. Arnold to Davidson, August 14, 1908, Davidson Papers; Colonel Oliver Munson to Arnold, August 19, 1908, Davidson Papers.

51. Ekern to LaFollette, September 2, 1908, Ekern Papers; W. L. Houser to Ekern, September 3, 1908, Ekern Papers; Ekern to Thomas A. Roycraft, September 4, 1908, Ekern Papers; Ekern to Houser, September 5, 1908, Ekern Papers.

52. The name of the *Skandinaven* agent has been variously spelled by contemporaries, ranging from Grytenhohen to Grytten Holms to Gefauholun. Nevertheless, the agent's important role in distributing, and perhaps writing, the political circulars for *Skandinaven* is indicated in the Arcadia *Leader*, October 23, 1908; Ekern to LaFollette, September 11, 1908, Ekern Papers; unsigned letter from Eau Claire, Wisconsin, writer to Ekern, October 11, 1908, Ekern Papers; unsigned letter from Ashland, Wisconsin, writer, October 20, 1908; clipping from *Badger State Banner*, October 1, 1908, in James Davidson Scrapbooks, Volume 9, State Historical Society of Wisconsin, Madison.

53. English translation printed in the local Democratic newspaper, the Arcadia *Leader*, October 23, 1908. Evidently, this represented but one of several similar circulars being distributed among Norwegian communities of Trempealeau county and elsewhere.

54. Trempealeau *Gazette*, September 4, 1908; J. T. Qualley to Ekern, September 3, 1908, Ekern Papers; Ekern to LaFollette, September 2, 1908, Ekern Papers. The list of his principal enemies was modified on later occasions. In a letter to John Strange, Oshkosh, Wisconsin, the very next day, for example, Ekern said he was defeated by a combination of "outside liquor interests and insurance companies aided by the local stalwarts and governor." And in a September 4 letter to C. F. Stout, Westboro, Wisconsin, he added the invidious factor of "nationality prejudice" to the list. He did privately concede, however, that he was partly to blame through neglect of his political organization at home while engaged in state politics. Ekern to Irvine Lenroot, September 3, 1908, Ekern Papers.

55. Ekern to LaFollette, September 2, 1908, Ekern Papers; V. S. Keffel to Ekern, September 2, 1908, Ekern Papers; Ekern to Walter Houser, September 5, 1908, Ekern Papers; Ekern to L. N. Clausen, September 5, 1908, Ekern Papers; A. M. Hellekson to Ekern, September 22, 1908, Ekern Papers; Robert Cowie to Davidson, August 21, Davidson Papers.

56. Blair *Press*, October 29, 1908; Milwaukee *Sentinel*, November 4, 1908; Ekern to LaFollette, September 28, 1908, Ekern Papers.

57. Ekern to William Gibson, October 5, 1908, Ekern Papers; Trempealeau *Herald*, October 9, 23, 1908; Trempealeau *Gazette*, October 16, 23, 1908; Blair *Press*, October 29, 1908, and its campaign supplement, Fall, 1908; Independence (Wisconsin) *News-Wave*, October 31, 1908.

58. Blair *Press*, October 29, 1908.

59. LaCrosse *Daily Chronicle*, October 21, 1908; Blair *Press*, October 29, 1908, and its campaign supplement, Fall, 1908; Trempealeau *Gazette*, October 23, 1908.

60. Milwaukee *Sentinel*, October 29, 1908; Galesville *Republican*, November 5, 1908.

61. Blair *Press*, October 29, 1908; Hawkenson to Ekern, October 24, 1908, Ekern Papers.

62. Independence *News-Wave*, October 31, 1908; Milwaukee *Sentinel*, October 29, 1908.

63. According to one observer, in these circumstances Davidson showed himself to be a better mixer than the senator in that, while he could not begin to approach the speaking ability of LaFollette, his modest plainspoken manner appealed to the people in a homely way that made them feel at one with him. From Milwaukee *Sentinel*, undated article, in Davidson, Scrapbooks of Newspaper Clippings; E. A. Edmonds to Davidson, October 29, 1908, Davidson Papers; Ekern to Roycraft, November 2, 1908, Ekern Papers; Ekern to E. S. Turner, November 2, 1908, Ekern Papers.

64. Blair *Press*, October 29 issue and its Campaign Supplement, Fall, 1908; Trempealeau *Herald*, October 30, 1908; T. J. Saed to Ekern, October 20, 1908, Ekern Papers; Ekern to L. K. Underheim, October 27, 1908, Ekern Papers; Milwaukee *Sentinel*, undated article in Davidson, Scrapbooks of Newspaper Clippings, Davidson Papers.

65. This is based on admittedly slim data. Pigeon township and Preston township plus Blair village were heterogeneous in dialect; and townships where one dialect prevailed included Albion township plus Eleva village, Unity township plus Strum village and Ettrick township. Classifications are drawn from Martin Ulvestad, *Norge i Amerika* (Minneapolis, 1901), and Haugen, *Norwegian Language in America*, II; 610–613. See also Haugen, 349, for discussion of this assimilative tendency among mixed Norwegian townships. No similar tendency, however, was found in the combined vote of Norwegian towns throughout the state: the 1906 primary vote for Davidson was 83.1 percent in eight mixed-dialect townships and 81.6 percent in twenty-nine more homogeneous townships.

66. Freng to Ekern, August 27, 1906, Ekern Papers; Ekern to Freng, August 28, 1906, Ekern Papers; letter of G. O. Linderman to Herman Ekern published in Galesville *Republican*, July 19, 1906.

CHAPTER 8

1. John L. Heaton, *Cobb of 'The World'* (New York, 1924), 270.

2. See Folwell, *History of Minnesota*, 3: 538–556; Robert I. Morlan, *Political Prairie Fire: The Nonpartisan League, 1915–1922* (Minneapolis, 1955); Chester H. Rowell, "The Political Cyclone in North Dakota" in *The World's Work*, 46 (July, 1923), 265–274; Christianson, *Minnesota: A History of the State*, 2: 367–370.

3. On the legal and political tactics employed against the League and the civil liberties implications of these events, see Carol E. Jenson, *Agrarian Pioneer in Civil Liberties: The Nonpartisan League in Minnesota during World War I* (New York, 1986), and her article, "Loyalty as Political Weapon: The 1918 Campaign in Minnesota," in *Minnesota History*, 43 (Summer, 1972), 43–57.

4. Minneapolis *Journal*, May 6, 1918.

5. On the League's wartime troubles, see O. A. Hilton, "The Minnesota Commission of Public Safety in World War I, 1917-1919," in *Bulletin of the Oklahoma Agricultural and Mechanical College*, Social Science Series Number 1 (Stillwater, 1951); Morlan, *Political Prairie Fire*, chapter 8. As for the heat of wartime emotions as it affected the League, examine almost any editorial page of the Minneapolis *Journal* during April through June of 1918.

6. *Thirteenth Census of the United States, 1910. Vol. I: Population*, 929.

7. The Norwegian attitude toward the war and that of other Scandinavian countries was discussed by Dr. M. F. Egan before the American Academy of Arts and Letters in *New York Times*, February 22, 1918; O. J. Storm, "Public Opinion in Norway During the War," reprinted from *France-Scandinavie* in *New York Times*, May 14, 1918.

8. Chrislock, *Ethnicity Challenged*, 68-72. Although Knute Nelson evidently took pride in his independent-minded "political maverick" image, he felt an intense antagonism toward those–especially fellow Norwegians–who spoke out against the country's prevailing social order. Be they Populists, progressives, or whatever, an intolerant Nelson judged them to be "kickers," "agitators," and radicals. See Gieske, "The Politics of Knute Nelson," 2: 382, and chapter 9 generally.

9. Impressed by what he had learned from a League organizer about their recruiting drives, a close advisor of Minnesota's Senator Knute Nelson wrote to the aging senator that the organizer "told me that he had charge of Brown, McLeod, Sibley and Nicollet Counties, that he had 28 workers under him in these counties and that they in turn have one or two men in each township. He showed me his record. He had a record of each farmer by town and range. He also had a blue print of each township with a notation on each 40 if they had a member of the league there. This is about the most perfect paper organization I have ever seen." Simon Michelet to Knute Nelson, June 18, 1918, Knute Nelson Papers, Minnesota State Historical Society, St. Paul, Minnesota.

10. Morlan, *Political Prairie Fire*, 152; Hilton, "Minnesota Commission of Public Safety," 26.

11. Morlan, *Political Prairie Fire*, 192; Bruce L. Larson, *Lindbergh of Minnesota: A Political Biography* (New York, 1971), 229-234; Cheney, *The Story of Minnesota Politics*, 44-45; Minneapolis *Journal*, May 4, 1918; L. M. Willcuts to Nelson, June 17, 1918, Nelson Papers. The full title of Lindbergh's book was *Why Is Your Country at War and What Happens to You After the War and Related Subjects* (Washington, 1917). It alleged that business interests and Wall Street had been responsible for the war.

12. J. A. A. Burnquist to Arthur LeSueur, March 11, 1918, quoted in Larson, *Lindbergh of Minnesota*, 222.

13. Letter from Nelson to Grevstad, October 21, 1920, quoted in Chrislock, *Ethnicity Challenged*, 116.

14. For a informative discussion of who joined the Nonpartisan League and why the League proved unable to develop a strong organization in Minnesota, based on an examination of League membership files and the 1918 farm labor and crop census as well as investigations of previous research on the subject, see Charles R. Lamb, "The Nonpartisan League and its Expansion into Minnesota," in *North Dakota Quarterly*, 49 (Summer, 1981), 108-143.

15. Prices of milk and dairy products in the early 1920s stayed roughly equal in purchasing power to what dairymen had enjoyed during the half-decade before World War I. To compensate in Wisconsin, the Nonpartisan League tried by coalition with labor and socialist organizations to expand beyond its several thousand

members in northern and southeastern sections of the state. But postwar voters found progressive rhetoric economically radical enough for them and devoted more attention to the issues of prohibition enforcement, Catholicism, tax reform, and economy in government. In Iowa, corn-belt farmers suffered acutely under the postwar agricultural depression, but worked their grievances out through the conservative Farm Bureau Federation and the Republican party. It was mainly through the spirited senatorial campaigns of Smith Brookhart, who emerged as a champion of the small farmer and of labor elements, that the victims of the depression politically expressed their discontent. In general, Republican hegemony remained supreme. See Baker, "Agricultural Regions of North America, Part V – The Hay and Dairying Belt," in *Economic Geography*, 4 (1928), 72–73, and his "Agricultural Regions of North America, Part IV – The Corn Belt," 462; Nesbit, *Wisconsin: A History*, 461–468; Sage, *History of Iowa*, 264–265.

16. Sageng to Nelson, December 20, 1917, Nelson Papers.

17. Benson (Minnesota) *Swift County Review*, February 26, 1918. Nevertheless, Swift county's Public Safety Commission went ahead and ordered that "the sheriff prevent any meetings of the Non-partisan League in the county by organizers not residents of this section." Appleton (Minnesota) *Press*, March 1, 1918.

18. *Swift County Review*, June 11, 1918.

19. William E. Leuchtenberg, *The Perils of Prosperity, 1914–1932* (Chicago, 1958), 128–129.

20. *Swift County Review*, June 4, 11, 1918.

21. Fergus Falls *Daily Journal*, November 4, 1918.

22. Fergus Falls *Free Press*, November 13, 1918.

23. Willmar (Minnesota) *Tribune*, October 10, 1917.

24. Letter from Nelson to Michelet, October 26, 1918, quoted in Chrislock, *Ethnicity Challenged*, 68.

25. *Nonpartisan Leader*, quoted in Morlan, *Political Prairie Fire*, 154.

26. Willmar *Tribune*, October 10, 1917.

27. Morlan, *Political Prairie Fire*, 156.

28. Fergus Falls *Free Press*, October 10, 1917.

29. Fergus Falls *Free Press*, October 10, 1917; Fergus Falls *Weekly Journal*, October 11, 1918. See also its issue of October 18.

30. Morlan, *Political Prairie Fire*, 156.

31. *Legislative Manual of the State of Minnesota, 1919* (Minneapolis, 1919), 318–322, 326–328, 796.

32. Fergus Falls *Weekly Journal*, June 20, 1918. Sageng's disenchantment with the League went back to at least 1917. See Sageng to James P. Boyle, February 19, 1917, Ole Sageng Papers, Minnesota State Historical Society, St. Paul, Minnesota.

33. Fergus Falls *Free Press*, March 27, 1918; Fergus Falls *Weekly Journal*, May 22, 1924.

34. Fergus Falls *Free Press*, March 27, 1918.

35. *Minnesota Legislative Manual*, 692, 712.

36. Willmar *Tribune*, April 24, May 1, 1918; Morlan, *Political Prairie Fire*, 197.

37. Willmar *Tribune*, June 5, 12, 1918. When Burnquist announced his candidacy for re-election, he declared that no political speeches would be made because they might divert public attention away from the war by "the stirring up of untimely issues in contests for public offices." Minneapolis *Journal*, May 6, 1918.

38. Willmar *Tribune*, June 19, 1918.

39. Willmar *Tribune*, June 19, 1918.

40. Willmar *Tribune*, June 19, 1918. The June 26 issue reports that the Willmar Commercial Club passed a resolution emphatically denying knowledge of any threats or violence contemplated against the farmers' parade that occurred the previous week, about which reports had "been extensively circulated and published throughout the farming communities."

41. Fergus Falls *Weekly Journal*, May 2, 9, 1918.

42. Fergus Falls *Free Press*, February 20, 1918. As editor Odland put it, "The bitter enemies of the League, including the Fergus Falls *Journal* and our friend Elmer, have diligently tried to convey the impression that the farmers who have joined the Nonpartisan League have nothing to say, and will have nothing to say, as to League affairs—that Townley is everything."

43. Fergus Falls *Weekly Journal*, March 21, 1918. That the League should "ignore two of the most faithful and able representatives that the farmers ever had in this county, Senator Ole Sageng and H. A. Putnam," the *Journal* cited as evidence that "Mr. Townley has got to have the right kind of men or he can not run things, and Sageng and Putnam are not his kind of farmers."

44. Fergus Falls *Weekly Journal*, May 30, June 6, 1918.

45. Fergus Falls *Weekly Journal*, June 13, 1918. See also R. K. Braugh to Nelson, June 15, 1918, Nelson Papers.

46. Fergus Falls *Weekly Journal*, June 13, 1918.

47. Fergus Falls *Weekly Journal*, June 20, 1918.

48. Letter to editor from J. L. Rots dated June 9, 1918, and printed in Fergus Falls *Free Press*, June 12, 1918. See also Sageng's partial response in the Fergus Falls *Weekly Journal*, June 20, 1918.

49. On postwar political dynamics, see Rowell, "LaFollette, Shipstead, and the Embattled Farmers: What's Happening in Wisconsin and Minnesota, and Why," in *The World's Work*, 46 (August, 1923), 408–420; "Where Democrats Vote Republican," in *The New Republic* (August 18, 1920), 334–335.

CHAPTER 9

1. Minnesota's League membership is cited in Morlan, *Political Prairie Fire*, 201, and Iowa's in Saloutos and Hicks, *Agricultural Discontent in the Middle West*, 189.

2. Morlan, *Political Prairie Fire*, 177; Saloutos and Hicks, *Agricultural Discontent*, 190.

3. This capsule summary of Harding's pre-1918 career is based on Visser, "William Lloyd Harding and the Republican Party in Iowa."

4. Nathaniel R. Whitney, "The First Three Liberty Loans in Iowa" in Benjamin F. Shambaugh, ed., *Iowa and War*, No. 15 (Iowa City, 1918), 2. See also Whitney's larger work in Shambaugh, ed., *The Sale of War Bonds in Iowa, Iowa Chronicles of the World War* (Iowa City, 1923), 30, 127–128, 148–149, 167–169.

5. Visser, "William Lloyd Harding," 236, 252.

6. Problems on the Mackey Telephone Line in Glidden are reported in the Decorah *Public Opinion*, May 1, 1918.

7. The conclusion that the proclamation was largely due to the governor's weakness of character and the forcefulness of his advisors rests partly on the contemporary observations of James Pierce, publisher of the *Iowa Homestead*. What is compelling in Visser's account is not his acceptance at face value of Harding's explanation for issuing the edict but his broader conclusion that without a "strong personality or group behind him" Harding was "rudderless." This weakness became especially pronounced after his close advisor, George D. Perkins of the Sioux City *Journal*, died in 1914. "From that point on," says Visser, Governor Harding

"accepted the advice of far lesser men, many of whom used him mercilessly for their own selfish ends." See Visser, "William Lloyd Harding," 315–316. This judgment corresponds closely to the views that Pierce expressed during the 1918 election campaign. Although the publisher had recently broken with Harding over certain issues, he had remained in general agreement with the governor's language proclamation. Harding's poor handling of the language matter, however, reinforced Pierce's doubts about the governor's qualities of leadership generally. In Pierce's estimation, Harding's advisors pushed him into issuing the language order, because "it is not the kind of thing that Governor Harding ever does of his own free will." Specifically, the publisher concluded that "the chairman of his council of defense, Lafe Young, with whom the subject had become an obsession, simply sneaked up on Governor Harding's blind side and wheedled him into it." *Iowa Homestead* (Des Moines), October 24, 1918.

8. The proclamation laid down four rules to be in effect for the war's duration. "First. English should and must be the only medium of instruction in public, private, denominational or other similar schools; Second. Conversation in public places, on trains and over the telephone should be in the English language; Third. All public addresses should be in the English language; Fourth. Let those who cannot speak or understand the English language conduct their religious worship in their homes." "Iowa War Proclamations," in Shambaugh, *Iowa and War*, No. 13, 43–46.

9. Excerpts from address by Governor Harding in H. C. Hurack, ed., *Proceedings of the Twenty-Fourth Annual Session of the Iowa State Bar Association Held at Des Moines, Iowa, June 27 and 28, 1918* (Iowa City, 1918), 170–172.

10. Cedar Rapids Evening Gazette, May 30, 1918. See also the staff editorial comments in the issues of May 26, 27, 1918.

11. The split between the Des Moines *Register* and Governor Harding had begun several years before 1918. In some respects the language controversy became simply one more phase of the struggle. The *Register* had particularly criticized Harding's lukewarm advocacy of prohibition and his 1916 move to sidetrack the "good-roads" movement. Consequently, William Lloyd Harding read little about himself in the columns of the Des Moines *Register* that rose above faint praise or unflattering comment.

12. For majority support behind Harding's edict see Ames *Evening Times*, June 29, 1918, and Sioux City *Tribune* staff editorial reprinted in the Des Moines *Register*, May 31, 1918.

13. The reported remarks had been to the effect that, despite having lived for years in the settlements of Shelby and Audubon counties, the young people when grown were still 100 percent Danish. For details see Peter L. Peterson, "Language and Loyalty: Governor Harding and Iowa's Danish-Americans During World War I," in *Annals of Iowa*, 42 (Fall, 1974), 411–415; Des Moines *Register*, August 8, 26, 1918.

14. All daily issues of the Des Moines *Register* between May 23 and November 10, 1918, were examined to identify the column inches of space given over to the language order.

15. Less than one percentage point separated the average fall in support by the two groups: Norwegian precincts declined by 38.73 percentage points and Danish precincts by 39.56. Average Republican voting levels in Danish settlements were figured on the basis of votes cast in five previous elections by a cluster of five precincts (Oakland township and Sharon township plus Kimballton village, in Audubon county; and Elkhorn township and village, Jackson township, and Monroe township in Shelby county).

16. From an interview by Harding quoted in "Huns Use Foreign Speaking Folk to Further Their Aims," in the Des Moines *Capital*, June 1, 1918.

17. From an editorial on "The Fight for Americanism," in the Des Moines *Capital*, June 4, 1918.

18. Nelson to Bernhard E. Bergesen of Seattle, August 22, 1918, quoted in Chrislock, *Ethnicity Challenged*, 82.

19. English translation in the Des Moines *Register*, June 1, 1918.

20. Gustav Amlund to Nicolay Grevstad, December 22, 1917, quoted in Chrislock, *Ethnicity Challenged*, 75. According to Chrislock, 82, 156 (notes 95, 98), *Decorah-Posten's* criticism of the language order became more pronounced over time.

21. Sioux City *Tribune* staff editorial reprinted in Des Moines *Register*, May 31, 1918.

22. The English language newspapers of five counties where Norwegians were most concentrated (Winnebago, Winneshiek, Worth, Story, and Hamilton) were examined, including all issues of all newspapers between May 23 and November 15, 1918, for which copies exist at either the Iowa City or the Des Moines libraries of the Iowa State Historical Society. The eleven newspapers, listed in alphabetical order, are: Ames *Evening Times* (daily); Decorah *Journal*; Decorah *Public Opinion*; Decorah *Republican*; Forest City *Summit*; Osage *Mitchell County Press*; *Manley Signal and the Kensett News*; Story City *Herald*; Webster City *Freeman*; Northwood *Worth County Index*.

23. Letter to the editor printed in Forest City *Summit*, June 6, 1918.

24. Decorah *Public Opinion*, June 26, 1918; see also its issues of July 3, 17, and 24, 1918.

25. How this education program had worked locally was described in the article, which indicated how wartime propaganda reached Norwegian-American citizens. It read: "As an evidence of how the [federal] government looks at the question, one may take the placards that are posted in public places throughout the country stating in Norwegian and German, as well as in English, 'Why We Are At War.' Coming closer to home, we may take the case of President C. K. Preus, of Luther College, who at the request of the government, made two speeches in the Norwegian language in Allamakee county so that the older Americans of Norwegian birth could readily grasp the fundamental principles of the third Liberty Loan drive. We might also cite the fact that Prof. Oscar L. Olson, also of Luther College, was requested to head an organization in the state of Iowa for the dissemination of information in the Norwegian language among forty thousand citizens of the state regarding the Liberty Loan."

26. Des Moines *Capital* staff editorial, reprinted in Decorah *Journal*, September 18, 1918.

27. Decorah *Journal*, September 18, 1918.

28. Decorah *Journal*, November 13, 1918.

29. Nelson, *The Lutheran Church Among Norwegian-Americans*, 2: 241-253. See also Chrislock, *Ethnicity Challenged*, 25-26.

30. *Lutheran Church Herald*, 2 (1918), 360-361. Those in the Norwegian Lutheran Church of America who favored a more rapid transition found their position expressed in the church's weekly publication, the *Lutheran Church Herald*. Published in the English language, this official organ had been established several years earlier to quicken the steps toward greater English use that were proceeding upward through Sunday School, young people's societies, instruction for confirmation, and finally church services and business meetings. Editors of the *Herald*

persistently repeated the view that "the Norwegian language should be considered merely temporary" in carrying out church work.

31. *Lutheran Church Herald*, 2 (1918), 360–361. See also further editorial comments in the issues of November 26, 1918, 760–761, and December 17, 1918, 801. Seven items appeared in the *Herald* during 1918 regarding governmental measures to bar the use of foreign languages.

32. Discussion of proceedings at the Fargo Convention relies on a report titled "Fargo Convention," in *Lutheran Church Herald*, 2 (1918), 371–372, and a report reprinted from the Fargo *Forum* by the Forest City *Summit*, June 13, 1918. Considerable discussion about changing the name of the church had preceded the Fargo meeting. Ten articles appeared in the *Lutheran Church Herald* between April 19 and August 2, 1918.

33. Fargo *Forum* report reprinted in Forest City *Summit*, June 13, 1918.

34. The 1916 remark by President Preus is quoted in the Swift county (Minnesota) *Review*, March 14, 1916.

35. *Lutheran Church Herald*, 2 (1918), 372.

36. Nelson, *The Lutheran Church*, 249. See also Chrislock, "Name Change and the Church," in *Norwegian-American Studies*, 27 (1977), 194–223. Two years later, with wartime fears gone, sentiment so reversed itself that, by a vote of 377 to 296, the convention rejected any name change.

37. *Lutheran Church Herald*, 2 (1918), 417.

38. Forest City *Summit*, August 8, 1918.

39. Decorah *Journal*, October 9, 1918. See also Decorah *Republican*, October 9, 1918, and Decorah *Public Opinion*, October 9, 1918. As circumstances dictated, Governor Harding seemed to retreat from or vigorously defend his proclamation. Unyielding resistance is visible in a reprint of a Harding letter contained in the Ames *Evening Times*, June 15, 1918. Other examples of explanations that ranged from clarification to near capitulation are as follows: staff editorial entitled "Be Fair With Governor," in Ames *Evening Times*, August 8, 1918, which reprints Harding's letter to a county attorney inquiring about prosecutions relating to violations of the language order; Cedar Rapids *Evening Gazette*, May 29, 30, 1918; Ottumwa *Courier* editorial reprinted in the Des Moines *Register*, June 6, 1918.

40. *Iowa Homestead*, October 24, 1918.

41. Cedar Rapids *Evening Gazette*, October 29, 1918.

42. See, for example, Ames *Evening Times*, October 25, November 4, 1918; Cedar Rapids *Evening Gazette*, October 25, November 5, 1918; Des Moines *Register*, November 3, 1918.

43. The statewide level of voter turnout dropped ten percentage points from the average combined vote of the past three off-year elections (1914, 1910, 1906), while the vote of Norwegian precincts fell only four percentage points from the previous levels.

44. The Republican vote of Norwegian precincts from 1901 to 1916 averaged 79.9 percent and that of Iowa as a whole 52.6 percent. In 1918 Governor Harding's vote held at 50.6 percent while that of Norwegian precincts fell to 37.3 percent.

45. Where Harding's majority over his opponent of two years before had been abnormally large, this year it was abnormally small—slightly less than fourteen thousand votes. This was an uncomfortably narrow margin for a party accustomed to majorities of twenty thousand or more. All agreed that the governor's language proclamation had cost him the most votes. See Des Moines *Register*, November 6, 1918; Cedar Rapids *Evening Gazette*, November 7, 1918; Decorah *Public Opinion*, November 13, 1918; Webster City *Freeman*, November 11, 1918.

46. Similar votes marked Norwegian townships in Winnebago and Worth

counties and dissimilar votes characterized those of Winneshiek and Hamilton counties. In Winnebago county, the Harding vote in five out of seven Norwegian voting units closely clustered about the 30 percent mark while in neighboring Worth county, though showing less precinct uniformity, five out of six Norwegian precincts voted more strongly for Harding than did their counterparts in Winnebago county. The weaker vote for Harding in Winnebago county precincts may be partly due to the agrarian influence of the *Iowa Homestead*. This influential agricultural newspaper had broken with Harding over his indecisive handling of cases where farmers' rights had been violated by would-be patriots. But more importantly, the editor linked Harding to those who wanted to suppress activities of the Nonpartisan League – a movement with which the editor and many Winnebago grain farmers sympathized.

The impact of county or state influences over local forces loses persuasiveness as an explanation where sharp differences among Norwegian precincts arose within the same county, as was the case in Winneshiek and Hamilton counties. Support for Harding tumbled drastically in three Norwegian precincts of Winneshiek county (Madison, 10 percent; Glenwood, 20 percent; Springfield, 24 percent), but the governor suffered far less in two others (Highland, 51 percent; Pleasant, 45 percent). Similarly in Hamilton county, while two southeastern townships gave a majority and near majority for Harding (Lincoln, 54 percent; Ellsworth, 47 percent), adjoining Scott township could muster only 23 percent of its vote for the governor. Quite obviously, for some counties, circumstances *within* Norwegian localities strongly influenced the vote.

47. Two possible explanations initially came to mind. One is that the diverging votes simply reflected, in exaggerated form, long-standing tendencies for some precincts to be weaker in their Republicanism than others. A second possibility was that some precincts proved more sensitive than others to accusations of Norwegian-American disloyalty to the war effort. Testing the first possibility revealed no association between the 1918 gubernatorial vote and the average Republican vote given in the three previous general elections for governor. As for the second idea, that some resented more than others the aspersions being cast on Norwegian-American loyalty, the assumption was that the more militant precincts would also have voted more heavily for Congressman Gilbert N. Haugen. The Norwegian-American congressman's loyalty had been seriously questioned because of his vote against preparedness legislation during the previous session. But a comparison of the votes cast for Governor Harding and Congressman Haugen within the Fourth Congressional District revealed no such associated voting pattern.

48. Decorah *Republican*, November 14, 1918. See also Ames *Evening Times*, October 25, November 4, 1918.

49. Attempts to go one step further and learn whether or not the more "Americanized" church precincts – that is, those with proportionately greater numbers of English language servies – were less offended by the language proclamation produced inconclusive results. Statistics on numbers of English and Norwegian language services were obtained from *Beretning om Den norsk lutherske kirke* (Minneapolis, 1918), 580–586.

50. Most precincts defied analysis because they either contained several Norwegian churches with several pastors or the rate of pastoral turnover was such that specific influence on the part of any one minister could not be presumed.

51. Pastor Thore Olson Tolo served Big Canoe and Highland Norwegian Evangelical Lutheran churches. Pastor Martin Norstad served three churches: (1) Bethesda, in Jewell; (2) Clear Lake and Ellsworth, 8 miles southwest of Jewell,

and (3) Zion, 7 miles northwest of Jewell. Locations of Norwegian churches and their pastors were derived from *Norsk lutherske menigheter i America*, 1:329–331; 2:520; and *Beretning om Den norsk lutherske kirke*, 580–586; Rasmus Malmin, Norlie, and O. A. Tingelstad, trans. and comps., *Who's Who Among Pastors in All the Norwegian Lutheran Synods of America, 1843–1927* (3rd rev. ed., Minneapolis, 1928), 422, 600.

CONCLUSION

1. Nelson to Grevstad, October 21, 1920, quoted in Chrislock, *Ethnicity Challenged*, 116.

2. Fergus Falls *Globe*, March 26, 1904.

3. Bogue, Clubb, and Flanigan, " 'The New Political History," 203.

4. Kleppner, "Immigrant Groups and Partisan Politics," in *Immigration History Newsletter*, 10 (1978), 3; Hays, "Modernizing Values in the History of the United States," in *Peasant Studies*, 6 (1977), 70.

5. The "always-and-everywhere" portrayal of ethnic politics is a feature now also decried by Kleppner in *The Third Electoral System*, 359–360.

6. Even the general Republican thrust of Norwegian-American allegiances was not uniform. In the state of Montana, for example, the Democratic party attracted many Norwegian Americans. See Bergmann, *Americans from Norway*, 109.

7. Samuel P. Huntington, "Paradigms of American Politics: Beyond the One, the Two, and the Many," in *Political Science Quarterly*, 89 (1974), 22–26.

8. Elazar, *The Generational Rhythm of American Politics*.

9. This is consistent with findings that reject the emphasis in "critical elections" theory on key elections as having converted voters from one party to another. See Clubb, Flanigan, and Nancy H. Zingale, *Partisan Realignment: Voters, Parties, and Government in American History* (Beverly Hills, California, 1980); Allan J. Lichtman, "Political Realignment and 'Ethnocultural' Voting in Late Nineteenth Century America," in *Journal of Social History*, 16 (Spring, 1983), 55–56. A similar instance of differing party alignment by a later immigrant generation appears to have occurred with the Dutch when the 1870s Sioux county, Iowa, settlement became Republican in contrast to the Democratic voting pattern of the Pella, Iowa, settlement, which had established itself before the Civil War. See Kleppner, *Third Electoral System*, 167–168.

10. Paul B. Du Chaillu, *Land of the Midnight Sun: Summer and Winter Journeys Through Sweden, Norway, Lapland and Northern Finland*, 1 (New York, 1899), 402, 423.

11. Quoted in Draxten, *Kristofer Janson in America*, 19.

12. Thorstein Veblen, "Farm Labor for the Period of the War," in *The Public* (July 20, 1918), 920–921. See also his discussion of the "Country Town" in *Absentee Ownership and Business Enterprise in Recent Times: The Case of America* (New York, 1923), 142–165.

13. Dykstra, "Town-Country Conflict," 195–204; Stanley B. Parsons, *The Populist Context: Rural Versus Urban Power on a Great Plains Frontier* (Westport, Connecticut, 1973), 35–59.

14. With Norwegian Americans disproportionately marching into agricultural third-party and left-of-center politics, it might be tempting to reconsider the socioeconomic interpretation of American political history. Here the argument would be that socioeconomic concerns superceded ethnocultural predispositions among Norwegian Americans, who then voted their agrarian anti-monopolism, which demanded state intervention on behalf of wresting vulnerable free enter-

prise from the grip of irresponsible monopolies over money and banking, railroads, and land. One might speculate whether Norwegian-American anti-monopolist sympathies stemmed from agrarian Old-World suspicions or, as one writer claims, from a Norwegian folk heritage impelling them toward a cooperative common-wealth, or perhaps from a conspiratorial "devil" theory of history somehow equating the power of economic monopoly with Catholicism. Whatever the reason, the fact that thousands of Norwegian-American farmers found such socioeconomic rhetoric attractive is a telling indication worthy of study.

To some observers of midwestern voting patterns, however, economic factors have been paramount only during brief periods. Jensen, for example, offers a "dual politics" version in his *Winning of the Midwest*, xiii. He reasons that ethnocultural conflicts ordinarily absorbed voters' attention, while economic discontents held sway during times of "economic crisis." A variation of this for the Norwegian-American electorate might be that agrarian radicalism motivated them during hard times and anti-Catholicism motivated them during other times. There is some truth to these propositions, but the contrary can equally be demonstrated by recalling that anti-Catholicism among Norwegian Americans especially asserted itself during the hard times of the 1890s and that economic radicalism especially flourished during the agriculturally prosperous years of World War I. Furthermore, the Republican vote continued to sag in the settlements of northwestern Minnesota for years after the political vehicle of Populism evaporated following the hard times of the nineties.

To go to the opposite extreme, however, and contend that left-of-center Republicanism or radical politics was the "natural level" to which Norwegian Americans aspired would be clearly to overstate the case. One need only recall that orthodox Republicanism apparently prevailed among Iowa's Norwegian settle-ments and that neither Populism nor the Nonpartisan League drew many adher-ents in the settlements of Wisconsin. Moreover, in southeastern Minnesota during Populist and Nonpartisan League times, the average vote of Norwegian settle-ments aligned itself with that of the surrounding region in firmly rejecting candi-dates of these movements.

15. Fergus Falls *Globe*, June 11, 1898.

16. Lindberg, "Pastors, Prohibition and Politics," 23.

17. Kleppner, *The Cross of Culture*, 73.

18. Letter from Swierenga to author, January 22, 1980.

19. Dawley, "E. P. Thompson and the Peculiarities of the Americans," 40.

20. Kleppner, *Third Electoral System*, 360.

21. Morris Rosenberg discusses this "block-booked" characteristic of sociologi-cal variables, which in themselves mean a great many things and cannot be properly understood without taking account of the fact that other variables are as-sociated with them (each acting as an extraneous, component, intervening, antece-dent, suppressing, or distorting influence). See his *The Logic of Survey Analysis* (New York, 1968), 26–27.

22. Thompson, *Making of the English Working Class*, 194; reprint of "The Peculiarities of the English," in his *Poverty of Theory*, 85.

23. Cantor, "Introduction," in *American Workingclass Culture*, 3, 11. See also Richard Oestreicher, "Urban Working-Class Political Behavior and Theories of the American Electoral Politics, 1870–1940," in *Journal of American History*, 74 (March 1988), 1258–1266.

24. Rogin, *The Intellectuals and McCarthy*, 118–119. The class components of cultural divisions are brought out in Green, "Behavioralism and Class Analysis," 96–98.

25. van den Berghe, *The Ethnic Phenomenon*, 242-244.

26. Fergus Falls *Globe*, November 5, 1904.

27. Interview with Harald Boen, Wadena, Minnesota, September 4, 1970; Fergus Falls *Globe*, October 10, 31, 1896.

28. *Skandinaven*, translated in *North* (Minneapolis), September 14, 28, 1892.

29. Rowell, "LaFollette, Shipstead, and the Embattled Farmers," 408.

30. The need to apply "situational analysis" to the social analysis of political history is emphasized in Hays, "New Possibilities for American Political History: The Social Analysis of Political Life," in Lipset and Hofstadter, eds., *Sociology and History: Methods* (New York, 1968), 197-202. See also his "A Systematic Social History," in George Athan Billias and Gerald N. Grob, eds., *American History: Retrospect and Prospect* (New York, 1971), 326-328; and Robert F. Berkhofer, Jr., *A Behavioral Approach to Historical Analysis* (New York, 1969), chapters 2, 3.

Bibliography

MANUSCRIPTS

Des Moines. Iowa State Historical Department, Division of Museum and Archives. Census of the State of Iowa, 1895.

Madison. State Historical Society of Wisconsin. Census of the State of Wisconsin, 1905.

Madison. State Historical Society of Wisconsin. "Cultural-Ethnic Backgrounds in Wisconsin: A Retabulation of Population Schedules from the Wisconsin State Census of 1905." Department of Rural Sociology and Agricultural Economics, University of Wisconsin, 1937–1940.

Madison. State Historical Society of Wisconsin. James O. Davidson papers.

Madison. State Historical Society of Wisconsin. Herman L. Ekern papers.

Madison. State Historical Society of Wisconsin. Robert M. LaFollette papers.

Madison. State Historical Society of Wisconsin. Presidential and Gubernatorial Primary Election Returns.

St. Paul. Minnesota State Historical Society. Agricultural Census of the State of Minnesota, 1922.

St. Paul. Minnesota State Historical Society. Census of the State of Minnesota, 1895.

St. Paul. Minnesota State Historical Society. Census of the State of Minnesota, 1905.

St. Paul. Minnesota State Historical Society. Elmer E. Adams papers.

St. Paul. Minnesota State Historical Society. Charles W. Brandborg and Family papers.

St. Paul. Minnesota State Historical Society. Ignatius Donnelly papers.

St. Paul. Minnesota State Historical Society. James Manahan papers.

St. Paul. Minnesota State Historical Society. Knute Nelson papers.

St. Paul. Minnesota State Historical Society. Presidential Election Returns.

St. Paul. Minnesota State Historical Society. Jacob A. O. Preus papers.

St. Paul. Minnesota State Historical Society. Ole O. Sageng papers.

Washington, D.C. National Archives. Record Group 29. Federal Population Census for Iowa, Minnesota and Wisconsin, 1880.

COUNTY RECORDS

Chippewa County, Minnesota. "Personal Property Tax Lists, 1905." Montevideo, Minnesota.

Clay County, Minnesota. "Personal Property Tax Lists, 1905." Moorhead, Minnesota.

Dunn County, Wisconsin. "Personal Property Tax Rolls, 1905." Menomonie, Wisconsin.

Fillmore County, Minnesota. "Personal Property Tax Lists, 1908, 1915." Preston, Minnesota.

Freeborn County, Minnesota. "Personal Property Tax Lists, 1905." Albert Lea, Minnesota.

Goodhue County, Minnesota. "Personal Property Tax Lists, 1905." Red Wing, Minnesota.

Houston County, Minnesota. "Personal Property Tax Lists, 1905." Caledonia, Minnesota.

Kandiyohi County, Minnesota. "Personal Property Tax Lists, 1905." Willmar, Minnesota.

Norman County, Minnesota. "Personal Property Tax Lists, 1905." Ada, Minnesota.

Otter Tail County, Minnesota. "Personal Property Tax Rolls, 1905." Fergus Falls, Minnesota.

Pierce County, Wisconsin. "Personal Property Tax Rolls, 1900." River Falls, Wisconsin.

Swift County, Minnesota. "Personal Property Tax Lists, 1905." Benson, Minnesota.

Trempealeau County, Wisconsin. "Personal Property Tax Rolls, 1900." La-Crosse, Wisconsin.

Vernon County, Wisconsin. "Personal Property Tax Rolls, 1900." Viroqua, Wisconsin.

FEDERAL AND STATE DOCUMENTS

Iowa Secretary of State. *Census of Iowa.* Des Moines, 1885, 1895, 1905, 1915, 1925.

Iowa Secretary of State. *Iowa Official Register.* Des Moines, 1881–1924.

Minnesota Secretary of State. *Fifth Decennial Census of the State of Minnesota by Major and Minor Civil Divisions.* St. Paul, 1905.

Minnesota Secretary of State. *Fourth Decennial Census of the State of Minnesota by Counties, Towns, Cities and Wards.* St. Paul, 1895.

Minnesota Secretary of State. *Legislative Manual of the State of Minnesota.* St. Paul, 1880–1924.

U.S. Bureau of the Census. *Special Reports: Religious Bodies: 1906, Part I: Summary and General Tables. Washington, 1910.*

——. *Religious Bodies, 1916: Part I: Summary and General Tables.* Washington, 1919.

——. *Religious Bodies: 1926. Volume II: Separate Denominations.* Washington, 1929.

U.S. Census Office. *United States Census, Population.* Washington, 1880, 1890, 1900, 1910, 1920, 1930.

Wisconsin Department of State. *The Blue Book of Wisconsin.* Madison, 1880-1924.

Wisconsin Department of State. *Tabular Statements of the Census Enumerations and the Agricultural, Dairying and Manufacturing Interests of the State of Wisconsin.* Madison, 1906.

NEWSPAPERS

Ada (Minnesota) *Norman County Herald.* 1888, 1890.

Ada (Minnesota) *Puhler's Red River Valley Journal.* 1885.

Ames (Iowa) *Evening Times.* October 17, 1917, May 23–November 13, 1918.

Appleton (Minnesota) *Press.* 1918.

Arcadia (Wisconsin) *Leader.* 1901–1910.

Battle Lake (Minnesota) *Review.* 1890–1892, 1894, 1896.

Blair (Wisconsin) *Press.* 1908.

Cedar Rapids (Iowa) *Evening Gazette.* 1918.

Chicago (Illinois) *Skandinaven.* 1906, 1908.

Decorah (Iowa) *Journal.* October, 1917; May–November, 1918.

Decorah (Iowa) *Public Opinion.* October–November, 1916, 1918; October–November, 1920–1924.

Des Moines (Iowa) *Capital.* May–November, 1918.

Des Moines (Iowa) *Iowa Homestead.* 1918.

Des Moines (Iowa) *Register.* 1917, 1918.

Fergus Falls (Minnesota) *Daily Journal.* 1912.

Fergus Falls (Minnesota) *Free Press.* 1917–1918, 1920, 1922, 1924.

Fergus Falls (Minnesota) *Globe.* 1890–1904.

Fergus Falls (Minnesota) *Independent.* 1881–1883.

Fergus Falls (Minnesota) *Rodhuggeren.* November, 1893–January 1895.

Fergus Falls (Minnesota) *Weekly Journal.* 1883–1904, 1912, 1916–1924.

Forest City (Iowa) *Independent.* September–November, 1917; May–November, 1918.

Forest City (Iowa) *Summit.* October–December, 1917; May–November, 1918.

Galesville (Wisconsin) *Republican.* 1897–1908, 1911–1912.

Independence (Wisconsin) *News-Wave.* 1906, 1908.

LaCrosse (Wisconsin) *Daily Chronicle.* September–November, 1908.

LaCrosse (Wisconsin) *Tribune.* October–November, 1908.

Manley (Iowa) *Signal and the Kensett News.* May–June, September–November, 1918.

Milwaukee (Wisconsin) *Journal*. 1908.

Minneapolis (Minnesota) *Irish Standard*. 1892–1895.

Minneapolis (Minnesota) *Journal*. May–June, 1918.

Minneapolis (Minnesota) *Loyal American and the North*. 1893–1895.

Minneapolis (Minnesota) *Lutheran Church Herald*. April–November, 1918.

Mitchell County (Iowa) *Press*. May–November, 1918.

Montevideo (Minnesota) *American*. 1918.

Northwood (Iowa) *Worth County Index*. September–October, 1917; May–November, 1918.

Norwegian Attitude toward the War and that of other Scandinavian countries discussed by Dr. M. F. Egan before American Academy of Arts and Letters. New York *Times*, February 22, 1918, 6.

Perham (Minnesota) *Bulletin*. 1891–1894.

Preston (Minnesota) *Republican*. 1918.

Rushford (Minnesota) *Star*. 1883–1900.

St. Paul (Minnesota) *Great West*. May–June, 1892.

Storm, O. J. "Public Opinion in Norway During the War." New York *Times*, May 14, 1918, 14.

Story City (Iowa) *Herald*. May–July, October–November, 1918.

Swift County (Minnesota) *Monitor*. 1888–1896.

Swift County (Minnesota) *Review*. 1916–1918, 1920.

Trempealeau (Wisconsin) *Gazette*. 1903–1909.

Trempealeau (Wisconsin) *Herald*. 1895–1913.

Webster City (Iowa) *Freeman*. May–November, 1918.

Willmar (Minnesota) *Tribune*. 1917–1918.

GENERAL WORKS

Alden, Ogle and Company. *Album of Biography: Of the Famous Valley of the Red River of the North and the Park Regions*. Chicago, 1899.

Andersen, Arlow William. *The Immigrant Takes His Stand: The Norwegian Press and Public Affairs, 1847–1872*. Northfield, Minnesota, 1953.

——. *The Norwegian-Americans*. Boston, 1975.

——. "Senator Knute Nelson: Minnesota's Grand Old Man and the Norwegian Immigrant Press," in Odd S. Lovoll, ed., *Makers of an American Immigrant Legacy: Essays in Honor of Kenneth O. Bjork*. Northfield, Minnesota, 1980.

——. *Rough Road to Glory: The Norwegian-American Press Speaks Out on Public Affairs, 1875–1925*. Philadelphia, 1990.

Anderson, Perry. *Arguments Within English Marxism*. London, 1980.

Anderson, Rasmus B. *The Life Story of Rasmus B. Anderson*. 2nd revised ed., Madison, 1917.

Babcock, Kendric Charles. *The Scandinavian Element in the United States*, Vol. 3 of the University of Illinois Studies in the Social Sciences. Urbana, 1914.

Bang, Per. *Norway La Norvege*. New York, 1971.

Benson, Lee. *The Concept of Jacksonian Democracy: New York as a Test Case*. Princeton, 1961.

Bergmann, Leola M. *Americans From Norway*. Philadelphia, 1950.

Berkhofer, Robert F., Jr. *A Behavioral Approach to Historical Analysis.* New York, 1969.

Beyer, Harald. *A History of Norwegian Literature*, trans. and ed. by Einar Haugen. New York, 1956.

Bjanes, O. T. *Norwegian Agriculture.* Oslo, 1926.

Blegen, Theodore C. *Minnesota: A History of the State.* Minneapolis, 1963.

———. *Norwegian Migration to America*, 2 vols. Northfield, Minnesota 1931, 1940.

———. "The Scandinavian Element and Agrarian Discontent" (Abstract of Paper), *Annual Report of the American Historical Association for the Year 1921.* Washington, D.C., 1926.

———. ed. *Land of Their Choice: The Immigrants Write Home.* Minneapolis, 1955.

Bodnar, John. *The Transplanted: A History of Immigrants in Urban America.* Bloomington, Indiana, 1985.

Bogue, Allan G. *From Prairie to Cornbelt.* Chicago, 1963.

Bojer, Johan. *The Emigrants*, trans. by A. G. Jayne. New York, 1925.

Brown, Robert H. and Philip L. Tideman. *Atlas of Minnesota Occupancy.* St. Cloud, Minnesota, 1961.

Brye, David L. *Wisconsin Voting Patterns in the Twentieth Century, 1900 to 1950.* New York, 1979.

Cannon, J. Vennerstrom. *Watershed Drama: Battle Lake, Minnesota.* Berkeley, 1943.

Cantor, Milton. "Introduction," in M. Cantor, ed., *American Workingclass Culture.* Westport, Connecticut, 1979.

Caton, John Dean. *A Summer in Norway . . . .* 2d ed., Chicago, 1880.

Center for Continuation Study. *Democratic Folk Movements in Scandinavia.* Minneapolis, 1951.

Cheney, Charles B. *The Story of Minnesota Politics: Highlights of Half a Century of Political Reporting.* Minneapolis, 1947.

Chrislock, Carl H. *The Progressive Era in Minnesota 1899–1918.* St. Paul, 1971.

———. *Ethnicity Challenged: The Upper Midwest Norwegian-American Experience in World War I.* Northfield, Minnesota, 1981.

Christianson, Theodore. *Minnesota: A History of the State and Its People*, Vol. 2. Chicago, 1935.

Clubb, Jerome M. "Party Coalitions in the Early Twentieth Century," in Seymour Martin Lipset, ed., *Emerging Coalitions in American Politics.* San Francisco, 1978.

———, William H. Flanigan, and Nancy H. Zingale. *Partisan Realignment: Voters, Parties, and Government in American History.* Beverly Hills, California, 1980.

Cohen, Abner. "Introduction: The Lesson of Ethnicity," in A. Cohen, ed., *Urban Ethnicity.* London, 1974.

Cole, Cyrenus. *A History of the People of Iowa.* Cedar Rapids, 1921.

Crichton, A. and H. Wheaton. *Scandinavia*, Vol. 2. New York, 1841.

Curti, Merle. *The Making of an American Community: A Case Study of Democracy in a Frontier County.* Stanford, 1959.

Curtiss-Wedge, Franklyn and Eben Douglas Pierce. *History of Trempealeau County Wisconsin.* Chicago, 1917.

Cyclopaedia of Temperance and Prohibition. New York, 1891.

Derry, Thomas K. *History of Modern Norway.* Oxford, 1973.

Desmond, Humphrey J. *The A. P.A. Movement: A Sketch.* Washington, D.C., 1912.

Destler, Chester McArthur. *American Radicalism 1865–1901.* 1946. Reprint, Chicago, 1966.

Dorfman, Joseph. *Thorstein Veblen and His America.* 1934. Reprint, New York, 1966.

Drake, Michael. *Population and Society in Norway, 1735–1865.* London, 1969.

Draxten, Nina. *Kristofer Janson in America.* Boston, 1976.

Du Chaillu, Paul B. *The Land of the Midnight Sun: Summer and Winter Journeys through Sweden, Norway, Lapland and Northern Finland,* Vol. 1. New York, 1899.

Dykstra, Robert R. "Stratification and Community Political Systems: Historian's Models," in Allan G. Bogue, ed. *Emerging Theoretical Models in Social and Political History.* Beverly Hills, California, 1973.

Dykstra, Robert R., and David R. Reynolds "In Search of Wisconsin Progressivism, 1904–1952: A Test of the Rogin Scenario," in J. H. Silbey, A. O. Bogue, and W. H. Flanigan, eds. *The History of American Electoral Behavior.* Princeton, 1978.

Eckstein, Harry. *Division and Cohesion in Democracy: A Study of Norway.* Princeton, 1966.

Elazar, Daniel J. *American Federalism: A View from the States.* New York, 1966.

———. *Cities of the Prairie: The Metropolitan Frontier and American Politics.* New York, 1970.

———. *The Generational Rhythm of American Politics.* Philadelphia, 1976.

Epstein, Leon D. *Politics in Wisconsin.* Madison, 1958.

Falnes, Oscar J. *National Romanticism in Norway.* New York, 1933.

Fenton, John H. *Midwest Politics.* New York, 1966.

Flom, George T. *A History of Norwegian Immigration to the United States.* Iowa City, 1909.

Folwell, William Watts. *A History of Minnesota,* Vol. 3. St. Paul, 1926.

Foner, Eric. *Free Soil, Free Labor, Free Men: The Ideology of the Republican Party Before the Civil War.* New York, 1970.

Galenson, Walter. "Scandinavia," in Walter Galenson, ed., *Comparative Labor Movements.* New York, 1952.

Garborg, Arne. *Peace,* translated by Phillips Dean Carleton. New York, 1929.

Gastil, Raymond D. *Cultural Regions of the United States.* Seattle, 1975.

Gienapp, William E. *The Origins of the Republican Party, 1852–1856.* New York, 1987.

———. "The Republican Party and the Slave Powers," in Robert H. Abzug and

Stephen E. Maizlish, eds., *New Perspectives on Race and Slavery in America*. Lexington, Kentucky, 1986.

Gjerde, Jon. *From Peasants to Farmers: The Migration from Balestrand, Norway, to the Upper Middle West*. Cambridge, 1985.

Gjerset, Knut. *History of the Norwegian People*. New York, 1915.

Gutman, Herbert. "Work, Culture, and Society in Industrializing America," in M. Cantor, ed., *American Workingclass Culture*. Westport, Connecticut, 1979.

Hale, Frederick, ed. *Their Own Saga: Letters from the Norwegian Global Migration*. Minneapolis, 1986.

Handlin, Oscar. *The Uprooted: The Epic Story of the Great Migrations that Made the American People*. New York, 1951.

Hansen, Marcus Lee. *The Immigrant in American History*. Cambridge, 1941.

Hart, John Fraser. *The Look of the Land*. Foundations of Cultural Geography Series. Englewood Cliffs, New Jersey, 1975.

Hartman, W. A., and J. D. Black. "Economic Aspects of Land Settlement in the Cut-Over Region of the Great Lakes States." *United States Department of Agriculture Circular No. 160*, Washington, D.C., 1931.

Haugen, Einar. *The Norwegian Language in America: A Study of Bilingual Behavior*, 2 vols. 2nd ed., Bloomington, 1969.

Haugen, Eva Lund and Einar, eds. and trans. *Land of the Free: Bjørnstjerne Bjørnson's America Letters, 1880–1881*. Northfield, Minnesota, 1978.

Haugen, Nils P. *Pioneer and Political Reminiscences*, Joseph Schafer, ed. Madison, 1929.

Hays, Samuel P. "New Possibilities for American Political History: The Social Analysis of Political Life," in Seymour Martin Lipset and Richard Hofstadter, eds., *Sociology and History: Methods*. New York, 1968.

———. "Political Parties and the Community-Society Continuum," in William Nisbet Chambers and Walter Dean Burnham, eds., *The American Party Systems*. New York, 1967.

———. "Politics and Society: Beyond the Political Party," in *The Evolution of American Electoral Systems*. Westport, Connecticut, 1981.

———. *The Response to Industrialism: 1885–1914*. Chicago, 1957.

———. "A Systematic Social History," in George Athan Billias and Gerald N. Grob, *American History: Retrospect and Prospect*. New York, 1971.

Haystead, Ladd, and Gilbert C. Fite. *The Agricultural Regions of the United States*. Norman, Oklahoma, 1955.

Heaton, John L. *Cobb of 'The World'*. New York, 1924.

Heber, Mrs. Reginald. *The Life of Reginald Heber, D.D. . . . together with A Journal of His Tour in Norway, Sweden, Russia, Hungary and Germany . . .* , Vol. 1. London, 1830.

Hicks, John D. *The Populist Revolt: A History of the Farmers' Alliance and the People's Party*. 1931. Reprint, Lincoln, Nebraska 1961.

Higham, John. *Strangers in the Land: Patterns of American Nativism 1860–1925*. New York, 1963.

Hilton, O. A. "The Minnesota Commission of Public Safety in World War I, 1917–1919," *Bulletin of the Oklahoma Agricultural and Mechanical College*, Social Science Series No. 1. Stillwater, 1951.

Hofstadter, Richard. *The Age of Reform: From Bryan to F.D.R.* New York, 1955.

Holt, Michael F. *Forging a Majority: The Formation of the Republican Party in Pittsburgh, 1848-1860.* New Haven, 1969.

Hovde, Brynjolf J. "Norwegian-Americans" in Francis J. Brown and Joseph Slabey Rousek, eds., *Our Racial and National Minorities.* New York, 1939.

——. *The Scandinavian Countries, 1720-1865: The Rise of the Middle Classes,* 2 vols. Boston, 1943.

Hurack, H. C., ed. *Proceedings of the Twenty-Fourth Annual Session of the Iowa State Bar Association Held at Des Moines, Iowa, June 27 and 28, 1918.* Iowa City, Iowa, 1918.

Jensen, Richard. *The Winning of the Midwest: Social and Political Conflict 1888-1896.* Chicago, 1971.

Jenson, Carol E. *Agrarian Pioneer in Civil Liberties: The Nonpartisan League in Minnesota during World War I.* New York, 1986.

Jorgenson, Theodore, and Nora O. Solum. *Ole Edvart Rolvaag: A Biography.* New York, 1939.

Jungman, Nico. *Norway.* London, 1905.

Kamphoefner, Walter D. *The Westfalians: From Germany to Missouri.* Princeton, 1987.

Kaye, Harvey J., and Keith McClelland, eds. *E. P. Thompson: Critical Perspectives.* Philadelphia, 1990.

Keyes, Charles F., ed. *Ethnic Change.* Seattle, 1981.

Kinzer, Donald L. *An Episode in Anti-Catholicism: The American Protective Association.* Seattle, 1964.

Kleppner, Paul. *The Cross of Culture: A Social Analysis of Midwestern Politics, 1850-1900.* New York, 1970.

——. "From Ethnoreligious Conflict to 'Social Harmony': Coalitional and Party Transformations in the 1890s," in Seymour Martin Lipset, ed., *Emerging Coalitions in American Politics.* San Francisco, 1978.

——. "Partisanship and Ethnoreligious Conflict: The Third Electoral System, 1853-1892," in *The Evolution of American Electoral Systems.* Westport, Connecticut, 1981.

——. *The Third Electoral System, 1853-1892: Parties, Voters, and Political Cultures.* Chapel Hill, 1979.

Knaplund, Paul. *Moorings Old and New: Entries in an Immigrant's Log.* Madison, 1963.

Koht, Halvdan, and Sigmund Skard. *The Voice of Norway.* New York, 1944.

LaFollette, Robert M. *LaFollette's Autobiography: A Personal Narrative of Political Experience.* 1913. Reprint, Madison, 1960.

Laing, Samuel. *Journal of a Residence in Norway During the Years 1834, 1835, and 1836.* London, 1837.

Larsen, Karen. *A History of Norway.* New York, 1948.

Larson, Henrietta. *The Wheat Market and the Farmer in Minnesota, 1858-1900,* Vol. 122 of Columbia University Studies in History, Economics, and Public Law. New York, 1926.

Larson, Laurence M. *The Changing West and Other Essays.* Northfield, Minnesota, 1937.

———. *The Log Book of a Young Immigrant.* Northfield, Minnesota, 1939.

Latournette, Kenneth. *Christianity in a Revolutionary Age*, Vol. 2. New York, 1958.

Lawson, Victor E., and Martin E. Lew. *Illustrated History and Descriptive and Biographical Review of Kandiyohi County, Minnesota.* St. Paul, 1905.

Leiren, Terje I. *Marcus Thrane: A Norwegian Radical in America.* Northfield, Minnesota, 1987.

Leuchtenburg, William E. *The Perils of Prosperity, 1914–1932.* Chicago, 1958.

Lewis Publishing Company. *Biographical History of LaCrosse, Trempealeau and Buffalo Counties, Wisconsin.* Chicago, 1892.

The Life of Reginald Heber, D. D., Lord Bishop of Calcutta, By His Widow, With Selections From His Correspondence, Unpublished Poems, and Private Papers; Together with a Journal of His Tour in Norway, Sweden, Russia, Hungary, and Germany, and A History of the Cossaks, Vol. 1. London, 1830.

Lipset, S. M., P. F. Lazarsfeld, A. H. Barton, and J. Linz. "The Psychology of Voting: An Analysis of Political Behavior" in Gardner Lindzey, ed., *Handbook of Social Psychology*, Vol. 2. Reading, Massachusetts, 1954.

Lipset, Seymour Martin. *Political Man: The Social Bases of Politics.* 1960. Reprint, New York, 1963.

———. "Religion and Politics in the American Past and Present," in Robert Lee and Martin E. Marty, ed., *Religion and Social Conflict.* New York, 1964.

Lovoll, Odd Sverre. *A Folk Epic: The* Bygdelag *in America.* Boston, 1975.

Luebke, Frederick C. *Immigrants and Politics: The Germans of Nebraska, 1880–1900.* Lincoln, 1969.

McDonald, Grace. *History of the Irish in Wisconsin in the Nineteenth Century.* New York, 1976.

Malmin, Rasmus, O. M. Norlie, and O. A. Tingelstad, trans. and comps. *Who's Who Among Pastors in All the Norwegian Lutheran Synods of America, 1843–1927*, 3rd ed. rev. of *Norsk Lutherske Prester i Amerika.* Minneapolis, 1928.

Margulies, Herbert F. *The Decline of the Progressive Movement in Wisconsin, 1890–1920.* Madison, 1968.

Mason, John W., ed. *History of Otter Tail County, Minnesota*, 2 vols. Indianapolis, 1916.

Maxwell, Robert S. *LaFollette and the Rise of the Progressives in Wisconsin.* Madison, 1956.

Merrill, Horace S, *The Bourbon Democracy of the Upper Middle West, 1865–1898.* 1953. Reprint, Seattle, 1967.

Mitau, G. Theodore. *Politics in Minnesota.* 2d rev. ed., Minneapolis, 1970.

Morlan, Robert L. *Political Prairie Fire: The Nonpartisan League, 1915–1922.* Minneapolis, 1955.

Munch, Peter A. "Social Class and Acculturation," in *The Strange American Way: Letters of Caja Munch from Wiota, Wisconsin, 1855–1859, with An American Adventure (excerpts from "Vita Mea," with an autobiography written in 1903)*, trans. by Helene Munch and Peter A. Munch. Carbondale, Illinois, 1970.

———. *A Study of Cultural Change: Rural-Urban Conflicts in Norway.* Oslo, 1956.

———. "Pastor Munch of Wiota, 1827–1908," in Odd S. Lovoll, ed., *Makers of An*

American Immigrant Legacy: Essays in Honor of Kenneth O. Bjork. Northfield, Minnesota 1980.

Nelson, E. Clifford, and Eugene L. Fevold. *The Lutheran Church Among Norwegian-Americans,* 2 vols. Minneapolis, 1960.

Nelson, Olof N. *History of the Scandinavians and Successful Scandinavians in the United States.* Minneapolis, 1901.

Nesbit, Robert C. *Wisconsin: A History.* Madison, 1973.

Nichol, Todd W., ed. and trans. *Vivacious Daughter: Seven Lectures on the Religious Situation Among Norwegians in America.* Northfield, Minnesota, 1990.

Nordic Emigration: Research Conference in Uppsala, September, 1969. Uppsala, Sweden, 1970.

Nordskog, John Eric. *Social Reform in Norway: A Study of Nationalism and Social Democracy,* No. 9 of University of Southern California School of Research Studies. Los Angeles, 1935.

Norlie, Olaf M. *History of the Norwegian People in America.* Minneapolis, 1925.

——. *Norsk lutherske menigheter i America, 1843–1916,* 2 vols. Minneapolis, 1918.

Norway: Official Publication for the Paris Exhibition, 1900. Kristiania, 1900.

Norwegian Lutheran Church of America. *Beretning om den Norske Lutherske Kirkes . . . , 1917.* Minneapolis, 1918.

——. *Beretning om den Norske Lutherske Kirke i Amerika 1923.* Minneapolis, 1923.

Parsons, Stanley B. *The Populist Context: Rural Versus Urban Power on a Great Plains Frontier.* Westport, Connecticut, 1973.

Pollack, Norman. *The Populist Response to Industrial America.* Cambridge, Massachusets, 1962.

Popperwell, Ronald G. *Norway.* New York, 1972.

Preus, J. C. K., ed. *Norsemen Found a Church: An Old Heritage in a New Land.* Minneapolis, 1953.

Qualey, Carlton C. *Norwegian Settlement in the United States.* Northfield, Minnesota, 1938.

Raney, William F. *Wisconsin, A Story of Progress.* New York, 1940.

Reigstad, Paul. *Rolvaag: His Life and Art.* Lincoln, Nebraska, 1972.

Rice, John G. *Patterns of Ethnicity in a Minnesota County, 1880–1905.* Umeå University Geographical Reports Number 4. Umeå, Sweden, 1973.

Robinson, Edward Van Dyke. *Early Economic Conditions and the Development of Agriculture in Minnesota.* Minneapolis, 1915.

Rogin, Michael Paul. *The Intellectuals and McCarthy: The Radical Specter.* Cambridge, Massachusetts, 1967.

Rokkan, Stein. "Geography, Religion and Social Class: Cross Cutting Cleavages in Norwegian Politics," in S. M. Lipset and S. Rokkan, eds., *Party Systems and Voter Alignments.* New York, 1967.

——, and Henry Valen. "Regional Contrasts in Norwegian Politics: A Review of Data from Official Statistics and from Sample Surveys," in E. Allardt and S. Rokkan, eds., *Mass Politics: Studies in Political Sociology.* New York, 1970.

Rølvaag, O. E. *Giants in the Earth*, trans. by Lincoln Colcord and O. E. Rølvaag. New York, 1929.

——. *Peder Victorious*, trans. by Nora Solum and O. E. Rølvaag. New York, 1929.

——. *Pure Gold*, trans. by Sivert Erdahl and O. E. Rølvaag. New York, 1931.

——. *Their Fathers' God*, trans. by Trygve M. Ager. New York, 1931.

Rosenberg, Morris. *The Logic of Survey Analysis*. New York, 1968.

Sage, Leland L. *A History of Iowa*. Ames, 1974.

Saloutos, Theodore, and John D. Hicks, *Agricultural Discontent in the Middle West, 1909–1939*. Madison, 1951.

Semmingsen, Ingrid. *Norway to America: A History of the Migration*, trans. by Einar Haugen. Minneapolis, 1978.

Shannon, Fred. *The Farmers' Last Frontier: Agriculture 1860–1897*. 1945. Reprint, New York, 1968.

Silbey, Joel H., and Samuel T. McSeveney, eds. *Voters, Parties and Elections: Quantitative Essays in the History of American Popular Voting Behavior*. Lexington, Massachusetts, 1972.

Skårdal, Dorothy Burton. *The Divided Heart: Scandinavian Immigrant Experience through Literary Sources*. Lincoln, Nebraska, 1974.

Storing, James A. *Norwegian Democracy*. Boston, 1963.

Sundby-Hanson, Harry, ed. *Norwegian Immigrant Contributions to America's Making*. New York, 1921.

Swansen, H. Fred. *The Founder of St. Ansgar: The Life Story of Claus Laurits Clausen*. Blair, Nebraska, 1949.

Tavuchis, Nicholas. *Pastors and Immigrants: The Role of a Religious Elite in the Absorption of Norwegian Immigrants*. The Hague, 1963.

Taylor, Bayard. *Northern Travel: Summer and Winter Pictures, Sweden, Denmark and Lapland*. Rev. ed., New York, 1881.

Thistlethwaite, Frank. "Migration from Europe Overseas in the Nineteenth and Twentieth Centuries," in *Xle Congres International des Sciences Historiques, Stockholm 1960, Rapports, V: Histoire Contemporaine*. Gothenburg, 1960.

Thompson, Edward P. *Making of the English Working Class*. New York, 1952.

——. *Poverty of Theory & Other Essays*. London, 1978.

Ulvestad, Martin. *Norge i Amerika*. Minneapolis, 1901.

United States Brewers' Association. *The Year Book with Proceedings of the Fifty-Third Annual Convention Held in Atlantic City, N.J.* New York, 1914.

Valen, Henry, and Daniel Katz. *Political Parties in Norway: A Community Study*. Oslo, 1967.

van den Berghe, Pierre L. *The Ethnic Phenomenon*. New York, 1981.

Veblen, Thorstein. *Absentee Ownership and Business Enterprise in Recent Times: The Case of America*. New York, 1923.

Weaver, John C. *American Barley Production: A Study in Agricultural Geography*. Minneapolis, 1950.

Wefald, Jon. *A Voice of Protest: Norwegians in American Politics, 1890–1917*. Northfield, Minnesota, 1971.

Weiner, Richard R. *Cultural Marxism and Political Sociology.* Beverly Hills, 1981.

Wentz, Abdel Ross. *The Lutheran Church in American History.* Philadelphia, 1923.

Whitney, Nathaniel R. "The First Three Liberty Loans in Iowa," in Benjamin F. Shambaugh, ed., *Iowa and War,* No. 15. Iowa City, 1918.

——. *The Sale of War Bonds in Iowa. Chronicles of the World War,* ed. by Benjamin F. Shambaugh. Iowa City, 1923.

Woolley, John G., and William E. Johnson. *Temperance Progress in the Century.* London, 1903.

Youngdale, James M., ed. *Third Party Footprints: An Anthology from Writings and Speeches of Midwest Radicals.* Minneapolis, 1966.

Zempel, Solveig, ed. and trans. *In Their Own Words: Letters from Norwegian Immigrants.* Minneapolis, 1991.

ARTICLES

Acrea, Kenneth. "The Wisconsin Reform Coalition: LaFollette's Rise to Power." *Wisconsin Magazine of History,* 52 (Winter 1968-1969), 132-157.

Ander, Fritiof. "The Swedish-American Press and the American Protective Association." *Church History,* 6 (1937), 165-179.

Babcock, Kendrick C. "The Scandinavian Contingent." *Atlantic Monthly,* 77 (1896), 660-670.

——. "The Scandinavians in the Northwest." *Forum,* 14 (1892), 103-109.

Baker, Oliver E. "Agricultural Regions of North America." *Economic Geography,* 3 (1927), 447-465; 4 (1928), 44-73, 399-433.

Bergmann, Leola N. "Norwegians in Iowa." *Palimpsest,* 40 (1959), 289-368.

Bocock, John P. "The Irish Conquest of our Cities." *Forum,* 17 (1894), 186-195.

Bogue, Allan G. "United States: The 'New' Political History." *Journal of Contemporary History,* 3 (1968), 5-27.

——, Jerome M. Clubb, and William H. Flanigan. "The New Political History." *American Behavioral Scientist,* 21 (1977), 201-220.

Boyesen, Hjalmar H. "The Scandinavian in the United States." *North American Review,* 155 (1892), 526-535.

Brye, David L. "Wisconsin Scandinavians and Progressivism, 1900-1950." *Norwegian-American Studies,* 27 (1977), 163-193.

Burnham, Walter Dean. "The Changing Shape of the American Political Universe." *American Political Science Review,* 59 (1965), 7-28.

——. "Quantitative History: Beyond the Correlation Coefficient, A Review Essay." *Historical Methods Newsletter,* 6 (1972), 17-26.

Campbell, Ballard C. "Did Democracy Work? Prohibition in Late Nineteenth-Century Iowa: A Test Case." *Journal of Interdisciplinary History,* 8 (1977), 87-116.

Carlsson, Sten. "Scandinavian Politicians in Minnesota Around the Turn of the Century." *Americana Norvegica,* 3 (1971), 237-271.

Chrislock, Carl H. "The Alliance Party and the Minnesota Legislature of 1891." *Minnesota History,* 35 (1957), 297-312.

——. "A Cycle in the History of Minnesota Republicanism." *Minnesota History*, 39 (1964), 93–110.

——. "Name Change and the Church, 1918–1920." *Norwegian-American Studies*, 27 (1977), 194–223.

Clark, Dan Elbert. "History of Liquor Legislation in Iowa." *Iowa Journal of History and Politics*, 6 (1908), 55–87, 339–374, 503–608.

Converse, Philip E. "Of Time and Partisan Stability." *Comparative Political Studies*, 2 (1969), 139–144.

Coutts, W. A. "Agricultural Depression in the United States." *Publications of the Michigan Political Science Association*, 2 (1896–1897), 1–65.

Creel, George. "Our Aliens–Were They Loyal or Disloyal?" *Everybody's Magazine*, 40 (1919), 3.

Dawley, Alan. "E. P. Thompson and the Peculiarities of the Americans." *Radical History Review*, 19 (Winter 1978–1979), 33–59.

Derr, Nancy. "The Babel Proclamation." *The Palimpsest*, 60 (July/August 1979), 98–115.

Dieserud, Juul. "Norwegians in the Public and Political Life of the United States." *Scandinavia*, 1 (1924), 49–58.

Dykstra, Robert R. "Town-Country Conflict: A Hidden Dimension in American Social History." *Agricultural History*, 38 (1964), 195–204.

Emerick, C. F. "An Analysis of Agricultural Discontent in the United States." *Political Science Quarterly*, 11 (1896), 439.

Engesæter, Aage. "Poverty, Overpopulation, and the Early Emigration from Sogn." *Norwegian-American Studies*, 32 (1989), 31–51.

Farmer, Halle. "The Economic Background of Frontier Populism." *Mississippi Valley Historical Review*, 11 (1925), 469–489.

Fevold, Eugene L. "Norwegian Immigrant and His Church." *Norwegian-American Studies*, 23 (1967), 3–16.

Gedicks, Al. "The Social Origins of Radicalism Among Finnish Immigrants in Midwest Mining Communities," *Review of Radical Political Economics*, 8 (1976), 1–31.

Gjerde, Jon. "Conflict and Community: A Case Study of the Immigrant Church in the United States." *Journal of Social History*, 19 (Summer 1986), 681–697.

Green, James R. "Behavioralism and Class Analysis: A Review Essay on Methodology and Ideology." *Labor History*, 13 (1972), 89–106.

Guterman, Stanley S. "The Americanization of Norwegian Immigrants: A Study in Historical Sociology." *Sociology and Social Research*, 52 (1968), 252–270.

Hale, Frederick. "Anticlericalism and Norwegian Society Before the Breakthrough of Modernity." *Scandinavian Studies*, 52 (1980), 245–263.

——. "An Embattled Church." *Scandinavian Review*. 69 (March 1981), 52–60.

——. "Transatlantic Norwegian Religion and Ethnicity." *Fides et Historia*, 17 (Fall-Winter 1984), 6–24.

Hansen, Jean Skogerboe. "*Skandinaven* and the John Anderson Publishing Company." *Norwegian-American Studies*, 28 (1979), 35–68.

Hays, Samuel P. "History as Human Behavior." *Iowa Journal of History*, 58 (1960), 193–206.

———."Modernizing Values in the History of the United States." *Peasant Studies*, 6 (1977), 68–79.

———. "The Social Analysis of American Political History, 1880–1920." *Political Science Quarterly*, 80 (1965), 373–394.

Hjellum, Torstein. "The Politicization of Local Government: Rates of Change, Conditioning Factors, Effects on Political Culture." *Scandinavian Political Studies*, 2 (1967), 69–93.

Hicks, John D. "The Origin and Early History of the Farmers' Alliance in Minnesota." *Mississippi Valley Historical Review*, 9 (1922), 203–222.

———. "The People's Party in Minnesota." *Minnesota History Bulletin*, 5 (1924), 531–560.

Huntington, Samuel P. "Paradigms of American Politics: Beyond the One, the Two, and the Many." *Political Science Quarterly*, 89 (1974), 1–26.

Hvamstad, Per, comp. "The Letters of Mons H. Grinager: Pioneer and Soldier" translated by C. A. Clausen. *Norwegian-American Studies*, 24 (1970), 29–77.

Janson, Kristopher. "Norsemen in the United States." *Cosmopolitan*, 9 (1890), 678–686.

Jenson, Carol E. "Loyalty As a Political Weapon: The 1918 Campaign in Minnesota." *Minnesota History*, 43 (Summer 1962), 43–57.

Johnson, C. R. "Minnesota and the Nonpartisan League." *New Republic*, 20 (1919), 290–293.

Kleppner, Paul. "Immigrant Groups and Partisan Politics." *Immigration History Newsletter*, 10 (1978), 1–5.

Lamb, Charles R. "The Nonpartisan League and its Expansion into Minnesota." *North Dakota Quarterly*, 49 (Summer 1981), 108–143.

Larson, Agnes M. "The Editorial Policy of *Skandinaven*, 1900–1903." *Norwegian-American Studies and Records*, 8 (1934), 112–135.

Legreid, Ann M., and David Ward. "Religious Schism and the Development of Rural Immigrant Communities: Norwegian Lutherans in Western Wisconsin, 1880–1905." *Upper Midwest History*, 2 (1982), 13–29.

Lichtman, Allan J. "Political Realignment and 'Ethnocultural' Voting in Late Nineteenth Century America." *Journal of Social History*, 16 (Spring, 1983), 55–82.

Lindberg, Duane R. "Norwegian-American Pastors in Immigrant Fiction, 1870–1920." *Norwegian-American Studies*, 28 (1979), 290–308.

———. "Pastors, Prohibition and Politics: The Role of Norwegian Clergy in the North Dakota Abstinence Movement, 1880–1920." *North Dakota Quarterly*, 49 (Autumn, 1981), 21–38.

Lowell, Lindsay B. "Sociological Theories and the Great Emigration." *Norwegian-American Studies*, 32 (1989), 53–69.

Luebke, Frederick C. "Main Street and the Countryside: Patterns of Voting in Nebraska During the Populist Era." *Nebraska History*, 50 (1969), 257–275.

McCormick, Richard L. "Ethno-Cultural Interpretations of Nineteenth-Century American Voting Behavior." *Political Science Quarterly*, 89 (1974), 351–377.

McSeveney, Samuel T. "Ethnic Groups, Ethnic Conflicts, and Recent Quantitative Research in American Political History." *International Migration Review*, 7 (1973), 14–33.

Margulies, Herbert F. "Anti-Catholicism in Wisconsin Politics, 1914–1920." *Mid-America*, 44 (1962), 51–56.

——. "Political Weaknesses in Wisconsin Progressivism, 1905–1909." *Mid-America*, 41 (1959).

Morlan, Robert L. "The Nonpartisan League and the Minnesota Campaign of 1918." *Minnesota History*, 34 (1955), 221–232.

Munch, Peter A. "Authority and Freedom: Controversy in Norwegian-American Congregations." *Norwegian-American Studies*, 28 (1979), 3–34.

——. "Segregation and Assimilation of Norwegian Settlements in Wisconsin." *Norwegian-American Studies and Records*, 18 (1954), 102–140.

——. "Social Adjustment Among Wisconsin Norwegians." *American Sociological Review*, 14 (1949), 780–787.

——. and Robert B. Campbell. "Interaction and Collective Identification in a Rural Locality." *Rural Sociology*, 28 (March 1963), 18–34.

Nelson, Knute. "The Unelected President." *The Norseman* (no. 1, 1971), 14–17.

Nicholas, E. H. "Mr. Creel and the Nonpartisan League." *Weekly Review*, 1 (1919), 101.

Nixon, Herman C. "Economic Basis of the Populist Movement in Iowa." *Iowa Journal of History and Politics*, 21 (1923), 373–396.

——. "The Populist Movement in Iowa." *Iowa Journal of History and Politics*, 24 (1926), 3–107.

Oestreicher, Richard. "Urban Working-Class Political Behavior and Theories of American Electoral Politics, 1870–1940." *Journal of American History*, 74 (March 1988), 1257–1286.

O'Hara, Frank. "The Grievance of the Spring Wheat Growers." *Catholic World*, 66 (1917), 380–387.

Osterud, Oyvind. "The Transformation of Scandinavian Agrarianism: A Comparative Study of Political Change Around 1870." *Scandinavian Journal of History*, 1 (1976), 201–213.

Peterson, Peter L. "Language and Loyalty: Governor Harding and Iowa's Danish-Americans During World War I." *Annals of Iowa*, 42 (Fall 1974), 411–415.

Pomper, Gerald M. "From Confusion to Clarity: Issues and American Voters, 1956–1968." *American Political Science Review*, 66 (1972), 415–428.

Repass, David E. "Issue Salience and Party Choice." *American Political Science Review*, 66 (1972), 415–428.

Rowell, Chester H. "LaFollette, Shipstead, and the Embattled Farmers." *The World's Work*, 46 (August 1923), 408–420.

——. "The Political Cyclone in North Dakota." *The World's Work*, 46 (July 1923), 265–274.

Ryder, Norman B. "The Cohort as a Concept in the Study of Social Change." *American Sociological Review*, 30 (1965), 843–861.

Saloutos, Theodore. "The Agricultural Problem and Nineteenth-Century Industrialism." *Agricultural History*, 23 (1948), 156–174.

Sandaker, Arvid. "Emigration from Land Parish to America, 1866–1875," trans. and ed. by C. A. Clausen. *Norwegian-American Studies*, 26 (1974), 49–74.

Saul, John S. "The Dialectic of Class and Tribe." *Race & Class*, 20 (Spring, 1979), 347–372.

"The Scandinavians and the Presidential Nominations." *Scandinavia*, 1 (1884), 277–278.

"The Scandinavians in the Late American Elections." *Scandinavia*, 1 (1883), 26–26.

Semmingsen, Ingrid. "The Dissolution of Estate Society in Norway." *Scandinavian Economic History Review*, 2 (1954), 166–203.

——. "Emigration from Scandinavia." *Scandinavian Economic History Review*, 20 (1972), 45–60.

——. "Norwegian Emigration in the Nineteenth Century." *Scandinavian Economic History Review*, (1960), 150–160.

Smemo, Kenneth. "The Immigrant as Reformer: The Case of the Norwegian-American." Paper read at Sixty-Sixth Annual Meeting of the Organization of American Historians, April 13, 1973, at Chicago, Illinois. Mimeographed.

Smith, Guy-Harold. "Notes on the Distribution of the Foreign-born Scandinavian in Wisconsin in 1905." *Wisconsin Magazine of History*, 14 (1930), 419–436.

——. "The Population of Wisconsin." *Geographical Review*, 18 (1928).

Spitzer, Alan B. "The Historical Problems of Generations." *American Historical Review*, 78 (1973), 1353–1385.

Stinchcombe, Arthur. "Agricultural Enterprise and Rural Class Relations." *American Journal of Sociology*, 67 (1961), 165–176.

Sunde, Rasmus. "Emigration from the District of Sogn, 1839–1915." *Norwegian-American Studies*, 29 (1983), 111–126.

Svalestuen, Andres A. "Emigration from the Community of Tinn, 1837–1907: Demographic, Economic, and Social Backgrounds," translated by C. A. Clausen. *Norwegian-American Studies*, 29 (1983), 43–88.

Swierenga, Robert P. "Ethnocultural Political Analysis: a New Approach to American Ethnic Studies." *Journal of American Studies*, 5 (1971), 59–79.

Taylor, G. "Enforcing English by Proclamation." *Survey*, 40 (1918), 394–395.

Tønnesson, Kåre. "Popular Protest and Organization: The Thrane Movement in Pre-industrial Norway, 1849–55." *Scandinavian Journal of History*, 13 (1989), 121–139.

Veblen, Thorstein. "Farm Labor for the Period of the War." *The Public* (July 20, 1918), 918–922.

Vecoli, Rudolph. "Contadini in Chicago: A Critique of *The Uprooted*." *Journal of American History*, 51 (1964), 404–417.

Vincent, John Martin, and Milton Offutt. "Norway's Decisive Vote to Repeal Prohibition." *Current History*, 25 (1926), 422–423.

Warner, Donald F. "Prelude to Populism." *Minnesota History*, 32 (1951), 129–146.

Weaver, John C. "Changing Patterns of Cropland Use in the Middle West." *Economic Geography*, 30 (1954), 1–18.

Weibull, Jörgen. "The Wisconsin Progressives 1900–1914." *Mid-America*, 47 (1965), 191–221.

Wilcox, Benton H. "An Historical Definition of Northwestern Radicalism." *Mississippi Valley Historical Review*, 26 (1939), 377–394.

Workman, J. Brooke. "Governor William Larrabee and Railroad Reform." *Iowa Journal of History*, 57 (1959), 231–266.

Wright, James E. "The Ethnocultural Model of Voting." *American Behavioral Scientist*, 16 (1973), 653–674.

Wyman, Roger E. "Agrarian Working Class Radicalism? The Electoral Basis of Populism in Wisconsin." *Political Science Quarterly*, 89 (1975), 825–847.

——. "Wisconsin Ethnic Groups and the Election of 1890." *Wisconsin Magazine of History*, 51 (1968), 269–293.

Zeitlin, Maurice. "Political Generations in the Cuban Working Class." *American Journal of Sociology*, 71 (1966), 493–508.

THESES AND DISSERTATIONS

Belgum, Gerhard Lee. "The Old Norwegian Synod in America 1853–1890." Ph.D. dissertation, Yale University, 1957.

Brandes, Stuart Dean. "Nils P. Haugen and the Wisconsin Progressive Movement." Master's thesis, University of Wisconsin, 1965.

Chrislock, Carl H. "The Politics of Protest in Minnesota, 1890–1901, From Populism to Progressivism." Ph.D. dissertation, University of Minnesota, 1954.

Dyste, Arvid Gerald. "Causes of Religious Conflicts Among the Immigrants in America." Master's thesis, University of Minnesota, 1989.

Erlebacher, Albert. "Herman L. Ekern: The Quiet Progressive." Ph.D. dissertation, University of Wisconsin, 1965.

Flint, John T. "State, Church and Laity in Norwegian Society: A Typological Study of Institutional Change." Ph.D. dissertation, University of Wisconsin, 1957.

Gieske, Millard L. "The Politics of Knute Nelson, 1912–1920." Ph.D. dissertation, University of Minnesota, 1965.

Hynes, Mary Callista. "The History of the American Protective Association in Minnesota." Master's thesis, Catholic University of America, ca. 1939.

Lalim, Cathryne Christine. "The Response of the Red River Valley Norwegian-American Newspapers to Populism in the 1890's." Master's thesis, University of North Dakota, 1971.

Lindberg, Duane Rodell. "Men of the Cloth and the Social-Cultural Fabric of the Norwegian Ethnic Community in North Dakota." Ph.D. dissertation, University of Minnesota, 1975.

Lundvall, Howard Carl. "The American Protective Association: A Study of an Anti-Catholic Organization." Master's thesis, State University of Iowa, 1950.

Naftalin, Arthur. "A History of the Farmer-Labor Party in Minnesota." Ph.D. dissertation, University of Minnesota, 1948.

Paulson, Arthur Christopher. "The Norwegian-American Reaction to Ibsen and Bjørnson 1850–1900." Ph.D. dissertation, State University of Iowa, 1933.

Rugland, Sigvart L. "The Norwegian Press of the Northwest, 1885–1900." Master's thesis, State University of Iowa, 1929.

Saam, Gretchen. "The Immigrant in the Novels of Rolvaag and Cather." Master's thesis, State University of Iowa, 1941.

Schou, John T. "Decline of the Democratic Party in Iowa, 1916–1920." Master's thesis, University of Iowa, 1960.

Sorenson, Charles Somner. "A Comparison of the Views of Hamsun, Rolvaag, and Feikema on Rural Society." Master's thesis, State University of Iowa, 1955.

Spetland, Olaf H. "The Americanizing Aspects of the Norwegian Language

Press in Wisconsin, 1847–1865, With Particular Reference to its Role in Local, State, and National Politics." Master's thesis, University of Wisconsin, 1960.

Stauffer, Alvin Packer Jr. "Anti-Catholicism in American Politics, 1865–1900." Ph.D. dissertation, Harvard University, 1933.

Swanson, H. Fred. "The Norse in Iowa to 1870." Ph.D. dissertation, University of Iowa, 1936.

Visser, John E. "William Lloyd Harding and the Republican Party in Iowa, 1906–1920." Ph.D. dissertation, University of Iowa, 1957.

Wyman, Roger E. "Voting Behavior in the Progressive Era: Wisconsin as a Case Study." Ph.D. dissertation, University of Wisconsin, 1970.

APPENDIX

Description of Method

Since all investigations proceed on the basis of certain assumptions that guide the selection of facts and their presentation, it is appropriate that I address prominent features of my research approach. A central aim of my investigation was to identify Norwegian-American voting patterns in diverse settings to discover the central tendencies, range of variation, and possible sources of differences expressed.

Selection of settlements for study

I selected 189 predominantly Norwegian minor civil divisions from among rural settlements of Wisconsin, Iowa, and Minnesota to serve as indicators of rural Norwegian political patterns. Of them, Wisconsin provided 48, Iowa 32, and Minnesota 109. This distribution roughly approximates the proportion of Norwegian-American citizens found within each state in 1910, according to population figures published in Volume I of the Thirteenth United States Census. Take Minnesota, for example. This state contained 58 percent of the total population of Norwegian origin in the three states, and 57 percent of the 189 political units were selected from this state. Wisconsin was slightly under-represented (25 percent of the political units and 31 percent of the three-state Norwegian-American population), while Iowa was slightly over-represented (17 percent of the political units compared to 13 percent of the population).

As to what constituted a "predominantly Norwegian" settlement, I concerned myself with small rural political units (townships and incorporated towns and villages) that contained 50 percent or more Norwegian-American potential voters, according to manuscript schedules of the 1880 United States Census. A township's Norwegian voters I defined as every male age twenty-one or older if he or his father had been born in Norway. Wisconsin provided the only exception. Based on the 1905 state census, I counted an adult "family head" as a potential Norwegian voter if he or either of his parents were born in Norway.

I also verified the continued homogeneous character of these selected voting units in the manuscript schedules of both the 1895 state census of Iowa and the 1905 state censuses of Minnesota and Wisconsin. For Wisconsin, I drew information about the ethnic character of voting units mainly from "Cultural-Ethnic Backgrounds in Wisconsin: A Retabulation of Population Schedules from the Wisconsin State Census of 1905." This is an unbound typescript prepared in the 1930s by the departments of Rural Sociology and Agricultural Economics at the University of Wisconsin and is on file at the State Historical Society of Wisconsin, Madison.

I also included among the 189 selected voting units a few Norwegian precincts that were either formed after 1880 (such as in northwestern Minnesota) or later reached 50 percent or more of the locality's population according to when, by inter-census interpolation, I estimated that they met the aforementioned conditions.

A final consideration involved making sure that the boundaries of a political unit in 1880 remained constant throughout the period under study. In some cases this required combining certain township, town, and village units in order to achieve the necessary comparability over time. For these purposes, I relied on boundary changes identified in footnotes of population tables for minor civil divisions published in volumes of the United States Census, 1880–1930.

Votes examined

The study is based on ballots cast for candidates for governor and president in general elections between 1880 and 1924. With but very few exceptions, time limits did not permit me to consider the results of primary elections. I recognize that the impact of Republican factionalism often worked itself out in these contests, but I chose to sacrifice this in the interests of expanding the number of years being considered in the study. Most voting returns I derived from the Wisconsin *Blue Book*, the Minnesota *Legislative Manual*, and the Iowa *Official Regis-*

ter. Minnesota's precinct votes for president, however, came from unbound returns on file at the Minnesota State Historical Society. I
turned to local county newspapers for precinct returns for most races
other than for governor and president, and for any that could not be
found in the biennial volumes published by each state.

Procedure used to estimate voter turnout

My base-line data at the precinct level came from the federal manuscript census schedules of 1880, the Iowa state census of 1895, the Minnesota and Wisconsin state censuses of 1905, and the 1930 population
figures published in the Fifteenth United States Census. The job of estimating the number of potential voters in Iowa's precincts (people age
twenty-one or older) proved quite easy. Several published decennial
state censuses in Iowa through 1925 identified the number of males by
age, which made reliable inter-census estimates possible.

Estimates for Minnesota and Wisconsin constituted another story,
however. Since fully twenty-five years separated the 1905 precinct-
level information in the two states from the 1930 federal census information, I devised another method for estimating potential voters
there. Published federal censuses of 1910 and 1920 provided county-
level figures on the age of citizens. I computed the percentage of the
potential voters in the total county's population for 1910 and 1920 and
determined the difference between the two percentages. By interpolation, I converted that result to an average number of annual percentage point changes in potential voters between the two years. I then
took each estimated annual percentage of a county's potential voters
and multiplied it by the estimated total population of each of its
precincts. This yielded annual estimates of potential voters within
each precinct.

The method seems to work, at least for rural counties. When I
checked the estimates computed by this method against my own
known counts from the 1905 state manuscript censuses, I found that
those derived from county level percentages did not vary from my own
precinct level counts by more than 3.5 percentage points, with the
average variation being only 2.0 percent.

In spite of apparently adequate procedures for making estimates,
between-state comparisons of voter turnout rates proved impossible.
This is because Iowa's state censuses were plagued by constant under-
reporting of population. Unlike Minnesota and Wisconsin, which
mounted separate organizations especially to conduct their census,
Iowa merely thrust this additional burden onto the workload of the

township assessor and county auditor. Consequently, less attentive coverage resulted and this showed in my computations, which yielded consistently high levels of voter turnout—sometimes exceeding 100 percent. For this reason, throughout my study voter turnout levels in Norwegian-American townships have been compared only to that given by other political units *within* each state.

Estimating synod predominance of Norwegian Lutheran membership in a political unit

Here I relied on information gathered by Olaf Morgan Norlie and published in his *Norsk lutherske menigheter i America 1843–1916* (Minneapolis, 1918). I based my estimates on the way things looked as of 1892. It is difficult to be precise about the synod affiliations of Norwegian Lutheran residents of a township, town, or village. This is because Norlie's information is given by congregation, not township. In lieu of the impossibly time-consuming task of determining for 189 voting units whether or not members of a congregation lived in one township or nearby in another, certain assumptions had to be made. Mainly, in the absence of information to the contrary, I assumed that the residences of church members clustered in a circular pattern around each congregation that Norlie had identified on maps. To the extent that the membership appeared to spill beyond the borders of the political unit in question, I assigned a percentage of it to the adjoining township(s). After doing this for all Norwegian congregations either within or near the political unit, I combined all estimated members living within the precinct. Then I computed which percentage of this total was associated with each synod.

I used these percentages for calculating partial and multiple correlations and performing regression analyses. For purposes of classifying units according to their predominant synod (that is, Hauge's Synod, United Lutheran Church and Lutheran Free Church, mixed Norwegian Synod and pietist congregations, or Norwegian Synod), I assigned each to a class based on whether 50 percent or more of the estimated membership aligned themselves with one or another synod.

Additional comments on the selection of settlement characteristics

In nearly all cases I have selected a cultural, social, or economic indicator at one point during the period and measured its relationship to the votes throughout the period under study. The major precaution taken was to select attributes for Norwegian townships that held nearly constant from one township to another over the years. I included, for example, percentage of farm acreage in corn because the Norwegian-American townships that produced low amounts of corn in the 1880s were also those at the low end of corn production in the 1920s. The following is a list of the independent variables considered in the study. I have noted, where applicable, the state and year of the information derived, if I found it available for only one or two of the states.

1. Percentage of adult Norwegian males.

2. Estimated Norwegian Lutheran church predominance.

3. Estimated average years of population residence as of 1895.

4. Predominant region of origin in Norway (east Norway, mixed east and west Norway, and west Norway).

5. Percentage of farm renters (Minnesota, 1922; Wisconsin, 1905).

6. Average value per acre (Minnesota, 1899; Wisconsin, 1905).

7. Percentage of improved acreage per farm (Minnesota, 1922; Wisconsin, 1905).

8. Average value of rural personal property (Minnesota, 1905; Wisconsin, 1900–1905).

9. Coefficients of variability in value of rural personal property (Minnesota, 1905; Wisconsin, 1900–1905).

10. Percentage of crop acreage in wheat (Minnesota, 1922; Wisconsin, 1905; Iowa 1895).

11. Percentage of crop acreage in corn (Minnesota, 1922; Wisconsin, 1905; Iowa, 1895).

12. Percentage of crop acreage in minor grains (buckwheat, rye, barley) (Minnesota, 1922; Wisconsin, 1905; Iowa, 1895).

13. Percentage of crop acreage in hay (Minnesota, 1922; Wisconsin, 1905; Iowa, 1895).

14. Percentage of crop acreage in oats (Minnesota, 1922; Wisconsin, 1905; Iowa, 1895).

15. Percentage of crop acreage in other crops (Minnesota, 1922; Wisconsin, 1905; Iowa, 1895).

16. Percentage of urban population (in incorporated towns, villages, and cities as of 1910).

17. Relative peripherality of minor civil unit (an index based on combining three variables: value per acre, percentage of urban population, distance to county seat) for Minnesota and Wisconsin only.

18. Percentage of turnover of potential voters, 1895–1905 (Minnesota).

19. Distance to county seat (measured from center of township).

20. Region of location within the state.
    a. Southeast Minnesota (Fillmore, Houston, Goodhue, Dodge, Freeborn, Faribault counties).
    b. West-central Minnesota (Meeker, Kandiyohi, Chippewa, Swift counties).
    c. Northwestern Minnesota (Otter Tail, Wilkin, Becker, Clay, Norman, Polk, Clearwater counties).
    d. Central Wisconsin (Dane, Green, Iowa, Waupaca, Washara, Portage, Adams counties).
    e. Southwest Wisconsin (Vernon, Crawford, Monroe counties).
    f. Western Wisconsin (Trempealeau, Jackson, Buffalo, LaCrosse counties).
    g. Northwest Wisconsin (Pierce, St. Croix, Dunn, Shawano counties).
    h. Northeast Iowa (Winneshiek, Fayette, Clayton, Mitchell, Worth counties)
    i. Central Iowa (Story, Hamilton, Hardin counties).
    j. North-central Iowa (Winnebago, Humboldt, Emmet counties).

Index